CENTRIPETAL POLITICS

CENTRIPETAL POLITICS

Government and the New Centres of Power

Ghiţa Ionescu

Hart-Davis, MacGibbon   London

Granada Publishing Limited
First published in Great Britain 1975 by Hart-Davis, MacGibbon Ltd
Frogmore, St Albans, Hertfordshire AL2 2NF and
3 Upper James Street, London W1R 4BP

ISBN 0 246 10854 1
Printed in Great Britain by W & J Mackay Limited, Chatham

Sovereignty in the sense in which Parliament understood the term was already disappearing...There were sections of society with such power that they could and might render government by consent impossible...and members of the European Economic Community would have to solve them together because they required the same kind of answers.

T. Lawson, MP
(Motherwell, Lab.)
The Times, 29 November 1973

Contents

Idem semper

Acknowledgements

Inasmuch as the long preparation of this book has fallen into two phases I am dividing my acknowledgements in the same way.

For the first phase, I wish to thank Andrew Shonfield and John Pinder for their valuable comments on an earlier draft of the manuscript. Frequent discussions with three of my friends in the Department of Government of the University of Manchester, S. E. Finer, K. Medhurst and Roger Williams, and with Mrs Helen Wallace of UMIST gave me the benefit of their views on some aspects of the subject. Michael Dempsey, then senior editor at Hart-Davis, Mac-Gibbon, encouraged me with unfailing enthusiasm. Above all I want to thank Isabel de Madariaga and Ernest Gellner, whose advice was invaluable.

These two friends continued to assist me in the second phase of my work in which the final version of this book took shape. Not only did they discuss my ideas, but they read and commented on the manuscript. Sibyl Grundberg, who succeeded Michael Dempsey at Hart-Davis, MacGibbon as my work was nearing completion, has given most welcome and necessary assistance in preparing it for the press. I must record my gratitude for the patience and understanding she has constantly showed me.

I want to thank very warmly M. Emile Noel, the Secretary General of the EEC, and his two assistants, Messrs Henri Etienne and G. Ciavarini-Azzi, as well as the staff of the Secretariat of the European

Commission for their frequent help, advice, and expert information during my research on the policy-making of the Community, a subject which forms part of the argument of this book. The research was made possible by a one-year grant from the Social Science Research Council, which I am happy to acknowledge here. I am grateful to Messrs Raymond Barre, F. Malfatti, John Davies and George Thompson for their kindness in allowing me to interview them at length while I was engaged in that research.

Mrs Joan Titterton, my secretary at the University of Manchester, and Mrs Hicks acquitted themselves most valiantly of the task of typing the many versions of this manuscript.

My wife bore the brunt of the work, both intellectually and domestically. My gratitude is equalled only by my admiration.

G.I.

Introduction

This study begins with the premise that government – as we know it in the Western societies – has reached a crossroads. Indeed, it will argue that important choices must be made if our societies are not to succumb to pressures and trends which would seem bent on rendering the industrial states ultimately ungovernable. These pressures, which recently have become increasingly identifiable and disruptive, are the direct effect of the growing impact of the industrial-technological revolution on the political structures, as well as the economies of the countries in which it has occurred. From within and from without, new forces and new centres of power have come to exert an influence on the course of events.

From within a given country the corporate forces (professional corporations such as trade unions, commercial and industrial corporations such as national and multinational enterprises, and administrative corporations such as cities and regions) have accrued sufficient power and autonomy to impose their sectional decisions on the rest of the community.

From without, the technological revolution has brought about such close international interdependence that all representative governments, and most especially those of the medium and small-sized states, find their national policies constantly being blown off course, and international developments well outside their control playing havoc with these national policies.

Faced with the prospect of increasingly ungovernable societies, and with the ultimate threat of national disintegration, the representative governments relinquish their positions as unique national policy-makers and seek 'partnerships' or 'contracts' with each of those corporate forces in modern society without which that society would cease to function. They seek a social partnership, or contract, with the unions. They seek industrial and financial partnership with the national or multi-national enterprises. They seek political-administrative partnership with the regions by way of constitutional devolution. By doing so, the representative governments (that is to say, parliaments and the governments which they form) agree to put themselves on a new footing with the corporations concerned, and acknowledge the fact that the decisions which they take in these conditions are the bilateral product of two independent centres of decision. But because the government must form partnerships with *each* of these corporations, and because the interests of these corporations are more often than not opposed to each other, so the government may often sink in the difficult role of go-between, or re-emerge in its classic role of umpire.

In external relations, representative governments seek partnership with each other, in order to gather sufficient strength through the sharing of power and responsibilities to the pressure of international developments which are too powerful for each of them to stand up to alone. The representative national governments, that is to say the bearers of national sovereignty, recognize that the decisions they take in this way are the joint product of two formerly separate centres of decision, themselves and the supra-national community, and that these decisions are binding on all members of this supra-national partnership.

It is further suggested here that the aggregation of the new partnerships, and the disseverance of the previously unique centre of government, will inevitably be accompanied by the coming of politics of a new and unrehearsed kind, that is to say of new and un-rehearsed political processes and institutions. The successes of each of the two partnerships, the socio-economic and the supra-national, are interdependent: a national economic policy agreed upon by all corporate interests in the society would still fail if it met with adverse international conditions too strong for one state alone to cope with; and decisions taken by a supra-national centre would be void if they were not implemented by the national communities in the member states. Thus the purpose of the new politics must be to co-ordinate such decisions, and to rally, for their making and implementation, the participation of the majority, as in all representative politics. In order to visualize what kind of politics these politics will be, and what kind of techniques these politics will use, it will be useful to introduce here the expression 'centrifugal politics'.

What this term means deserves some explanation. The reader will notice how frequently the expression 'centre' recurs in the course of this discussion. This is only natural if we remember that the principal object of the inquiry is the problem of government – one of the most straightforward definitions of government is that it is the centre of decision-making of the community. It is also true that the most usual descriptions of the kinds and ways of government derive etymologically from the word centre: thus central v. local; centralized v. decentralized; centralistic v. polycentric; centric v. eccentric; concentration v. deconcentration. But when it comes to political processes, there is a less popular but opposite pair of expressions which have been hitherto overlooked: centrifugal-centripetal.

The *Concise Oxford English Dictionary* defines centrifugal in its laconic way as 'flying, tending to fly from centre'; and centripetal as 'tending towards centre, opposite to centrifugal'. Though brief, these definitions are more than adequate to underline the importance of these expressions when given a political connotation, more especially in the context of this essay. For if the modern industrial-technological society is characterized, as we surmise, by the increased socio-economic emancipation of the corporations, then that society is a particularly centrifugal society. (Inflation, for instance, the syndrome of the modern industrial-technological society, is a characteristically centrifugal process.) And if politics is, as Bernard Crick put it, 'the activity by which different interests within a given unit of rule are conciliated by giving them a share in power', then politics is centripetal, as opposed to society, which is centrifugal. And further, the more centrifugal the society, the more centripetal its politics should be.

Neither the expression, nor the idea proposed here is entirely original.[1] But in order to understand better the sense in which 'centripetal politics' is used here, it will be useful to contrast it with five other concepts; namely, the politics of the centre, the politics of centralism, the politics of consensus, the politics of power and the politics of concertation.

In the summer and autumn of 1974 the expression 'the politics of the centre' (always of great importance in West Europe) was the most frequently heard slogan in British politics. Mr Heath, Mr Thorpe, Mr Mayhew, and Mr Jenkins have all spoken of the 'centre' as of the Mecca. The trouble is that the centre in politics is not the same as the centre of decision-making in the nation as a whole. The centre in politics is to be found at a point in the semi-circle of parliamentary parties: between the Left and the Right. Now, the search for this centre is a most legitimate preoccupation, and the political leaders and commentators who have devoted their time to seeking out the situations which would favour it are fully justified. But the centre of decision-making is no longer to be found in the centre of national representation. In the case of decisions about internal matters, it has been displaced to somewhere between the world of political representation and the world of the corporate forces – unions, companies and regions. In external relations, it has been displaced to somewhere hovering between British sovereignty and parts of the international world without the assent of which major British decisions would be inoperative. In this sense, government-in-partnership is a coalition government formed of the national parliament and these extra-parliamentary forces.

1. Arendt Lijphart, the originator of the theory of 'consociotional democracy' has used these very terms with different meanings, thus: 'We shall refer to the homogeneous and stable democracies as *centripetal*...and to the fragmented and unstable ones as the *centrifugal*...democracies'. 'Consociotional democracy', *World Politics*, vol. 21, no. 2, p. 220, Princeton, 1959. But the interpretations with which a theory of centripetal politics might best be compared are Harry Eckstein's theory of 'congruence', and Stein Rokham's theory of 'corporate pluralism' (see pp. 23–4 below and H. Eckstein, *Division and Cohesion in a Democracy: A Study of Norway*, Princeton, 1966, pp. 225–88).

But here we come to the two great dangers which might lie in government-in-partnership. The first great danger is that the national majority might become irrelevant. A decision rationalized by the argument, 'This is the common decision of the government and of partner A, B or C as well as of the direct pressure which the government and the respective corporate force, A, B or C, can exert on society as a whole', might leave the numerical majority of the population without much say in the matter. To calculate the effective opposition of the majority, with these kinds of techniques of government, might become an exercise of interest only to nostalgic psephologists.

But government-in-partnership can be frustrated in a different way. This can occur when the 'partners' clash with each other. Take, as an example of such a situation in Britain, the problems arising around North Sea Oil. Here the region demands to be given its monopoly; the unions demand that the monopoly should go to the British state; the multinational corporations demand that they should handle the oil since they invested the capital; and the European Community demands that the oil should be shared with the Community. The danger here is of total stalemate, the situation of 'no-decision' so characteristic of representative governments rendered powerless by the formidable sectional interests.

We come now to the contrast between 'centripetal' and 'centralistic' politics. Here it is important to remember that the latter term refers to a central government. Centralistic politics is based on the politics or political techniques of power, hierarchically and vertically oriented. The politics of power is common to all kinds of centralistic governments which form a wide spectrum. At one end of this spectrum are the centralistic but benevolent liberal states; at the other, as a terrible caricature but also as a warning, are the old totalitarian governments. It remains to be seen whether the centralistic or the decentralized system will cope best with the problems of an industrial-technological society. It may well happen – and this is one of the alternatives discussed in the conclusions – that the liberal industrial societies will collapse because of their self-defeating centrifugalism. And it may happen that the authoritarian industrial societies of the right or left will again succeed in making their societies work by fear and terror, on the assumption that any kind of order is better than total disorder. On the other hand, there are increasing signs – such as the feverish search for economic reform (by, among other means, decentralization), technological backwardness, and the self-assertion of the technical intelligentsia – that the Marxist-Leninist regimes are finding it increasingly difficult to cope with the problems of an advanced society. The Czechoslovak crisis of 1968 highlighted all these difficulties.

When we come to the difference between the 'politics of consensus' and 'centripetal politics', we should remember that the theory of consensus assumes that the forces of cohesion in society will prevail over the forces of disruption. The theory of consensus entails a commitment to the maintenance of an existing constitution, as well as to the maintenance of the given nation-state which it guarantees. In its search for the new centres of a complex society, centripetal politics must however be prepared to change, not merely to amend, the constitution. While consensus presupposes that by sheer reason and public spirit society will remain stable, centripetalism accepts that by its very nature society is unstable. It visualizes politics, and its incessantly rejuvenated rules, as the rallying and converging activity by which a dynamic stability is assured. The word dynamic is operative. Whereas consensus is ultimately static, centripetalism is essentially dynamic.

In order to distinguish further between centripetal politics and the 'politics of power', special mention should be made of Saint-Simon, the first political philosopher to concern himself with the adaptation of politics to the industrial society, long before Marx, Weber, Schumpeter and the Fabians. I do not intend to overburden this introduction with a recapitulation of his theory.[1] At two essential points, however, a theory of centripetal politics intersects Saint-Simon's intuitions at the beginning of the nineteenth century.

1. See my 'Saint-Simon and the politics of the industrial society' in *Government and Opposition*, vol. 8, no. 1, pp. 24–28, and *The Political Thought of Claude Henri de Saint-Simon*, forthcoming.

One is his belief that politics is perennial, and perennially adaptable, and therefore would have to adapt to the industrial-technological society as well. This seems simple and acceptable. Yet it is worth remarking that this is one of the points on which Marx, the disciple, parted company with Saint-Simon, his acknowledged master. Marx thought that the future classless society of the workers would dispense with politics, which were for him merely the reflection of class conflict. But Saint-Simon, who never departed from his belief that politics were perennial, sought to foresee what kind of political organization, processes and rules of the game the industrial society would require.

The second point of intersection is at Saint-Simon's attitude to power. The striking characteristic of the industrial-technological society is the diffusion of power within it. If this is not the way Saint-Simon would have put it, the idea itself can be detected in his work. He was the first to assert, seemingly against Machiavelli and Hobbes, that there would come a society, the industrial society, in which politics would no longer be the politics of power and society would be administered, not governed. In that society, the politics of power (*du pouvoir*) would be replaced by the politics of abilities (*des capacités*). He was not speaking of a sudden and inexplicable cessation of power in industrial society. But having analysed what today is described in political science as the 'distribution of power and the lines and amount of conflicts'[1] in industrial society, he came to the conclusion that power would be widely diffused among all those who produced or provided any kind of goods or services indispensable to the functioning of this particularly interdependent society. Furthermore, just as no one could force any member of society to provide those goods or services, neither had anyone enough power to run the society from above. It followed that, as power would be so diffused among those who had the ability that it would be *everywhere*, it would by the same token also be *nowhere*. Power, *pace* Machiavelli and Hobbes, does not disappear or

1. Brian M. Barry, 'The economic approach to the analysis of power and conflict,' in *Government and Opposition*, vol. 9, no. 2, Spring 1974, p. 189.

7

transform itself into other forms. But power neutralizes itself by its own diffusion.

Saint-Simon's 'politics of abilities' is perhaps better described in conjunction with the current fashionable and highly useful concept of 'politics of concertation', which also comes nearest to the concept of centripetal politics put forward here. The expression 'concertation' is used specifically in modern French politics and increasingly in the European Community. 'Politics of concertation' is the technique of policy-making in which the horizontal process of consultation-commitment replaces the vertical process of command-obedience. All the sectional groupings in the new division of labour in society converge on a new point of intersection. And they make their decisions, not on the basis of an imposed, pre-established centralized order, but by means of a convergence towards mutually acceptable agreements, which later on may be institutionalized in partnerships. Thus it is only by applying new *techniques* and *styles* of politics, that forces previously centrifugal will be made to tend towards a newly located 'centre' or 'centres' (it is significant that the *Oxford English Dictionary* does not refer to *the* centre but to *centre*, without the article). Moreover, as centres change and shift, so the politics of concertation (which are inherently centripetal, tending towards centre) serves to seek out the centres wherever they may be temporarily or permanently located. 'Centre' is wherever the real lines of decision-making converge.

Does this mean that a new corporate system of decision-making is replacing the old system of national representation? If the answer were an unqualified yes, this would only confirm the anti-parliamentary theories of Marxism-Leninism or fascism. Both these theories denounce parliaments as 'hot air factories' and political representation as a façade of the bourgeois state. They both proclaim direct government by the *Volk* or the masses, the communes or the corporations, under the unopposed inspiration of one party and leader alone. They were both wrong, and on both counts. Legislatures have throughout history assumed different forms and played different roles, but they have been preserved. As for abolishing political representation in favour of direct government or direct administration, this is and will always remain sheer Utopia. All kinds of decision-making processes are ultimately based on representation. One can too easily forget, for instance, that the trade unions themselves are no more than organs of representation.

The alternative to the hypothesis put forward above is the combination of the system of political representation with the system of political partnership. The representative government might share some of its national prerogatives with the corporations and some of its international prerogatives with the neighbouring states. The representative government, whose function was always to mediate, might no longer act alone, but jointly with other partners. This new mediating role of representative government can already be clearly discerned in the workings of a parliamentary democracy like Sweden. Indeed, government-in-partnership might be described, to paraphrase Clausewitz, as the continuation of parliamentary democracy by other means. National parliaments would remain an essential political factor in the new partnerships, and political representation would remain the basic political system. At the same time the national representative government might waive some parts of its sovereignty, at home and abroad, to make these indispensable partnerships work.

Such a development might, moreover, be seen as the continuation of a trend which is characteristic of western European political culture. Since the Second World War the welfare state has become the expression of the Western European political system and of the mixed economy, the peculiarly Western European combination of public and private sector. Looked at in retrospect, it is more than evident that from the beginning the *raison d'être* of the welfare state was to accommodate the changes in the system of decision-making brought about by the industrial-technological revolution while maintaining political freedom.

Political freedom is not measurable only by the independence of Parliament. It is the combination of freedom of communication (press and media), of association (parties and opposition), of expression (meetings and demonstrations). While this general ambience prevails, what is essential in parliamentary democracy

9

remains safely protected. The welfare state, while answering to the need for economic and social reforms, has preserved this essential dualism against total state-socialism. What all the governments of Western Europe have in common, and the ultimate *raison d'être* of the European Community as a whole, is this goal of the preservation of political and national freedom, while finding new structures to cope with new economic and social problems.

The time may have come to 'continue' the welfare state by changing it into something else, perhaps into an unforeseeable model. But the continuity will lie in preserving the essential duality of the mixed economy and the welfare state, the essential interweaving of socio-economic dirigism and political liberalism which is the hallmark of the European political culture.

This study focuses on the changes which occurred in Britain in 1974, both in its internal politics and on the international plane, in its relationship to the European Community. During the last two months of 1973 and the first two months of 1974, the United Kingdom and the EEC underwent parallel political crises of exceptional intensity. As the causes of these crises were deeply interwoven, their effects too will continue to prove both reciprocal and far-reaching. In centring this discussion on the interlocked arenas of Britain and Europe, I have found the related events which occurred there during this period to be symptomatic of the problems of industrial-technological society generally.

The study has proceeded by analysing in its own light – that is to say, by singling out those aspects which are relevant to its working hypothesis, first the British crisis and then the European crisis, bringing both crises into a single perspective in its conclusions.

The greater part of this book is devoted to an analysis of the *political* causes of the general crisis of government in the United Kingdom and in Western Europe as a whole in the seventies. But the conclusions, some of which are provisionally presented in chapter five, include a discussion of the future of government in Britain and Western Europe if the trends detected in the analysis were to continue. Two possibilities can be envisaged: the abolition of representative government, or the continuation of representative government through new partnerships.

For the moment, I shall only sketch the outlines of what I see as the second possibility: that Britain and Europe should adapt their political systems to what has been called here 'centripetal politics'. In this case, British representative government, while continuing to function regularly, nevertheless would accept the double *partnership* which the political, social and economic processes of the industrial-technological societies by now so very clearly require. One potential and necessary partnership is with the corporate forces of society – social contracts with the trade unions, economic contracts with the enterprises, national contracts with the regions – thus creating a mixed representative-corporate kind of government. The other is with the European Community, creating a mixed national-supra-national government. British representative government would therefore continue to be *at* the centre of British decision-making, but it would work with other centres from which decisions concerning Britain would (indeed actually now do) originate. It is with this last parenthetical assertion that my argument begins.

Chapter One

Politics in an industrial-technological society

The first chapters of this study will concentrate on the internal political problems which have faced Britain since the beginning of the industrial-technological revolution. They will analyse, in the light of the crisis of 1973–4, the political dilemma inherent in industrial-technological society. Here we propose to examine the most intriguing relation in the politics of this new society – the relation between the corporate forces of the new society and the representative institutions of the old state. But first, what is an industrial-technological society?

Let me propose, as a provisional working definition, that an industrial-technological society is characterized by two new features. One is the rapid transition from manufacturing to service industries. The other is the application of theoretical knowledge to all phenomena of industrial life. Since the end of the Second World War most industrial societies have been undergoing such a transformation, especially those of the USA, the USSR, and, more slowly, of Japan and Western Europe.

But why industrial-technological society rather than industrial society (Aron), the new industrial state (Galbraith), post-capitalist society (Dahrendorf), industrialism (J R Hicks), corporate society (Robin Marris), and especially the popular post-industrial society (Daniel Bell)?[1]

1. Daniel Bell, *The Coming of Post-Industrial Society*, London, 1974, pp. 160–1. Daniel Bell's book is to date the most complete sociological treatise on the general subject of the new industrial society. But a further debt to Daniel Bell must be acknowledged for his 'Notes on the post-industrial society', which when it appeared in the New York journal *The*

I chose to call this society industrial-technological in preference to post-industrial for two major reasons. One is that while it is easy to understand why Dahrendorf should call the society he describes 'post-capitalist', implying an *industrial* post-capitalist society, it is less easy to understand Bell's choice of the term 'post-industrial'. Industrial society replaced feudal or agricultural society in the nineteenth century. Since then it has undergone several economic and technological transformations. The most important of these, and the one which provokes the fiercest argument, is the capitalist era.

The fact that non-capitalist, or indeed anti-capitalist, industrial societies like that of the USSR, have many characteristics in common with the capitalist industrial societies proves beyond doubt that industrial society is (as Raymond Aron was right to stress) the 'genus', and capitalist or communist, advanced or developed societies are 'species' of this genus. Whereas everything that Daniel Bell says in support of his theory that a new society is about to be, or is already born, is right in general, none of the major tenets of his argument prove that the 'coming' post-industrial society will be other than a further, albeit highly original, phase or transformation of the industrial society as we have known it.[1]

Public Interest (nos 6 & 7) in 1967 gave a new impetus and direction to the study of industrial society. A summary bibliography of 20th century works should include the studies of: Emile Durkheim, *Socialism*; Joseph Schumpeter, *Capitalism, Socialism and Democracy*; Raymond Aron, *Eighteen Lectures on Industrial Society* and *Democracy and Totalitarianism*; J. K. Galbraith, *The New Industrial State*; Ralf Dahrendorf, *Class and Class-Conflict in an Industrial Society*; Andrew Shonfield, *Modern Capitalism*; François Perroux, *L'Europe sans rivages*, and *l'Indépéndence de la nation*; Samuel H. Beer, *Modern British Politics*; David E. Apter, *Choice and the Politics of Allocation*; Robin Marris, *The Corporate Economy* and *The Corporate Society*; and Anthony Giddens, *The Class Structure of the Advanced Societies*.

1. 'In what way does a post-industrial society differ from previous society? In an historical sense, Professor Tominaga is right: the post-industrial society is a continuation of trends unfolding out of industrial

The second reason for my choice of the term 'industrial-technological' is that I find it impossible to use 'post-industrial' in an inquiry devoted to Great Britain and Western Europe. One sees in the very light of the statistics he uses that while Bell's five 'dimensions' of the post-industrial society apply satisfactorily to the United States, they do not accurately characterize the less technologically advanced countries of Western Europe. (See Tables 1 and 2.) And politically the states of Western Europe, unlike the USA, have been welfare states since the Second World War. This latter difference will prove particularly relevant to a study which, like the present one, concentrates on the political aspects of the Western European welfare states.

Table 1
Labour force and GNP in Western Europe and US by sectors 1969

Country	Agriculture		Industry		Services	
	% of GNP	% of Labour	% of GNP	% of Labour	% of GNP	% of Labour
West Germany	4.1	10.6	49.7	48.0	46.1	41.4
France	7.4	16.6	47.3	40.6	45.3	42.8
Britain	3.3	3.1	45.7	47.2	51.0	49.7
Sweden	5.9	10.3	45.2	41.1	48.9	48.8
Netherlands	7.2	8.3	41.2	41.9	51.6	49.8
Italy	12.4	24.1	40.5	41.1	57.7	45.1
United States	3.0	5.2	36.6	33.7	60.4	61.1

One of the ways of approaching the study of politics in a changing society is by assessing the impact on the characteristic organizations of the old (in this case, welfare) state of the characteristic organizations of the new (in this case, industrial-technological) society. I shall

society...Yet for *analytical* purposes one *can* divide societies into pre-industrial, industrial and post-industrial and see them in contrast along many different dimensions'. Bell, op. cit., pp. 115–16.

15

Table 2

Comparison of the Research & Development Effort of the United States with that of other Western States and Japan

State	GNP in billions of dollars 1964	GNP per apital in cdollars	Popula-tion (in millions) 1964	R & D Expenditure (in millions of dollars)	GNP %	Year	Qualified R & D personnel (a) Total	Number per 10,000 popula-tion	Year
Germany	103.98	1,774	58.2	1,436	1.4	1964	33,382	6	1964
France	88.12	1,674	48.4	1,299	1.6	1963	32,382	7	1963
Italy	49.58	897	51.1	290	0.6	1963	19,415	4	1963
Belgium	15.44	1,502	9.3	123	0.9	1963	5,536	6	1963
Nether-lands	16.86	1,385	12.1	314	1.9	1964	9,227	8	1964
EEC excluding Luxem-bourg	273.98	—	179.7	3,462	1.4	1963-4	99,942	—	1963-4
United Kingdom	91.90	1,700	54.2	2,159	2.3	1964-5	59,415	11	1965
Sweden	17.47	2,281	7.6	253	1.5	1964	16,425	22	1964
Japan	69.08	622	96.9	892	1.5	1963	114,839	12	1964
Canada	43.54	2,109	19.2	425	1.0	1963	13,525	7	1963
United States	638.82	3,243	192.1	21,323	3.4	1963-4	474,900	25	1965

Source: OECD, *Reviews of National Science Policy: United States* (1968), p. 32, In Bell, op. cit., pp. 9–10.
(a) Full-time equivalent
(b) Estimated according to OECD standards and not according to those of the NSF.

here call the former organizations the representative institutions[1] and the latter the corporate forces. The three representative institutions in the national political process are the political parties, the parliament and the government. The three principal, but by no means

1. The original inspiration can be found in Raymond Aron's essay, 'Les sociologues et les institutions representatives,' in *Ecrits politiques*, Paris, 1974.

sole, corporate forces of the industrial-technological society are the trade unions, the enterprises, and the regions and other units of local administration.

These three categories of organizations, although fundamentally different in their purposes, functions and roles in society, are nevertheless all corporations. The term derives from the Roman 'corpora' and from the medieval 'corporatio' (also called in the different vernaculars of the period, *confreries*, *guilds*, *Innungen*, *gilden* or *gremios*). But then as now they were either professional (unions, syndicats, colleges, etc.) or commercial-industrial (enterprises) or territorial-administrative (communes, boroughs, districts, provinces, regions).

One common denominator of corporations is that they are functional – that they define themselves by their role in society. This role is to produce goods or provide services indispensable to the society. This is why, on the one hand, corporations are generally associated with the producers in society. Even such odd products as 'information' can be supplied by corporations – as for instance the characteristic case of the British Broadcasting Corporation. This, on the other hand, is why the difference between *public* and *private* corporations has a relatively small significance from the purely functional viewpoint of the relations between corporations and society, or between corporations and consumers.

A second common denominator of corporations is the fact that their intrinsic functional principle is the search for autonomy. Historically this principle is central to their development: it was during the middle ages that communes, merchant firms and crafts began to assert their autonomy against the feudal kings. But from the fourteenth century onwards, with the dawn of the nation-state, they began to lose it again. When the first sovereign nation-state focused on the representation of the will of the people emerged – the state set up in France by the French Revolution – one of its first laws banned the craft unions. Both intrinsically and functionally the corporations are agents of decentralization, and intrinsically and functionally they are opposed to the centralizing agent of the society, the state.

Durkheim more than any other sociologist has stressed this fundamental aspect of autonomy in the concept of the corporation and thus helped to bridge the gap between the medieval significance of the term and its modern meaning. His approach is particularly illuminating because instead of insisting on the obsolescence of medieval meanings and institutions, and merely contrasting them with modern institutions, he tried to detect the positive continuity of these institutions across the ages. 'The point is made that to ask for a corporative organization for industry and commerce is to demand that we retrace the course of history,' he says in his preface to the second edition of *The Division of Labour in Society*. 'This argument would carry weight if we proposed artificially to resuscitate the old corporations as they existed in the Middle Ages. But the problem is not presented in that light. It is not a question of discovering whether the medieval institutions can identically fit our contemporary societies, but whether the needs which they answered are not always present although they must, in order to satisfy them, change according to the times.'[1] The need which in Durkheim's view the corporations would answer was precisely the need to increase and to establish on a solid basis the participation required in a modern society threatened by disintegration. 'A nation can be maintained only if, between the state and the individual, there is intercalated a whole series of secondary groups near enough to the individuals to attract them strongly into their sphere of action and drag them in this way into the torrent of social life'. Beyond this, Durkheim stressed two fundamental functions of modern industrial life, the economic and the political, which would ultimately lead to a reduction of the power of the state. Of the economic function he says: 'Neither political society in its entirety nor the state can take over this function, economic life, because it is specialized and grows more specialized every day, escapes their competence and their action.' The political function he describes as follows: 'From various quarters it is asked that elective assemblies should be formed by

1. Emile Durkheim, *The Division of Labour in Society*, New York, 1968, pp. 7 and 28.

professional occupation and not by territorial divisions: and certainly in this way political assemblies would more exactly express the diversity of social interests and their relations.'

What Durkheim therefore poses as a conceptual prerequisite of the notion of a corporation is its natural, logical opposition to the central power. The very concepts of government and corporations are in his view as logically opposed as are the concepts of central versus local, or national versus sectional.

This should help to clear the confusion deliberately created by Mussolini (and Franco after him) when he called his fascist state a 'corporate state'. The confusion has since been maintained, not only by fascist doctrinaires but also by some critics and opponents of fascism. The latter, being naturally opposed to anything that fascism stood for, failed sometimes to discriminate between what was genuinely intrinsic to fascism and what were merely propaganda gimmicks tacked on to its description. Mussolini corrupted the notion of corporation by pretending that it was an attribute of his fascist doctrine and of the state founded on it. This still prevents some people, for emotional reasons, from considering the corporation objectively either in its proper historical perspective or in its modern form.

And yet there is no more fundamental opposition than that between a corporation (or commune), primarily defined by its pursuit of the autonomy of the part, and the state, primarily defined by its attempt to achieve the global supervision of all its constituent parts. Elsewhere I have discussed the logical non-sequitur inherent in the Leninist notion of the Soviet, or commune-state.[1] But Lenin at least proclaimed that the purpose of communist revolution was the 'withering away of the state', or its dissolution at the hands of the communes (soviets) and of the social organizations. Moreover, the new Leninist state, described as the state of the dictatorship of the proletariat, was claimed to be the very tool through which the operation of liberating socialist society from the centuries-long domination of the (bourgeois) state would be carried out. The argument

1. 'Lenin, the commune and the state', in *Government and Opposition*, vol. 5, no. 2, 1970.

that the dictatorship of the proletariat was part of a dialectical transition between the present state-run and the future stateless society served as a logical link in the theory.

But in the case of the fascist revolution and its 'corporate' state, the trade unions, local and regional units of administration and large companies were taken over by the fascist state as part of its policy of dirigist centralization and were openly regarded as permanent servants of the totalitarian state (an expression which Mussolini, unlike Lenin or Stalin, did use). They were to be transmission belts of the state – an expression which Lenin, and especially Stalin, used to define the role of the trade unions and the soviets in the new Russian state, when the trade unions, after the crisis of the Workers' Opposition of 1919–21, were explicitly told that they were to be ancillaries to the party and to the state. In fascist Italy, all corporations in the fascist state were curbed to the exclusive advantage of the state. This was true not only of organized labour. It was true also of firms and industrial enterprises. At first, in Italy, the state allowed private capitalists to take an increased share of profits as a reward for severe handling of workers' organizations. But later, when the new state commercial and industrial corporations were set up, new conflicts of interest developed between industry and its state protector. It was then that the first state holding companies appeared in Italy. The regions, not to mention the smaller units of local administration, were also curbed under the dual central control of the state and the Fascist Party.

It is not the state which should be described as corporate, but society. Indeed, the more society tends to be corporate the less authoritative and powerful is the state. The wider the areas in which the corporations impose their unilateral decisions, the narrower is the area of decision- or policy-making by the state. Moreover, corporations can find direct lines for bargaining among themselves: what is called 'the inter-corporate dimension' which by-passes the constitutional centre of decision-making. The latter's activities are thus gradually restricted to endorsing, by legislative means, dispositions which were decided upon before the process of legislation was initiated.

The real model of a corporate society is not that of the Italian fascist society between 1922 and 1933. It is Swedish society from 1933 (or at any rate from 1938 when the Saltzjobäden industrial agreements between employers and employees were signed) until today. For it was in 1933 that the Swedish Socialist Party came to power and inaugurated the style of government which has helped it to remain in power ever since, and which has brought Sweden nearer to the image of a 'more-administered-than-governed society' (in the Saint-Simonian sense) than any other country in the contemporary world.

By this I mean that the separation of government from administration is built into the very structure of Sweden's government. Ministries and departments in Sweden are concerned only with the general overview. Public administration is in the hands of autonomous boards. Thus, the scope and the volume of what we call government is much more limited, and the autonomy of what we call administration is much stronger than in other European states. This Swedish trait prefigures the trends of the *administered* industrial society, with its characteristically impersonal authorities and a remote government, confined to a role of trustee and arbitrator between interests.

In the case of Swedish society, one can also distinguish between political and social organizations. 'The organisations and not the political parties actually deal with problems of distribution of income' remarks Nils Stjernquist,[1] who explains this by recalling that 'Swedish society today is pluralistic. The organizations favour compromise; they try to avoid state regulations and strikes and to come to terms with each other by bargaining.'

To what degree are these traits specific to Sweden, or common to the industrial-technological society?

It is true that in its tradition and political culture Sweden has shown a predisposition for functional organization. It is after all the only European society which had Four Estates, instead of three,

1. Nils Stjernquist, 'Sweden', in Robert A. Dahl, *Political Oppositions in Western Democracies*, New Haven, 1966, p. 130.

adding to the representation of nobles, the clergy and the burghers that of the peasants. It is relevant for our study that at the time the peasants were the only *producers* and their inclusion in the elementary processes of decision – and policy-making derived from this fact. It can be argued that ever since, Swedish society has acknowledged the importance of functional as well as political representation and has succeeded in obtaining high degrees of participation in both. A Swedish citizen participates in more social and political associations than any other citizen in the world (fifty-seven per cent of Swedish citizens belong to at least four categories of associations, a church, a union, a co-operative and a fourth different one). But he pays the price by giving to public activities a greater amount of his private time than any other contemporary citizen in the world. It can also be said that this high functionalization of society has led to the specialization of the role of each institution in Swedish public life – political parties, unions, and especially the press, which is free of state control and liberal in its attitudes.

It is also true that it was during and after the period of industrialization, which was particularly rapid in Sweden, that this highly functional tendency achieved its final crystallization and ultimate significance. Swedish society has become a complete functional grid cut across by lines of social status, income bracket, professional groups, religious and cultural ties and political and ideological affiliations. It has also fully accepted private ownership of at least ninety per cent of its industries – the state having no interest in nationalizing industries which are in any case forced by the pressures of powerful groups to serve the public interest.

By now, the Swedish corporate society, fully alive to its own direct power of decision-making, has increasingly and inevitably forced representative government to accept a more formal role. This affects particularly the role and importance of Parliament itself, and its indispensable institutional appendix parliamentary opposition, now threatened with extinction because of Sweden's electoral immobility. (The Socialist Party has been in power, although at times as a minority government, for forty years.)

Perhaps the best description of the political impact of corporate forces on a technological-industrial society was given by Stein Rokkan in 1965 in his essay, 'Norway: Numerical democracy and corporate pluralism'.[1]

> The extension of the franchise [says Rokkan] to all adults and the maintenance of a strict majoritarian rule of decision-making in the legislature made it possible for a movement of the hitherto underprivileged to rise to power. But the parallel growth of a vast network of interest organizations and the other corporate bodies made it impossible to rule by any simple 'fifty per cent plus' principle. To understand the strategies and counter-strategies of government and opposition we have to analyse the bargaining processes between giant alliances of such associations and corporations. The vote potential constitutes only one among many different power resources brought to bear in these bargaining processes: what really counts is the capacity to hurt or to halt a system of highly interdependent activities. In the triangular conflict between labour, the farm interest, and business no single group dares to rely exclusively on its electoral machinery. The efforts on the electoral front are paralleled at the level of organizational action and at the level of the mass media. The workers and the employers rely on their capacity to call strikes and to paralyse recalcitrant industries and service sectors. The farmers and fishermen have given top priority to the establishment of an efficient machinery for the control of production and marketing: one obvious purpose had been to increase their ability to withhold needed primary goods from the consumers and to force decisions on prices and subsidies. The managers, owners and financial interests rely on their power to call off investment plans, to withhold skills and to channel their initiatives to areas beyond the control of the unions and the national government. We have seen how these groups of organizations constitute the major poles in the system of electoral alignment. But none of

1. In Dahl, op. cit., pp. 106–7.

23

these groups can rely exclusively on the verdict of one-citizen, one-vote contests. Even if they lose out in the competition for votes and seats they can still bring their organizational resources to bear on the actual policy decisions of government. They need not actually use the weapons at their disposal, but the very fact that they can claim a measure of control over central factors in the national economy acts as a deterrent in the bargaining process. The crucial decisions on economic policy are rarely taken in the parties or in Parliament: the central area is the bargaining table where the government authorities meet directly with the trade union leaders, the representatives of the farmers, the smallholders, and the fishermen, and the delegates of the Employers' Association. These yearly rounds of negotiations have in fact come to mean more in the lives of rank-and-file citizens than the formal elections. In these processes of intensive interaction, the parliamentary notions of one member, one vote and majority rule, make little sense. Decisions are not made through the counting of heads but through complex consideration of short-term or long-term advantages in alternative lines of compromise.

In the next three chapters we shall analyse, in the light of the 1973-4 political crisis in Britain, the impact which each of the three major corporate forces, organized labour, the enterprises and the regions, had on the three representative institutions – the political parties, Parliament and Government – within the framework of the 'mixed economy' and the 'welfare state'.

Chapter Two

Organized labour and representative institutions in Britain

This chapter is concerned with the role which organized labour played in the political crisis in Britain in 1974, and with the antecedents of the crisis in British political history.[1] It is divided into three parts. The first, *The trade unions in pursuit of political autonomy*, discusses why and how organized labour's search for industrial autonomy was accompanied in the post-1968 era by a trend towards political emancipation. The second part, *The representative institutions in pursuit of national responsibility*, examines, in an inevitably simplified and *ad-hoc* way, the efforts of both Mr Wilson and Mr Heath, and their respective parties and governments, to bring the trade unions into the process of policy making in Britain. The third, *The confrontation of 1974*, retraces the main phases and evokes the main theme of the acute political struggle which led to the election of February 1974.

The trade unions in pursuit of political autonomy

The pursuit of autonomy by corporate forces is bound to affect the processes of national decision-making, particularly in an industrial-technological society, because of the close interdependence of its

1. This second, recapitulative, task is made much easier by the wealth of literature on the subject: Samuel H. Beer's *Modern British Politics* (London, 1965), for instance, is a full history of the interplay between the politics of the parliamentary political parties and what he calls the corporatist or collectivist politics of the groups in British society, from the seventeenth century to the 1960s. Republished in 1969 with an important

parts, and the primordial roles which knowledge and technological skill play in it. The techno-structure (to use Galbraith's expression in a Galbraithian context) is unique in possessing endlessly diversified and specialized technological skills and knowledge. Society is directly vulnerable to the pressures of specialized workers because their skills, be they of the least prestigious order in the chain of production, cannot be replaced as in previous phases of the industrial society when contingents of unskilled workers could be replaced by other similar contingents. Moreover, insofar as the national economy is more enmeshed than ever before – and more enmeshed with the international economy – any refusal to deliver goods or services will sooner or later bring the affected economies to a halt. To this, of course, must be added the formidable political and social strength of organized labour through its unions, and to some extent, through working-class political parties.

The impact of organized labour on the parliamentary system makes itself felt in the industrial-technological society in three ways:

1. The direct action of organized labour can force Parliament to renounce some legislative measure on which its majority would agree, or to repeal it, or to modify any change which has already been enacted.
2. The refusal by organized labour to implement measures already enacted by Parliament can render the measures ineffectual and impotent.
3. The political action of organized labour, through both parliamentary and extra-parliamentary means, directly challenges the purpose of Parliament, which is to bring

Epilogue, in which Beer tries to evoke the future of the representative-corporatist politics in Britain after the 'new stage of scientific and technological achievement has heightened the impact of rationalisation, tending to produce a "post-industrial" and possibly also a "post-collectivist" politics' (p. 392). Other pioneer works in this field are S. E. Finer, *The Anonymous Empire*, London, 1958 (see also his recent article 'The power of organised labour' in *Government and Opposition*, vol. 8, no. 4).

together under its national authority, and, as it were, in one national assembly, both responsible government and responsible opposition.

But industrial-technological society also reveals and accentuates the differences between the methods by which organized labour would make and implement decisions in an ideal system of its own and the methods by which decisions are made in the representative political system. Economic administration by organized labour would ideally consist of direct self-administration or self-management, with direct control and immediate implementation of decisions. This method of decision-making reduces representation to the point where it becomes indistinguishable from delegation and where the representative's mandate is indistinguishable from an imperative mandate. Economic and social power would thus be conveyed directly through decentralized management and administration, and would relegate the 'hot-air' institutions or 'illusions' of representation to the past – to the 'bourgeois' society which needed such political fictions to divert and mask the real economic and social struggle.

Autonomy, the common goal of all corporate forces, by definition entails decentralized and direct decision-making and implementation. There is therefore a fundamental contradiction between the two approaches to decision-making: representative by centralized means on the one hand, and direct by decentralized means on the other. The latter formula is not only the ultimate purpose to be achieved by revolution in Marxist-Leninist theory (and indeed the promise it has broken most flagrantly and consistently in practice), or of the guild-socialist political doctrine as expressed by G. D. H. Cole; it is also the fundamental political tenet of pure and perennial trade-unionist or syndicalist philosophy.[1]

1. 'The central tenet of their doctrine was self-government. They believed that working men and women could come together to run their own lives, not through representations, not by controlling management and governments, but directly and by themselves.' H. A. Clegg.; *A New Approach to Industrial Democracy*, Oxford, 1963, p. 5.

27

Here, incidentally, one enters the particularly unrewarding area of study of ideological and political motivations. It can be argued – it is indeed too often and too stridently argued – that behind the trade unions' social agitation there is the reality of a different political-ideological orientation; in other words, that the ultimate purpose of industrial opposition is the replacement of the Western democratic political system by a system organized on the model of the USSR and other East European socialist states. Students of communist influence in the European syndicalist movement are sometimes puzzled by the fact that the mass of industrial workers, impatient to attain the 'syndicalist dream' of self-management and control of industry through workers' councils, seem unaware of the danger that their actions might bring to power the most centralist party of all. This may be a secondary question but it will frequently recur.

Be that as it may, the fact remains that there is an inherent incompatibility between the syndicalist system and the representative political system. In turn, this incompatibility causes the former to become an 'irresponsible opposition' within the latter. The expression 'irresponsible opposition' should not be taken as pejorative, either in a political or in an economic sense.[1]

Irresponsible opposition in the political sense must be taken here to mean an operation which is not responsible to, and does not acknowledge Parliament. Syndicalist ideologies are all antiparliamentarian. Guild-socialism, for instance, made a frontal

---

1. 'These opposite styles say a good deal about the differences that divide European trade unionism. They are what I shall call the "responsible" styles; the words being used in a purely descriptive sense, not to denote value. Most European trade unions operate in one style or the other, or at any rate along a scale that runs between the two. Sweden and Germany provide the leading example of "responsible" trade unionism, France and Italy of the "irresponsible". Others lie somewhere between. (The British TUC can never make up its mind which it is. It is, for example, desperately anxious to get round the table with the Government on economic questions. From time to time it succeeds, but it somehow never manages to stay seated for long.)' Eric Jacobs, *European Trade Unionism*, London, 1973.

attack on British representative institutions. It was opposed in *wrong* principle to decision-making by representation and advocated a decentralized, corporate process of decision-making by self-management. Thus the old arguments on guild socialism put forward by G. D. H. Cole:

> Even the theory of democracy today is still largely of the 'consciousness' of consent type. It assigns to the ordinary citizen little more than a privilege – which is in practice mainly illusion – of choosing his rules, and does not call upon him, or assign to him the opportunity, himself to rule. This is the essential meaning of the doctrine of 'sovereignty of Parliament'...
> But as the purposes covered by political government expand, and more and more of social life is brought under political regulation, the representation which may once within its limitations have been real, turns into misrepresentation...As the workers acquire a greater sense of their industrial strength, they seek to turn it to more ambitious uses and attempt to employ it as an instrument in commercial government. This is essentially the meaning of 'Direct Action'.[1]

This exegesis, although seemingly rejected conclusively by McIver and Crosland,[2] came to life again in the sixties in the light of the crisis of participatory democracy in Britain, and was restated in contemporary terms by, for instance, Anthony Wedgwood Benn[3] and Michael Barrat Brown.[4]

But the expression 'irresponsible opposition' must be taken in the context of the present theory of British trade unionism as 'The

1. G. D. H. Cole, *Guild Socialism Restated*, London, 1920, pp. 14, 15 and 17.
2. C. A. R. Crosland, *The Future of Socialism*, London, 1956. 'Like all Utopian schemes guild socialism had a purely static quality and took no account of the dynamic problems of economic growth and sectional innovation' (p. 94). Robert McIver, *The Modern State*, New York, 1926, pp. 465–6.
3. *The New Politics: Socialist Reconnaisance*, London, 1970.
4. *From Labourism to Socialism*, London, 1972.

Opposition which cannot be a government'; i.e. an opposition which, while it opposes representative and *responsible* governments directly and politically, still does not want to assume alternative policies or governmental responsibilities. (In this respect it is analagous to the Tribune of the common people in Rome, who had the *Tribunicia Potesta*, the veto, but not the *Imperium*, the power to make decisions.)

This doctrine of the industrial opposition of the trade unions has been expounded by Professor H. A. Clegg, who has described its manifestation in the transition period of the fifties within a theory of 'Trade unions as an opposition which can never become a government'.

The 'irresponsible opposition' theory contrasts the industrial and parliamentary situations. One of these contrasts is that managers and workers are engaged in a common enterprise in which workers must take an active, if grudging, part, whereas 'many, perhaps most, electors, are passive in politics'. Another argument is that the forms of parliamentary democracy are unsuitable to industry 'because of being too slow and bureaucratic'. This is put forward as one of the main reasons for the adoption of the device of public corporations in nationalized industry. The final argument is that if the trade union is industry's opposition, it must use other methods than those of a parliamentary opposition whose aim is to replace the government. 'A trade union can never hope to become the *government of industry*, *unless the syndicalist dream is fulfilled*.'[1]

The 'syndicalist dream' means in this context the control and ownership of industry by the workers, organized in Trade Unions. This could be achieved by complete or immediate nationalization or by the nationalization in succession of the principal branches of industry, banking, trade, etc. This, in the words of the Labour Party manifesto of 1918, 'Labour and the new social order' – actually written by the Webbs – would amount to 'a combined national service...to be worked, unhampered by capitalist, private or purely

1. H. A. Clegg, *Industrial Democracy and Nationalization*, Oxford, 1957, p. 24. (My italics.)

local interest (and with a steadily increasing participation of the Organized Workers in the management both central and local) exclusively for the common good'. The syndicalist dream also assumes that worker-ownership of an industry, or even of a branch of industry, would subordinate the role of government to one of partnership, the state or government supplying the capital and the workers being in charge of management and production. The idea of partnership is the dialectical counterpart of the idea of autonomy. Not only organized labour, but also the enterprises and the regions or local administration presume that once empowered to control and manage their respective sectors of the economy, any kind of central or co-ordinating authority will have no choice but to work in partnership with them.

History, in its objectivity, has up until now proved the syndicalist dream to be unrealizable. The experience of total nationalization in the USSR has shown that it leads to the complete domination of the state and party over the producers and their corporations. Only in Yugoslavia (the example of which impressed Aneurin Bevan, whose thought still dominates the present ideology of the Labour Movement in Britain) has an attempt been made, at least on paper, to deny the state the right of ownership of the means of production, and to define it, theoretically and constitutionally, as 'public' or 'nobody's' or 'producers' ownership. The direct political effect of this would be decentralization and the inevitable diminution of power of the central organs. The dividing line between the communist-etatist systems and the 'socialist'-decentralized system is actually to be found in the adoption by the latter and the rejection by the former of the workers' councils in industry and communes in agriculture. The government of the USSR, and those inspired by it, explicitly ban workers' councils. Yet the workers councils remain the perennial form of the 'syndicalist dream'. Recently the European socialist parties have taken a new look at the problems of workers' participation in the industrial-technological society, and in this new light, they have taken a much more favourable attitude towards workers' councils and workers' control. Thus they have seized the counter-offensive against the communist parties on the very ground of revolutionary structural change. But of this more will be said later.

As for the piecemeal achievement of the syndicalist dream, the nationalization of certain branches of industry, such as coal, railways and electricity, the British experience has, up to now, been disappointing for all parties. The industries themselves have not progressed, or at least no more than the ones under private ownership. The public in whose interest the operation was supposed to have been performed has frequently felt the disadvantages rather than the advantages of the operation: strikes, high prices, inefficiency. As for the workers themselves, upon seeing how nationalization has helped to erect over their work yet another structure of centralistic bureaucratic control and yet another system of exploitation, they have strongly denied that this is or ever could be the embodiment of the 'syndicalist dream', and have held the present political and social system responsible for the failure.

It is this gap between the 'syndicalist dream' and the reality of a representative system of government which the Labour Party – which, to use Ernest Bevin's historic expression, – came out of the bowels of the trade union, was and is supposed to bridge. The intricate mechanism which it established for the collaboration between the two wings of the movement, as well as for the selection of its leadership, leads to the possibility of domination by the trade unions, through, for instance, their possession of the overwhelming majority of votes at the Conference. In practice the tone of Labour Party policies has been determined, since the Second World War, by the political position, whether Right-tending or Left-tending, of the unions – which in turn has depended on the trade union leaders who came from their ranks: after the more-to-the-right Attlee-Bevin leadership, there followed the more-to-the-left Wilson-Jones team. Moments of crisis, or indeed of rupture, occur in the Labour Movement when the trade unions take a new ideological turn which the Parliamentary Labour Party is not yet prepared to follow.

In a recent book[1] Bill Simpson, who has been chairman of the NEC and chaired the Inquiry Committee on Party Organization

1. Bill Simpson, *Labour, the Unions, and the Party*, London, 1973.

which produced the Simpson Report, studied the crisis of the period 1964–70. The crisis was thought to be so bad that 'some expressed the view that the Labour Party had had its day'. He believes that this happened because the union movement was conscious of not being consulted by the Party; that 'the malaise had bitten deep and confidence in the government was never quite the same again'.

Three trends were responsible for the enduring conflict of 1964–70 between the Party and the unions. Two of them affected all workers' parties throughout the world. One was specific to the situation in Britain.

The first of the international trends was the socio-economic emancipation of the corporate force, organized labour, owing to the technological revolution.

The socialist and communist parties have of course been particularly affected by this trend, because of their traditional almost functional association with the trade unions. When one looks at contemporary Italy, France, Sweden, Britain, and now Western Germany, a gradual estrangement of the trade unions from the party or parties with which they were traditionally associated seems to be a common danger. The same trend can be detected in Yugoslavia, and in the light of crises in 1968 in Czechoslovakia, and in 1970 in Poland. This increasing divorce between what those countries call the 'politicians' and 'the economy', although over-stressed by the abundant 'New Left' literature, is now considered by students of the Marxist-Leninist regimes to be of the highest significance.

It is abundantly clear that either by co-operation with the governments or by 'contestation' of the very political process in which political parties thrive, the trade unions in most constitutional pluralistic states in the West have become *directly* engaged in national processes of decision-making in the economic and social spheres.

The second trend consists of the ideological radicalization of the trade unions everywhere in Western Europe in the late sixties, due to the action of the new revolutionary 'groupuscules' of Maoist and Trotskyist origin. These small groups rapidly achieved a great influence and outbid and outflanked not only the socialist parties, but

33

also the communist parties, which by contrast with the revolutionary zeal of the new elements appeared reactionary. According to a French student of the comparative politics of the new European trade unionism:

> Because they are more permeable than the parties, which have rigid structures by which they can control their memberships, the trade unions must be much more aware of the constant rejuvenation of ideas caused by the militant workers. The trade union leaders try to succeed where the political leaders of the Left have failed.
>
> This new trade unionism goes beyond self-assigned limits or the limits assigned to it by the parties. The trade unions act politically, intervene in production, demand that new relations of power should be observed between employers and employees. They occupy more and more of the ground previously reserved to the parties. Subtler, quicker than the political apparat, basing itself on a techno-structure better adapted to the modern forms of rapid industrialization, the trade unions then become the most sophisticated expression of the new political class...Because they are born out of an original form of resolute contestation the trade unions revert to revolutionary methods...Leaving behind the parties which are bogged down in a narrow parliamentarism, the trade unions open new ground which might allow them to seize economic control. They believe that the parties have aged as much as their themes. The political themes which the trade unions introduce into the discussion are: intervention in economic policy-making, self-management, workers' councils in which they manipulate directly and on the spot.'[1]

To these remarks must be added the specific reasons for the particular estrangement of the trade unions from the socialist parties.

1. Philippe Bauchard; *Les syndicats en quête d'une revolution*, Paris, 1972, pp. 10–12.

One arises from the undeniable fact that the internal organization of socialist parties is more conducive to control by its members. The accountability of the representative is more closely defined and the relations between the party and the organization of the trade unions are essentially reciprocal. Whether, as in the case of the German Social Democratic Party or the Swedish Socialist Party, the individual member of the trade unions is also expected to be a subscribing member of the Party, or whether as in the case of the British Labour Party the trade unions directly finance the constituency parties and members of parliament thus asserting an immediate right of control on the way in which MPs acquit themselves of their mandate in Parliament or Government, the fact remains that all socialist parties are in one way or another responsible to the trade unions. This is the opposite of the relationship which has until now prevailed between the trade unions and the communist parties, in which the former were subordinated to the latter.

The risk for the socialist parties of tarnishing their image in the eyes of the working class while in power has been great ever since socialist parties first started to take part in government in industrial societies based on capitalist foundations. And although relations between these parties, the workers and the trade unions, have frequently been acrimonious and not lacking in mutual recriminations, the divorce between the two had never been so clearly considered and formally spelled out as after 1968. Indeed, the year of the French 'contestation' coincided with the crisis in the relationships between the political parties and the trade unions in most European countries. It was highlighted by the December 1968, 'Kirala' incidents in Sweden, the 1969–71 (Baden-Württemberg) incidents in West Germany, the Italian 'hot autumn' of 1969 and last but not least by the open opposition of the British trade unions to the statutory reform of industrial relations proposed by the British Labour Party in 1969.

But now we come to the third, more controversial trend. This is supposed to be the perception of a relative decline in the efficiency and success of successive British governments, and consequently of British political personnel as a whole since the end of the Suez

35

crisis. This critical situation, this permanent inability of the British nation-state to pursue an economic policy of continuity and efficiency, is neither exclusive to Britain, nor new in history. All European nation-states have been beset by financial problems, almost to the point of insolvency. Contemporary France, Italy, Germany, etc. – all of them of a size and of economic resources which no longer guarantee, at least not since the Second World War, independent, 'sovereign' policy making – have had to realize that their sovereignty was, to borrow an expression from modern international affairs, 'penetrated'. (As a matter of fact, Germany, the model of a 'penetrated sovereignty', quickly achieved economic efficiency, and indeed buoyancy, precisely because it was helped from outside, especially by its profound penetration by US capital and firms.) But Britain's sovereignty was the most intact, and therefore proud, and this was one of the reasons why it hesitated, and still hesitates, to follow the other European countries in trying to replace the traditional national sovereignty by a less rigid sovereignty. This problem will be discussed at greater length later in this book. It was introduced parenthetically here only because it helps to explain why centrifugalism is accentuated, indeed to a certain degree caused, by the *failure of the centre to fulfil its 'central' duties*. Corporate forces are in any case autonomous, hence centrifugal. But when the centre loses its functional magnetism, when the centre of the nation – government – loses its functional efficiency, and the institutions lose their authority by lack of efficiency, a new *objective* centrifugalism is created or added to the inherent one. It is in this sense that I have here discussed the argument of the disenchantment of the trade unions (and of the enterprises and regions) with the poor performance of the state.

The new eagerness of the British trade unions to take their fate into their own hands may therefore be due to a mixture of disappointment with a growing and visible lack of success of their government, and of their own belief that modern industrial society favours corporate self-government. From the latter point of view such developments as the further democratization of society, the rising appetite for power provoked by the partial and partly successful

36

nationalizations as well as by the dominant political position of socialist parties in national politics, the growth of public education, the widening and intensifying of communications media, the 'rising expectations' of a consumer society encouraged by commercial advertising, and finally the direct consultation of the trade unions practised by all post-war governments in matters of industrial policies – all these may have contributed to an aroused consciousness of the importance of industrial producers in national decision making.

From the former point of view, the low rate of growth, the high rate of inflation, and especially the coexistence and combination of these two phenomena are the characteristic syndrome of British economic policy in the last decade or so. To be sure, this was a general European predicament, but other European governments made earlier efforts to find new solutions by forming the European Community. Some of them brought their industrial relations into a formal and legal framework, while others tried to find new mechanisms such as Prices and Incomes boards to fight inflation.

Thus, the disillusionment of British producers with government was caused by the bitter realization that the producers' party, the Socialist Party, was as unsuccessful as the party of the conservatives, and by the further, global realization that a succession of alternating governments of either party amounted to a succession of 'stop' and 'go' policies and a continued decline in the country's external economic and political position as well as continuing inflation and rise in prices internally. This is not the same argument as the one so frequently heard after the Lincoln by-election of March 1973, according to which the electorate is, for reasons similar to those discussed here, weary of the two-party system. What is suggested here is that the industrial producers were becoming, for practical reasons, weary of representative government by politicians.

A sympathetic but objective student, Allan Flanders, accepts that there are two distinct phases in the relations between the trade unions and the state since the war, and places the watershed at around 1955. 'It was not until after the 1955 election', he writes, 'that a gradual worsening of the relations between the Government and the Unions

37

set in, and with it a decline in the political influence of the TUC General Council.'[1] The gradual worsening of these relations can be linked with two other developments. One was the change, in the mid-fifties, of the leadership of the trade unions: the passing of the Citrine–Deakin–Sam Watson generation of trade union leaders, and the coming of the leftist Jack Jones–Scanlon generation. The other was the trauma of British politics as a whole, culminating in the 1956 Suez crisis, its after-effects on British political psychology and on British influence abroad and at home.

Yet if one takes the year 1960 as the turning point one finds that there is a considerable difference between the attitudes of the workers during the fifteen years preceding it and during the fifteen years from 1960 to date. Since the sixties the interest of the industrial workers in the progress or failure of the national governments has been motivated by two considerations. On the one hand, as citizens they are interested in the welfare of the nation as a whole. On the other hand as the determining 'class' in the industrial society, they are interested in the furtherance of equality within the state. Equality is now directly measured in terms of their own real wage, adjusted to inflation but indirectly measured by comparing their standard of living with that of the other 'classes' and 'groups' in society.

The trade unions claim that since the sixties British governments have failed on both counts. To be sure, they do not take into consideration the impact of their own action in these developments: in the case of inflation, for instance, they deny the 'push' effect of the increase of wages. In consequence, since the sixties the politics of trade union co-operation with the government has been gradually replaced, under the impact of the deepening economic crisis and growing public dissatisfaction with stop-go techniques, by a mounting attitude of defiance and mounting claims for direct action. This has progressed from unofficial 'wild' strikes of shop stewards to widespread non-co-operation of entire unions and afterwards of the Trades Union Congress and the Trade Unions Council, which by now is controlled by the second militant generation of trade union

1. Allan Flanders, *Trade Unions*, London, 7th ed., 1967, p. 167.

38

leaders, former militant shop stewards themselves. It has also progressed from spontaneous strikes to official and picketing strikes, with direct attacks on the nerve centres of society, and with accompanying violence – and from individual strikes of one or another union to the combined strikes of several unions with the possibility of general strike in view. This double escalation has been accelerated by the reciprocal stiffening of government measures from, for instance, those proposed in the White Paper *In Place of Strife*, to those contained in the Industrial Relations Act, and from the Prices and Incomes bills to the counter-inflation bills. But the question of who started, and who is responsible for this escalation, the government or the unions, is as in the case of inflation a chicken-and-egg argument.

This brings us back to the problem of irresponsible trade union opposition – and to the quests of two prime ministers, Mr Wilson (1964–70) and Mr Heath (1970–4), for trade union acceptance of economic, social and political responsibilities to match their real power in society.

The representative institutions in pursuit of national responsibility

The crisis of British government had not gone unnoticed in political circles. It had been predicted, and when it started to develop it was watched most carefully. It is true that it was diagnosed mainly as either the result of the impact on domestic politics of the universal phenomenon of economic internationalization – or as the consequence of decolonization abroad and social emancipation at home. British politics were seen as bound by these historical developments. But within these bounds, they were thought to be functioning as well as could be expected owing to the solidity and flexibility of the system as a whole.

But from the mid-sixties a new critical dimension was added: gradually and slowly people began to wonder whether at least some of the causes and solutions could not be found in the political realm.

How slowly, and how late, can be seen, however, in a relatively recent confession (1972) by Reginald Maudling who, by his personal contribution to the Butler and post-Butler reforms in Conservative thinking, has been observing from close quarters the developments of the last quarter of a century. '*I am beginning to wonder*,' wrote Mr Maudling in a memorandum[1] which was prepared for his Cabinet colleagues but which he published only after he resigned from the Government in the summer of 1972, 'whether we have recognized how profound are the changes we are facing and how far we may have to pursue our search for remedies. I *suspect* that the problems we are facing are not economic but political. Economic factors operate within a political framework and the old orthodoxies of economics, however coherent and self-consistent, may not apply in a changed political situation. What determines the course of a country's society and its economy *is fundamentally political power and how it is used*' (my italics). And finally, 'We have seen in the last two decades an arising consciousness of the power of Organised Labour. The days when the community at large could provide skills to replace those of a striking union, e.g. of electric power workers have now passed. Society's defence is now political, not practical'.

On Labour's side Anthony Wedgwood Benn had preceded Mr Maudling's reorientation of his thinking from economics to politics by some two years in his Fabian tract, *The New Politics: Socialist Reconnaissance*.[2] He introduced it as 'a reconnaissance of some of the issues, arising from industrial and technical changes, *which may be moving into the centre of politics in the seventies*. Parliamentary democracy and the party system have in recent years been criticized not only for *their inability to solve* some of our problems but also for *their failure to reflect* others adequately' (my italics). The new power acquired by organized groups, especially Labour, is seen also by Mr Wedgwood Benn as a principal cause of change: 'Authoritarianism in politics or industry just doesn't work any more. Governments can no longer control either the organizations or the people by using the old methods.'

1. 'The Maudling memorandum on incomes', *The Times*, 12 Sept. 1972.
2. Benn, op. cit., pp. 1 and 71.

A new adjustment of the relations between government and organized labour as well as a new system of industrial relations was subsequently sought by both sides, the Right tending to go further right, and the Left further left. This coincided with an awareness that other corporate forces, such as the nationalized industries (an old *bête noire* of the Right) the multinational corporations (a new *bête noire* of the Left), and the regions, as in the dramatic case of Northern Ireland, had also accentuated their centrifugalism and by their actions were undermining the authority of representational government.

But for objective reasons (the assertiveness of the unions *is* one of the major causes of inflation, and strikes one of the major causes of economic unreliability of the country as a whole) and for subjective reasons (i.e. the social orientation of each of the two political parties) the problem of industrial relations was brought to the fore. This was due in part to the fact that on this issue the parties clashed head on. Whereas on the subject of Northern Ireland there was bipartisanship, on the subject of industrial relations and later, on the subject of entry into Europe, the two parties took opposite sides. This was a strange historical irony because the Labour Party had preceded the Conservative Party both in the quest for membership in the European Community, and in the attempt at a reconsideration of industrial relations.

For the sake of historical accuracy let us remember that at the beginning of this reconsideration, that is, in the sixties, the prevailing view was that the leadership of the trade unions was losing authority and that it was being actively challenged from below by spontaneous or organized groups led by individual shop stewards who could disrupt production, and orderly industrial relations, with 'wild-cat' strikes. This was the pressing reason to re-examine relations with the trade unions. By 1966 a Royal Commission on Trade Unions and Employers' Associations was set up under the chairmanship of Lord Donovan; it presented its report in 1968.

The Donovan Report can be regarded as a watershed in two ways. First it has proved to be the dividing line between the view previously entertained in Britain, that informal industrial relations worked with sufficient efficiency and flexibility to do without the intervention of the law, and the view of both the Wilson (1964–70) and Heath Governments (1970–4) that the law had, to some degree to be brought into play. In other words it forms the first step in the escalation: Donovan Report – *In Place of Strife* – Industrial Relations Act. It is also a watershed in the style of strikes, that is to say it coincides with the change from the unofficial strikes of the fifties to the official and massive strikes of the sixties and seventies in defiance of the anti-inflationary policies of Labour and Conservative Governments alike.

The Donovan Report recommended the registration of labour/management agreements with the Department of Employment and Productivity, and the setting up of an Industrial Relations Commission to supervise the implementation of the registered agreements and in general to oversee the state of industrial relations. But the Commission rejected any immediate legal enforcement of collective agreements. It would be stupid and unfair, it argued, to start by enforcing existing agreements which are so badly in need of reform. 'Why so great a reluctance, it may be asked, to turn to the law to enforce obligations? Because none of the parties in Britain really wanted to bring industrial disputes before the Courts if they could possibly avoid it, or lawyers *qua* lawyers into industrial relations.'[1] But one member of the Commission had reservations.[2]

1. Flanders, op. cit., p. 174.
2. In his 'Note of reservation', Mr Shonfield expressed the view that 'in a society which is increasingly closely knit, where the provision of services to meet the elementary needs of a civilised daily life depends more and more on the functional performance of inter-related work tools of a collective character, trade unions will be treated as if they had the right to be exempt from all but the most rudimentary legal obligations'. Shonfield proposed to change what he called the bias of English law and instead of making it complicated and difficult for unions to enter contractual obligations, he proposed to treat this as the main and normal thing to do. He saw the formation of the habit of entering into trading agreements as the main objective of the proposed reform. His general attitude was one of scepticism toward the hortatory and 'mending and improving' attitude of industrial circles. He argued that reform had been long overdue.

The results, during 1969, of the improved machinery for negotiation and conciliation proved to be insufficient. Industrial life continued to be disrupted by unofficial strikes by small groups of workers while industrial workers as a whole showed a growing antipathy towards the Government and its exhortations, even though it was a Labour Government. The White Paper *In Place of Strife*[1] was published on 17 January 1969. In this document the Government was given more direct power of control over industrial relations by means of the newly instituted right to order 'conciliation pauses'; indirectly it was given more control through the creation of a permanent Commission of Industrial Relations; finally, some penal measures were to be instituted.

Both sides of industry, employers and labour alike, disliked the White Paper. Politically this produced superficially paradoxical results. Whereas the Conservative Party approved of its orientation, almost half of the Labour Party, the Left, vehemently opposed it, and encouraged the trade unions to reject it. On 26 March the National Executive of the Labour Party voted against the White Paper by a majority of 16 to 5, although some three weeks before the Bill had had an easy passage through Parliament.

Mr Wilson, then Prime Minister, first announced that he would continue to ask Parliament to approve the Bill. But when on 5 June a special conference of the TUC decided by an enormous majority to oppose it, if necessary by industrial action, Mr Wilson abandoned the Bill and replaced it with a statement of intent by the General Council of the TUC to try to adopt new measures to bring into industrial relations. This soon proved to be illusory. Massive strikes continued. Moreover the TUC, now in full offensive, concentrated on divesting the Government of its right to seek to control wage increases. Mr Wilson fell from power, and Mr Heath triumphed in the elections of 1970.

Mr Heath's vision of British policy-making since 1971 can be described as bi-focal. One focus is the national political process, the other the European supra-national political processes. But in this

1. Cmnd 3888, HMSO

43

vision, whereas policy-making at the European level was desirable, or even inevitable, it was still tentative and ineffectual. British policy-making had, on the contrary, obvious power and immediate effectiveness. At this level he considered the problem of industrial relations his number one priority.

Mr Heath's general view of the politics of modern industrial Britain, as it can be summarized from his speeches and writings, does not differ very much from Burke's classical image of a traditional British society of citizens all holding equal rights, all enfranchised, aggregating in political parties and in interest groups – Burke's 'little platoons' – according to their occupations and their beliefs. In modern Britain, industry and organized labour are the two major aggregates of interest.

But society functions only if the economy is as free as the politics of the country. It is the incessant watch by the citizens, and not the control of the state, which will keep both the economy and society functioning freely and properly. 'Our purpose' Mr Heath said in a speech at Blackpool on 10 October 1970, 'is to bring our fellow citizens to recognize that they must be responsible for the consequences of their own actions and to learn that no one will stand between them and the results of their own free choice'. Parliament represents all citizens, political beliefs and interest groups. Government is the expression of Parliament. Thus Mr Heath's general political theory is a blending of modern understanding of the new conditions of the position of Britain in the post-1945 world and of the most traditional Toryism.

Mr Heath's conception of British economic policy-making at governmental level changed during his stay in power. The autumn of 1972 divided his attitudes on this question into two different phases. In the first period the Government was passive, watching the interplay between the two major industrial interests, labour and employers, within a legal context to be improved by a Parliamentary bill on Industrial Relations. Once Government and Parliament had provided the law, it was for the interested parties to make their arrangements under the eyes of the law. If the law was infringed by either of the parties, the Judiciary would see to it that this was rectified.

This was an essentially legalistic period. The fragility of its reasoning lay in the fact that it transferred, on the optimistic assumption that people were essentially law-abiding, the ultimate levers of authority from the Executive to the Judiciary. In other words the essential weakness of the legalistic strategy was that it presumed, or hoped, that the Law and the Judges would have more authority over unruly sectors of society than Government (both Labour and Conservative) and its administrative army had proved to have in the last decade or so. That ultimately, the equilibrium of any polity is maintained by the interrelation between its citizens and its laws – provided the laws are fair and the citizens law-abiding – is of course the basic truth of all politics. But in times when the equilibrium is broken and the interrelationship interrupted, recourse to the challenged laws or to the embattled citizens themselves has proved, throughout history, to be more often than not ineffective.

The Industrial Relations Act failed. It failed to persuade the most important unions to register; it failed to scare the unions by the bold fines imposed on them in the guise of sanction; one of its other provisions, that there should be a secret ballot of the members if a union contemplated strike action, failed dismally to reveal any serious differences of views between the leadership of the union and the rank-and-file. Finally, it failed to achieve the essential object of a law: it proved to be unenforceable, as in the case of contempt by the five dockers who remained in open defiance of the Court and the Act, and who had to be liberated at once, partly in order to avoid the risks of a general strike.

In the second period, from the autumn of 1972 – which by contrast with the legalistic period can be defined as interventionist – the Government was seen as an active partner in the national process of economic policy making. Contrary to the electoral manifesto of the Conservative Party, it was now acknowledged that Government could and should intervene. In fact, it had intervened during the first period: at Rolls Royce, in the Mersey Docks, and in the Upper Clyde. But now the Government was seen as intervening not alone, and not directly, but by consultation with the other two partners, to decide on a common agreement. This interventionist method of

45

policy-making was clearly defined by Mr Heath on 26 September 1972: 'What we have really embarked upon is the management of the economy by three parties, the Government, the CBI and the TUC. Of course the Government has direct responsibilities, but both other parties recognize that they have responsibilities as well.' Here again it was assumed that the sectional interests would assume the same responsibilities as the Government, to manage the economy of the country. But, failing this, the Government had, as in the legalistic period, no levers of its own to make the corporate forces accept their national responsibilities if they did not want to do so.

It is this theme of the responsibilities of all citizens which gives continuity to Mr Heath's general conception. Whether he offered the soft stick of the law, or the insufficiently attractive carrot of participatory consultation, what he seemed to expect to find at the other end was an ultimate sense of national responsibility. Inflation was the new angle from which he thought this process of interlocked responsibilities on the national and international planes could best be seen. On the national plane, the very mechanisms of inflation offered him the best demonstration of his political philosophy. Frequently, in his arguments over inflation, its causes and solutions, Mr Heath was seen to criticize the whole of contemporary society for its short-sighted hedonism. This is, of course, anathema in electoral politics.

In fact, one of the most distinctive characteristics of Mr Heath's politics is, as it were, its preceptive style. Mr Heath may well live in the history of the late parliamentary era as one of the few politicians who tried to uphold the right of Parliament (in Bagehot's words) to *teach* the nation. De Gaulle was another politician willing to take this risk, but then de Gaulle ignored parliament and taught the nation directly. Mr Heath's finest hour from this point of view occurred when, knowing that the entry of Britain into Europe was by its very intricacy a subject on which collective national judgements could be exerted only approximately (and indeed could be easily misled by demagogic over-simplifications) he nevertheless asked Parliament to *teach* the nation. If one links this with the resigned but premonitory tone of his last address after the February 1974 elections, and with his gloomy predictions of the effects of inflation, one finds that the common denominator of all his attempts at communication is the preceptoral approach. Mr Heath does take upon himself the risk of pointing out to a society cajoled by political and commercial advertisers alike its defects and shortcomings, or to use Machiavelli's terms, to warn it against its own 'corruption' or 'laziness'. This in the seventies was sufficient to give a politician the reputation of being, in Ibsen's sense, an 'enemy of the people'. Mr Wilson, on the other hand, belonging to a party that finds its origins in the division of social classes, prefers to depict society as divided into 'good' and 'bad' *sectors*, into the People, on the one hand, and the Establishment on the other – and in doing so equates social injustice with the Tory party.[1]

Be that as it may, the fact is that inflation, the typical syndrome of the industrial–technological society, was found by Mr Heath in the last part of 1972 to be the cause and the social and political (as against economic) epitome of the chronic malaise of the nation. A study by the National Institute of Economics and Social Research, and a severe warning by the Bank of England in the summer of 1972, concurred that the malaise was not *really* and *exclusively* economically motivated. ('As in a hysterical pregnancy we are all suffering the symptoms of rapid inflation without any of its normal causes', remarked the *Economist* in an apposite metaphor.) The conservative view after 1972 was that the real cause of inflation was political. The search now started in earnest for adequate political solutions to this essentially political predicament. Here in Mr Heath's eyes was a reason for throwing over the ballast of the laissez-faire Tory ideology on which he had fought the election of 1970, and asking for a new policy and new political institutions with which the government, in

1. Thus in a speech of 6 July 1968: 'Being a Labour Government means that you are fighting a hostile and embittered establishment, a deprived establishment soured by deprivation of office and power, which they had been brought up to believe were theirs by divine ordinance. But now their sourness and deprivation are giving way to a new sense of anxiety. For a year the Tory leadership and their allies in the Tory press have screamed their heads off in a campaign of distortion and representation.' *The Labour Government 1964–70 : A Personal Record*, London, 1971, pp. 543–4.

consultation with the two major interests, could steer the vessel of state through the storm. Inflation was also the simple symbol through which he hoped to convey his profound concern about the behaviour of society itself, and to explain his elementary theory about the law of mutual responsibility illustrated by such nightmarish examples of the potential effect of inflation on a political regime as the Weimar Republic whose collapse in 1933 precipitated Hitler's ascent to power.

Of the five generally accepted causes of inflation – excess demands, inflated expectations, frustrated growth in real income, structural excess demand and union pushfulness – he singled out the last as the principal one. Of the two poles of the basic equation contained in the term Prices and Incomes policy, he singled out the latter, arguing reasonably that the former was much more dependent on international than on national causes. And out of what this study describes as the three principal corporate forces in an industrial-technological society, he chose organized labour as the main culprit.

Mr Wilson too had long known that inflation was the main danger for contemporary society. Moreover he had himself tried, when Prime Minister, to solve the problem of inflation by a Prices and Incomes policy, at least since 19 July 1966.[1] But he also knew, even earlier, that the trade unions would oppose this policy. The first intimations of this major conflict came on 3 July 1966 when Frank Cousins resigned on the grounds that he could not accept the legislation foreshadowed in the Queen's speech of April 1966.[2] But

1. 'To help contain domestic inflation and to prevent increased costs and prices from hitting exports, I announced the staggering six-month standstill on wages, salaries and other types of income, followed by a further six months of severe restraints and a similar standstill on prices...Similar rules would apply for dividends and also for prices...', Wilson, op. cit., pp. 259–60.
2. 'It was not that he [Cousins] was opposed to any form of income policy. On the contrary he was ready to advocate a very simple approach under which we would impose a strict control of all significant prices...The view of my colleagues responsible for these matters confirmed my view of the impracticability of the idea and we were forced back on the legislation we

48

at the Labour Party conference in October 1966 the TGWU resolution opposing wage legislation was defeated. For some two years an equivocal compromise was thus maintained between the Labour Government and the trade unions, Mr Wilson believing, or hoping, that after October 1966 both Government and unions were following the same course. The following extract from his memoirs describing the occasion of the centenary of the trade unions, at Manchester in May 1969, is particularly important as it describes not only this basic equivocation, but also, and even more relevantly to this study, Mr Wilson's conception of the role of organized labour in contemporary British society.

I took the opportunity to draw the moral that with the accession of the trade unions movement over a century to the position of an estate of the realm, with inherent power and with the established right of consultation, it had the duty to show a responsibility with its power: 'The TUC has arrived [he said in his speech at the celebration of the Centenary]. It is an estate of the realm, as real, as potent, as essentially part of the fabric of our national life, as any of the historic estates. It is not easy for many within a movement that grew out of revolt to accept all the implications of a role that now is creative, consultative, and, in the central economic struggle in which this nation is involved, decisive. Influence and power carry with them the duties of responsibility. Never has this been more clearly illustrated than in the historic decision of the Trade Union Congress, fifteen months ago, to accept the need for an incomes policy...' I then drew the moral in terms of the parliamentary struggle over incomes legislation: while in the longer term the voluntary system alone provided the solution to our national problems, in the short-term we needed both the voluntary system and the backing of statutory

had announced. Frank could not accept it...At 11 a.m. on Sunday July 3rd he came to see me to say that he had decided to resign and it was clear that I could not talk him out of it.' ibid., p. 245.

safeguards. This part of my speech, it seemed to me, was less enthusiastically received.[1]

The last act of the drama between the Labour Government and the trade unions was played at the 18 June 1969 meeting of the Cabinet in which it was decided not to proceed with punitive legislation.[2]

When, in 1972, the Heath Government fell back on a Prices and Incomes policy (with the emphasis on the latter), Mr Wilson, as leader of the Opposition, was justifiably sceptical of the success of the 'new' measures. Above all, he was only too aware of the rapid emancipation of the trade unions, especially of their detectable emancipation from the political tutelage of the Labour Party. For tactical reasons, but more important still, out of a deep conviction which he shared with his party as a whole, he did not hesitate to align with the unions in opposition to the Government. He chose to try to defeat his *alter ego*, the new Prime Minister, in the same fight in which he as Prime Minister had been defeated five years earlier, because as a socialist he believed that the future of democracy in an industrial society 'rested with' the continuation of the partnership between the trade unions and the Socialist Party.

One may wonder whether the increasing domination of the Labour Party by the TUC is condoned by the leaders of the party. To be sure they try, and hope, to see in it only the inevitable collaboration between the two (industrial and political) wings of the same movement – the political having for obvious reasons the leading position in this partnership. But the question which is asked here is whether, if they were actually faced with the harsher alternatives of direct, political domination by the trade unions' leadership, most of the leaders of the Party would accept this alternative. For historical reasons the Labour Party can never forget that it owes its birth to

1. Ibid., p. 533.
2. The episode is described by Mr Wilson thus, 'For good or ill we had accepted the views of the TUC but only because, under the catalytic action of our legislative proposals they had "moved forty years in one month".' ibid., p. 662.

the trade unions' need for an organ of parliamentary representation.[1]

But it is in the future prospects of democracy that there lie the most poignant reasons why the doctrinaires of the British Labour Party from the Webbs to Aneurin Bevan would accept that the trade unions assume the supreme political responsibility. This is the tragic evidence that whenever the political party of the working class has taken absolute control of the politics of the movement and of government, both democracy and trade unions have lost out – and tyranny was born. Where, however, as in the Scandinavian countries, the trade unions played a major part in the policy-making of a socialist government, they prospered, as did the democratic regime of the country as a whole.

Here we return to the question raised in an earlier part of this chapter.[2] This is the question of to what extent the contemporary British trade unions continue on a genuine course towards social democracy, and to what extent some segments might be manipulated from within by another political party. By this we mean, of course, the Communist Party, the old rival of the Labour Party[3] which, in all the countries where it has come to power, has dissolved the

1. For the history of the relations between the two organizations see Beer, op. cit.
2. See p. 28.
3. Sometimes depicted by Wilson himself in sombre colours: 'The House will be aware that the Communist Party, unlike the major political parties, has at its disposal an efficient and disciplined industrial apparatus controlled from Communist Party headquarters. No major strike occurs anywhere in this country in any sector of industry with which that apparatus fails to concern itself. It may be because of the political impotence of the Communist Party that it has sought expression in industrial organizations. The bid that the Communists are making is directed to next year's conference at which the rules can be changed and at which steps can also be taken to change the full-time officers...also to secure what is at present the main political and industrial objective of the Communist Party – the destruction of the Government Prices and Incomes policy.' Harold Wilson's speech in the House of Commons, 20 June 1966, quoted in his *Memoirs*, op. cit., p. 308.

socialist parties and reduced the trade unions to an insignificant role.

Since the banning of the Workers' Opposition in Russia in 1920, the communist parties which toe the CPSU line have been opposed, for obvious reasons, to the institutionalization of workers' control and to the emancipation of the trade unions from the party's control. The functional emancipation of organized labour in industrial-technological societies thus presents a threat to the dictatorship of the communist parties in power. Many Western communist parties adopt a similar line, albeit not openly. This opens great strategic opportunities for the modern Socialist Parties. The Italian, French, German and Scandinavian socialist parties have already pronounced themselves in favour of workers' participation in industry. The British Labour Party, now more open than ever before to the influence of the trade unions, has put a new emphasis on nationalization and workers' control into its programmes and manifestoes, and has taken a definite turn towards the 'syndicalist' attitude of the trade unions. The question remains whether some communist-dominated British trade unions might not in reality favour the subordination of the Labour Party to the state. This would be a sad reward for those socialist leaders who would relinquish their power to the unions in order to further syndicalist freedom.

Be that as it may, what is sure is that the principal concern of the leadership of the Labour Party is to save the Labour Movement as a whole, under any circumstances and by whatever means.

But here one is faced with a dilemma of a perhaps different kind, but nevertheless crucial to the future evolution of the Labour Party and socialist parties in general. These parties, which were born as, and ultimately still are, the parliamentary representation of the trade unions, live and die by their association with Parliament, indeed with a powerful and active Parliament. A non-, extra-, or worse still, anti-parliamentary political party might be called a Party, but will be as different from the German, Swedish or current British socialist parties, as these latter are from the communist parties of Poland, East Germany or Czechoslovakia. It is Parliament, and its sense of pluralistic and competitive opposition, which gives real weight and significance to the *Parliamentary* Labour Party. Their association is more than reciprocal, it is their mutual *raison d'être*. No one would deny that political parties are by now a most important representative institution in the Western democracies. Nor would anyone deny that parliaments, even of the Westminster model, need modernization. But the legitimate exertion to save the Party, rightly seen as the agent of unity of the movement and as the vehicle of social democracy, must go together with parallel efforts to save Parliament as well.

It is significant that Mr Wilson chose as the motto of his book *The Labour Government 1964–1970* a passage from Aneurin Bevan's last speech in the House of Commons, the first paragraph of which states:

There is one important problem facing representative Parliamentary government in the whole of the world where it exists. It is being asked to solve a problem which so far it has failed to solve: that is, how to reconcile Parliamentary popularity with sound economic planning. So far, nobody on either side of this House has succeeded, and it is a problem which has to be solved if we are to meet the challenge that comes to us from other parts of the world and if we are to grout and to buttress the institutions of Parliamentary government in the affections of the population…

This raises the question of whether the Labour Party, being both a parliamentary and an extra-parliamentary body, would not have to sacrifice some of its traditional commitments to Parliament in order to follow the trade unions in their syndicalist ways. Mr Wedgwood Benn, for instance, in his *New Politics*, concentrates primarily on saving the Party, if necessary by further subordinating it to the extra-parliamentary body. Parliament itself would have to be adjusted to the new politics. When one follows Mr Benn's arguments further, one sees that it is Parliament, and the process of representation of which Parliament is the keystone and the symbol, which he singles out as the more obsolescent of the two institutions. To give only one example: 'Perhaps the hardest thing for politicians to understand is that government no longer rotates entirely around

Parliament and the old cycle of inner party policy formulation – intense electoral propaganda – voters' mandate and legislative implementation, important as they are'.[1] The work offers two immediate solutions by which some new blood of 'direct decision-making' could be injected into the exhausted parliamentary democracy; but the major, even if less immediate, solution lies in the rejuvenation of the party, seen as the major organizational link of the future.

Two immediate solutions are public referenda and a public opinion institute 'which should act as an independent agent for assessing and reporting the national view *before* Parliament reached its final decision on some issues' (his italics). But these two solutions have a rather negative relevance for the issue of the viability of Parliament. Parliament, already outflanked as the central embodiment of sovereignty by the extra-parliamentary decision-making of the corporate forces, and forced to compete with such other arenas of consultation as polls, televized debates, etc., would be handicapped still further if premonitory national consultations by computers were institutionalized.

After the Conferences of 1970–73, the Taverne case[2] and the un-

1. Benn, op. cit., p. 12.
2. Dick Taverne is the former Labour member of Parliament for Lincoln, now 'Social-Democrat' who won the seat in 1962 with the highest ever Labour majority in Lincoln, and again in 1966. He lost the seat in October 1974. In his book *The Future of the Left*, he states that ever since 1968 he has felt that the Prices and Incomes Policy was to become the most difficult problem to be solved by the Wilson Government, coinciding with the beginning of the domination of the Left wing of the Party. At the time, the request by the Wilson Government to join the European Community was not an apple of discord within the Labour Movement. 'The Lincoln Party knew I was strongly in favour. I came across no strong feelings against.' But when on 6 October 1971 the Labour Party Conference in opposition voted against the entry by 5 to 1, he voted in defiance of the Parliamentary Labour Party whip and together with 68 other members, for entry. He was dismissed on 16 June 1972 at a meeting of the Lincoln General Management Committee. He announced his resignation at the end of the 1972 Labour Party Conference: 'The Chairman, Anthony Wedgwood Benn, went out of his way to denounce me. Benn said...that

easy reconciliation effected during the joint opposition to the Heath Government and its Industrial Relations Act, it became clear that the Labour Movement had entered a phase in which the Parliamentary Labour Party was dominated by the trade unions. Today it is dominated directly by the imperative political statements of union leaders, and indirectly by the attitudes of unflinching solidarity with the unions shown by the leadership of the Party in general, especially by some 'left-wing' personalities from that leadership. In practice, decisions taken by the party Conference (where 700,000 members of the Labour Party are represented as against 6,000,000 members of the trade unions) are mandatory for the Labour Party as a whole, and for the Parliamentary Labour Party in particular; the decisions of the conference can only be altered by the next one, or by extraordinary conferences especially summoned. Thus, for the whole duration of the yearly mandate these decisions of the Conference are operative, whatever the circumstances of Parliamentary struggles and strategy, and whatever the pressures of unforeseen developments or new ideas thrown up during that year. The Parliamentary Labour Party as a whole is given an imperative mandate by the Conference and should therefore act in Parliament in such a way as to ensure that the interests of the Party prevail over those interests which might be presented as 'national' or 'public'.

As for the individual MP, apart from being bound by the decisions of the Conference, he is bound by the more direct mandate

---

I was a candidate invented by the media and that the Labour movement would take on and defeat this new threat to democracy...The printers should see to it that the truth was published...' He won the seat by a majority of 13,000 votes. He considers that this was a most significant development, first, in the continuing discussion on the right of the MP to be a *representative* and not simply a *delegate*, and secondly, in bringing into the open the domination of the Labour Party by the 'industrial wing'. 'The Party has almost become the voice of some of the union leaders. Indeed, sometimes it acts like a minor member of the Trade Unions Congress terrified of disciplined action.' (Dick Taverne, *The Future of the Left*, London, 1974, pp. 133-4).

of his constituents who made his election possible and who paid his expenses. Thus in principle he cannot modify or change his views on old or new issues, and only seldom, as in the case of some Labour MPs on the issue of Europe in November 1972, can he uphold his view of the 'national interest' in opposition to the views held by the Labour Movement. Even then, if his constituency chooses to take him to task he can come, like Taverne, to grief.

This of course does not run contrary to the tradition of the Labour Party. Even Attlee in 1945 acknowledged that the PLP had complete discretion in its conduct of Parliamentary business 'but within the programme adopted by the annual party conference'.[1] The question arises whether at this particular juncture of British politics, when the very structures of the parliamentary regime are challenged and when Party is frequently put above Parliament, the strong tendency towards political emancipation of the trade unions will not affect the Labour Party more than ever before.

Finally, it should be added that a possible break between the Party and the trade unions in Britain is unlikely to occur in the near future. This is so because of what might be called their solidarity in maintaining an old ideology. The fact is that the contemporary ideology of British socialism is state socialism, and until recently both the Parliamentary Labour Party and the trade unions have defined socialism as the means of achieving state ownership and control of the means of production, and of establishing on this basis an egalitarian society. It is only recently that syndicalism, or guild socialism or what Durkheim called workers' socialism, has come back into the doctrinal modulations of the Labour Movement. But the British trade unions do not seem to be worried by the inherent contradiction between the two brands of socialism which they simultaneously advocate – but which between them contain the great dilemma of contemporary Marxism-Leninism. For the time being the British trade unions seem to uphold 'nationalization' as their double postulate; i.e. nationalization of the industries under state-ownership, and national, as against international or European

1. Beer, op. cit., p. 89.

socialism. This double postulate is bound when applied to lead to a particularly intensive concentration of power in the hands of the state, the corollary of which, if successful, can only be the crushing of the corporate forces – including the unions – under its might. How aware the British trade unions already are of this danger to syndicalism, only the future will show.

The confrontation of 1974

When Mr Heath, in the autumn of 1972, offered the trade unions collaboration with the Government and with the CBI in direct economic policy-making, the chances that the unions would accept wholeheartedly were slim. This was true, firstly, because in the legalistic phase of his government Mr Heath had been defeated indirectly by the ineffectiveness of the Industrial Relations Act, and directly by the Wilberforce capitulation to the first miners' strike (January–February 1972). Secondly the trade unions, which generate a functional antipathy to any Government, had by then a special antipathy to Mr Heath's, because it had tried, in earnest, to curb their power, and had failed.

While the negotiations at No. 10 Downing Street between the three economic partners were proceeding, a new miners' strike was already looming on the horizon. Commentators have argued ever since about whether this was a political or an industrial strike – and it was on this issue that the leaders of the unions gave contradictory answers. The official versions from both sides, and especially from the side of the trade unions, varied considerably, thus leaving the public with the impression that the miners were divided between moderates (Mr Gormley) who held industrial views and militants (Mr McGahey) who held political views. Moreover it ultimately seemed that the principal dialogue had been held between the Prime Minister and the Communist Vice-President of the NUM – who allegedly told Mr Heath that the purpose of the strike was directly political and aimed at overthrowing his Government and the Prices and Incomes Policy.

For the purpose of this study it will be sufficient to quote here a statement made in March 1973 by the 'moderate' leader of the NUM, Mr Gormley, at the special TUC Conference in London.

We believe we can no longer carry on as a responsible organization, just expressing our opposition to Government policy and submitting alternatives, without having the necessary ambition to do something positive if it does not change the Government's direction.

Of course, there will be many critics who will say that this would be an attempt to get the trade union movement to use its industrial strength to defeat the Government and thereby bring about a General Election. But we see nothing that could be called anarchy in such a decision, because, after all, by our failure to approach the issues as a united body, we are not stopping strikes, and every strike at the moment is not really against the employers. It is against the Government policy and therefore can be termed a political strike, so that what we are asking is that if there is to be a political action of this kind it should be done on a completely united basis.

We believe the Movement is crying out for this type of lead, particularly when it sees such unions as the Civil Service unions, National Union of Teachers, and public employees and others now becoming involved in industrial action in an unprecedented way, because they are feeling very frustrated in the present political climate.

Therefore we believe that now...the time is ripe for the Congress to pass a resolution which would show the Government that we as a trade union movement really mean what we say when we make protestations of opposition to their policies. Without this expression of action we believe the trade union movement in general becomes more and more discredited and its opinions are not taken seriously enough.[1]

1. *The Times*, 6 March 1973.

The unlikelihood of the trade unions agreeing to collaborate fully and responsibly within a *statutory* Prices and Incomes Policy was accentuated in the autumn of 1973. The months of October 1973 to March 1974 were a political tornado for Western Europe and for Britain, the vortex of which was the Arab-Israeli war of October 1973. The war accelerated the Damoclean threat of sharp price rises and reductions in oil exports from the Arab states. In turn this caused the energy crisis, the principal factor both in Britain's economic and subsequent political crisis, and also in the structural crisis of the European Community. These world-wide developments gave a new and violently centrifugal twist to British and European politics, and increased the centrifugal trends already at work within each of these two spheres. The pressure from without exacerbated the pressures from within. In the British case, although it was clear to everyone that the energy crisis was an external and, rightly or wrongly, unforeseen development, its effect was to exacerbate the conflictual relations between the British trade unions and the Heath Government. Both sides seemed to become more fixated than ever before on the other and, as it were, to hold it exclusively responsible for developments which, in reality, were playing havoc with both of them from very far distant and more potent quarters. This brought the conflict rapidly to a dramatic end.

In the obsessive relationship thus created, both the National Union of Mineworkers and to some extent ASLEF, supported by the massive Trades Union Congress as a whole, and, on the other hand, the British Government supported by the majority of Parliament, played a cat-and-mouse game of tactical moves and countermoves. Each watched the other, preparing its next move well in advance in an inevitable escalation of measures.[1] Thus, when on 4 February, 81 per cent of the miners voted in favour of a strike, their ultimate point of escalation was reached. But on 7 February, Mr

1. For instance in July 1973, some good three months before Stage Three of the statutory Incomes and Price's Policy was announced, the National Union of Mineworkers' Conference resolved that a wage increase of 35% should be asked for Stage Three. It also asked for a change in government

Heath doubled his options, as he believed, by announcing that elections would be held on 28 February 1974.

In fact, the election was not fought on the miners' strike issue alone. The debate ranged from relations between Britain and Europe to world inflation, the world energy crisis, and international relations as a whole. It touched on the more chronic domestic problems, especially spiralling prices. But the issue to which the Government wanted to draw the attention of the electorate – the miners' strike – was not so much a special issue by itself as a symptom of the overall issue of relations between sectional and national interests and power groups. 'In a society such as ours,' Mr Robert Carr said during the electoral campaign, 'which is both free and highly industrialized, it is inevitable and in principle right that some sections possess such power. And in fairness to the miners it needs to be remembered that they are by no means the only people to have this degree of power. But with possession of such great power goes an awesome responsibility to use it with great caution and moderation. That is why the issue in this dispute goes beyond the normal scope of industrial conflict, raises the basic question at the heart of any democratic society, namely – who wields power and under what degree of constraint – who governs the country and by what means?'

The answer to this question in an industrial, half-representative, half-corporate society could not be given by means of electoral consultation. An election is a means, or indeed *the* means, of representation and deliberation. But direct action is the result of corporate action, and as such it is as unlikely to be impeached or countered by means of representation as an acute physical condition can be cured by psychological means. It is true that an overwhelming mandate

---

and elected Mr McGahey, a forceful Communist leader, as its Vice-President. The Government declared a state of emergency in November 1973 and on 13 December 1973 retaliated startlingly to the continuation of the overtime ban decided upon by the Executive of the NUM on 28 November, by instituting the three-day week with effect from 1 January 1974.

would have shaken the confidence of the strikers. But the mandate could not have been overwhelming because the strikes carried with them the workers' solid votes and those of the Left – and because of the very dilemma which was expressed in the popular phrase at the time: 'but even if the government is re-elected who will dig the coal, and who will run the trains?'

The great tactical advantage of corporate industrial action is that whereas those who conduct it can immediately affect society as a whole, society itself cannot affect them immediately; and if and when it does, society still hurts itself most, as the three-day week so dramatically proved.

Mr Heath lost the elections, but the Labour Party did not win them. No political institution won in the 'confrontation'. A comment made by Mr John Grigg in an article in *The Sunday Times* (7 April 1974) gave a perhaps overdramatized, but lucid interpretation of the event. Mr Grigg's final conclusion was that 'Mr Heath is the first British Prime Minister to have been brought down mainly by the political exploitation of industrial power. A big trade union has done to a Tory leader what big business could never have done to a Socialist'.

It is to 'big business' that we now turn.

Chapter Three

The enterprises and the national interest in Britain

Among British industrial, financial or commercial companies or enterprises the present study concentrates especially on those enterprises which because of their very large size and corporate organization have tried to adapt themselves to the new conditions for competitive industry and commerce, and which are often described as 'mature corporations'.

In a study of the hundred largest British corporate enterprises[1] Derek Channon shows that the process of adaptation consisted in enlargement, in product and geographic diversification and in a change to corporate management. The majority of large British enterprises have been able to diversify their production and to adopt a multi-divisional structure. This is particularly important in reducing the risk associated with a narrow range of products. Multi-divisional structure has also facilitated a more efficient use of resources, a better allocation of investments and a more effective use of modern managerial skills. These new conditions in turn enhanced technological development, of which most British industries were in great need. (With the exception of some sectors of the chemical, electrical, and engineering industries, British industries have been slower than their American, Japanese or Western German counterparts to profit from innovations arising from basic research.) Geographic diversification was more easily achieved than product diversification. Some of the largest traditional British industries such as drink, tobacco, or oil, remain in the category of single or dominant product, but are geographically diversified.

1. Derek F. Channon, *The Strategy and Structure of British Enterprises*, London, 1973.

This chapter, concerned with the part which enterprises play in the processes of national policy-making, includes in its consideration the major financial (as for instance banks) and commercial (as for instance chain-stores) corporations which not only compare favourably in terms of assets and size with the industrial corporations, but which possess or control manufacturing companies. It has also included the large public corporations which play such an important role in British industrial life. This is not an original departure. The public corporations are full members of the official representative organization of all British industries, the Confederation of British Industry (CBI, formerly FBI). Here is a list of the most prominent British enterprises, public and private.[1]

Private*	*Public*
British American Tobacco (M.G.)**	British Airports Authority***
British Insulated Callenders (M.D.)**	British Airways Corpn***
Plessey	British Railways Board***
Pilkington Brothers (M.D.)	British Steel Corpn***
†Bass Charrington (M.G.)	British Transports Dock Board***
†Distillers	British Waterways Board***
Tate and Lyle	Electricity Council and Boards***
†Imperial Tobacco (M.D.)	Gas Councils and Boards***
British Petroleum (M.D.)	National Bus Company***
Burmah Oil (M.D.)	National Coal Board***
Esso Petroleum (M.D.)	National Freight Corpn***
Shell Transport (Dutch-Br.) (M.D.)	Post Office***
British Leyland Motors (M.D)	Scottish Transport Group***
Ford Motor (M.D.)	Bank of England
†Rolls Royce (M.D.)	British Broadcasting Corpn
International Business Machine (M.D.)	Cable and Wireless
Cadbury Schweppes (M.D.)	

1. The private corporations are selected from Dr Channon's comprehensive and much longer list (op. cit.) pp. 52–63; the public corporations, from the list included in Merlyn Rees, *The Public Sector in the Mixed Economy*, London, 1973, pp. 125–6.

Private*	Public

Private*

H. J. Heinz (M.D.)

Nestle (M.G.)
Rank Hovis McDougall (M.D.)
†Unigate (M.D.)
Unilever (Dutch-Brit.)
Dunlop Pirelli (M.D.)
Fisons (M.D.)
Imperial Chemical Industries
   (M.D./M.G.)
Beecham Products (M.D./M.G.)
Rio Tinto Zinc (M.G.)
Guest Keen and Nettlefold (M.D.)
Hawker Siddeley Group
Tube Investment (M.D.)
General Electric (M.D./M.G.)
Courtaulds (M.D.)
Reed Paper
Rank Organization (M.D.)

Banks

Lloyds Bank
Barclays Bank
Westminster Bank
Midland Bank
Hill Samuel Bank
Hambro Bank
Schroders Bank

Public

Commonwealth Development
   Corpn
Covent Garden Market Authority
Housing Corpn
Independent Television Authority
National Dock Labour Board
National Film Finance Corpn
National Ports Council
National Research Development
   Corpn
New Town Development Corpn
Sugar Board

Electricity Board for Northern
   Ireland
Northern Ireland Housing Trust
Northern Ireland Transport Co.

North of Scotland Hydro-
   Electric Boards***
South Scotland Electricity Board
Scottish Special Housing Assn***

---

* It will be noticed that whereas most of the largest public corporations are listed here, only some fifty major private corporations have been included. **M.D. designates multi-divisional by product, M.G. multi-divisional by geography. ***Nationalized public corporations. †Refers to those corporations which are not multi-national.

What all these enterprises have in common, is that they are all by definition in pursuit of profit, or what is called in commercial language *maximizing return* and in the parlance of public corporations *'financial objectives'*.[1] A private enterprise lives or dies by its performance and efficiency. Similarly with the public enterprises: although most of the goods produced and most of the services delivered are considered to be essentially and primarily of 'public' or 'national' interest, it is still by its 'returns' or achievement of its financial objectives that a public corporation is ultimately assessed.

As the enterprise exists by its exterior performance it detaches itself from its collective interior substance, and becomes a juridical subject of its own. It is personified in its managers, or technostructure. The employees, who organize themselves within the enterprise as unions or workers' councils or both, see the enterprise as distinct from them, although they have a direct stake in its performance, and sometimes link their own existence with its geographic location, as in the case of Rolls-Royce in Derbyshire, Upper Clyde in Scotland, and mines in South Wales from which the workers refused to be 'redeployed'. Whether privately or publicly owned, the enterprise is also distinct from its owners, and is considered in juridical and political relations as an entity. Opinions differ here on the extent of this distinction. While J. K. Galbraith in his book *Economics and the Public Purpose*[2] again stresses that the power of the stockholders is nil, Robin Marris's theory of 'managerial capitalism'[3] is based on the principle that although the capitalists still influence the managers, it is the latter whose first concern is the growth and success of the firm, regardless of how much of its returns are shared afterwards among the stockholders. The

1. In turn defined in the 1961 White Paper on the 'Financial and economic obligations of the nationalised industries', as 'the aim to balance their accounts over a period of five years, after providing for interest and depreciation at historic cost.' Rees, op. cit., p. 178.
2. London, 1974.
3. *The Economic Theory of 'Managerial Capitalism'*, New York, 1964.

65

modern corporation's essential autonomy is conditional upon its success. This is true also of the public corporations which must have autonomy of action if they are to be accountable for their 'financial objectives', although the question of how 'autonomous' a public corporation should be is the perennial British constitutional dilemma ever since the Haldane Committee of 1919 on the 'machinery of government'. Moreover, and as sometimes happens in socialist countries even nationalized enterprises managed by workers' councils can oppose the interests of the socialist state, or the communist party, as a whole.

The national or public effect of the functioning of the enterprise is based on the classic assumption that both its products and its services originate from, and its profits come back to, the national economy and the national market as a whole. The identification of the enterprise with the national interest (Mr Charlie Wilson's contention that 'what is good for General Motors is good for the United States', or Mr John Davies's contention that 'the aggregation of profit produces that accretion to total wealth which is a principal objective of national or international policy'[1]) is founded on this assumption. This leads to explicit collaboration between the national economy – as represented by Government – and individual enterprise; to joint-ventures into opening or enlarging fields of production which are considered profitable from both points of view. It is from this angle that the term enterprise links directly with entrepreneur and entrepreneurship (in the sense that Schumpeter gave to these terms), whereby the private interest *undertakes*, or takes charge of, an operation for the benefit of society or the nation as a whole.

But this implicit assumption does not, on the one hand, change the ultimate purpose of the enterprise as enterprise: that of maximizing return. On the other hand, the growth and spread of the multinational corporations has helped more than anything else to show how fragile is the equation of nationally located enterprise and national interest. The very principle of the multi-national corpora-

1. Quoted in Edmund Dell, *Political Responsibility and Industry*, London, 1973, p. 48.

66

tion is to diversify geographically and by product in pursuit of the highest productivity and profit. For this purpose national boundaries are irrelevant, and obligations towards the respective nation-states secondary.

In a balanced study of the 'Politics of the multi-national corporations', Dennis Kavanagh outlined the following *potential* dangers for the nation-state in its relations with the multi-national corporations:

> First, by differential or transfer pricing across the states, companies are able to escape national fiscal controls, not least in the full payment of taxes...Second, states become too dependent for capital on the investment plans of large corporations...Third, there is the prospect that subsidiaries will be vehicles for the policies of the state in which ownership is incorporated. Restrictions on the independence of the host-state are clear-cut here and arise from the influence of US government policy on the parent company, and on the foreign state *via* subsidiaries. Fourth, there is the element of uncertainty. The subsidiaries of foreign owned companies are often located in sectors which are central to economic growth, technology or exports, while the traditional instruments for managing the national economy, such as tariffs, currency rates, monetary policy and so on are less effective. Finally by switching about their enormous sums of capital between different units of enterprise the corporations are able to undermine the strength of a country's currency. This tidal wave of international liquid funds or 'hot money' (exceeding the total money supplies of Japan or Britain) fuels inflation.[1]

In the course of this chapter the problem of the multi-national corporations will be discussed from different aspects. Their role in the political crisis of 1974 will also be discussed. Here these *potential*

1. Dennis Kavanagh, 'Beyond autonomy' in G. Ionescu (ed.) *Between Sovereignty and Integration*, London, 1974. But see also Hugh Stephenson, *The Coming Clash: The Impact of the International Corporation on the Nation-State*, London, 1971.

political dangers described by Kavanagh only show that multi-national corporations are 'potentially' the most centrifugal corporate force in the economy of the nation-state.

Parallel with the problem of the relations between enterprises and the nation-state runs the problem of capital – the investments required by enterprises in order to function adequately and to produce, only later, the profit which is the goal of both capital and enterprise. As with enterprise, it is assumed that the profit made by capital benefits the entire national economy. The higher the profit the better for the national economy to which it ultimately returns. (Hence the theory that US-based multi-national corporations benefit the American economy.) From the analysis undertaken by W. B. Reddaway in his *Effects of U.K. Direct Investment Overseas*,[1] it appears that the location of the greater part of direct investment made by the major British corporations was in the white Commonwealth countries and the USA. The industries which invested there were the slow-growth industries like food, drink, and tobacco, and especially older industries with a relatively low technological content, primarily interested in sources of raw materials.[2]

Although Britain spent more on Research and Development in the sixties than other countries, one of the major differences between British industry and its US or French and German counterparts was the failure of British capital to invest sufficiently and profitably in capital equipment. The average ratio of capital investment to numbers of employees in British industry remained low. One of the causes of this reluctance of national capital to invest in national industry, and therefore to modernize it, was, according to industrialists, the apprehension caused by the cyclic 'stop-go' economic policies, and the disorderly state of industrial relations. It is true that this was partly compensated by foreign investment, and especially by American investment (sixty-six per cent of all foreign investment in the UK and ten per cent of the total goods produced in Britain). But the rhythm slackened in the sixties because of the disappointing performance of British industry as a whole. Perhaps

1. Cambridge, 1967.   2. Channon, op. cit., p. 81.

the most significant trend of capital migration occurred in 1973, during the first and only year of wholehearted British participation in the European Community. Whereas British capital in quest of profit migrated actively to Germany, France, Belgium or Italy, very little European capital in quest of profit came into Britain.

Thus the functional necessity for both enterprises and capital to be assessed through *returns of profit or loss* renders enterprise, once the ultimate profit or wealth of the national economy as a whole is questioned, a relatively centrifugal body in society. This characteristic was accentuated by the appearance of the giant corporations. For whereas small and middle-size companies are in need of national protection and can easily be controlled and made accountable to government, the giant corporations, private or public, matching the smaller nation-states in wealth, see collaboration with the national government as a matter of choice, and are hardly controllable by representative institutions. The autonomy of the enterprises is fully visible in the action of the giant corporations. Like the other corporate force, organized labour, they can impose their own decisions on the national economy, by investing in one industry and not in another, or in one country and not in another, by opening or closing plants according to their own plans (which might coincide with or be opposed to a nation's economic plans). Yet when, as in the case of Rolls Royce, they have to go into liquidation (whether because of poor performance or because of disadvantageous links with foreign capital), the national economy has to intervene and help them continue to work.

This of course is even more the case with the nationalized industries and the public corporations – which are subsidized by the Government, but which ultimately, as the abundant literature on the subject shows,[1] are not properly accountable either to Government or Parliament. Although in the case of the nationalized industries the balance between the financial independence of the enterprise and dependence on the national economy tips towards the latter, that

1. See especially R. Kelf-Cohen, *British Nationalisation 1945-73*, London, 1973, which also contains an excellent bibliography.

does not mean that control by parliament of these enterprises is any more satisfactory. Moreover, the pressure of the workers and the unions is, for obvious reasons, more powerful and effective than in the private industries. The managers are exposed to opposing pressures from the government and the workers. This has of late produced a stronger tendency toward intervention and direct decision-making by the government in the nationalized industries.

But this tendency has not – at least not yet – improved the *performance* of the nationalized corporations as corporations; since most of them are still 'in the red'. (This is, of course, also due to the fact that some of the major industries which have been nationalized, like mining and railways, were old and declining industries in need of massive investment.) Thus such events have in turn, aggravated the process of inflation. But the dilemma is not specific to nationalized industries in Britain alone or indeed in capitalist countries as a whole. An analogous dilemma can be found at the very heart of the economic reforms experimented with in communist countries. There the very large modern enterprises, constantly enlarging in size because of the universal process of technological concentration and becoming giant 'trusts' or 'kombinats', seem destined to be, more than any socio-economic group including the still un-organized labour, the agents of an uncharacteristic process of hiving-off by the Marxist-Leninist state. This process might lead to an *ad hoc* economic decentralization, although it can also be argued that concentration at the top of the 'kombinats' can render the State and Party control easier. But the problem there is whether the new size and self-containment of the 'kombinats' would liberate them from the micro-economic controls of state and party, and whether their new effort to pave their own entrepreneurial way could still be reconciled with macro-economic socialist planning.

How enterprises influence decision-making

Modern enterprises influence in various ways the decision-making processes of national government in economic, financial and commercial matters which affect them. But modern enterprises also *impose* their own decisions by reducing, stopping, continuing or expanding their activities in the economic environment created by the policies of the government, *as well as* by modifying that environment by their own means.

Let us take first the processes of influence. When small and middle-sized enterprises represented the core of British manufacturing (now one hundred large enterprises account for sixty per cent of the net assets and sales of domestic manufacturing) they formed a community of interests and views usually described as 'business' or the 'business point of view'. The term is still in use, and still useful nowadays, although the business point of view is no longer the view of the majority of all the concerns, formulated by trade associations and councils, but is in reality the rarefied common views of the major corporations. In general, as far as attitude towards government and national economic policy is concerned, the fact that the expression of views is now more concentrated in the powerful Industrial Policy group formed by the chairmen of ICI, Dunlop, Shell, Distillers, etc. (and less representative of small business) does not make a great deal of difference. The fundamental attitudes of business towards government remain functionally perennial – and more often than not a small enterprise finds itself, with respect to government at least, in natural agreement with the views of big business.

The general philosophy of business, as expressed with continuity and clarity in journals such as *The Financial Times* or *The Economist*, is too well known to require lengthy exposition. It starts from the principle of necessary freedom for enterprise to consider its own profitability as the one objective criterion not only for enterprise, but also for the national interest. The state or government should watch the functioning of this spontaneous and mutual process, and *intervene* in it only in order to remove obstacles or interference which might obstruct it. The attitude of business towards governments and the other representative institutions is traditionally condescending and sceptical. Business believes that ultimately the welfare of the nation depends on itself – that politics, important and glamorous as it might be, is only the reflection of the real state of affairs of which business is or should be in charge. Government can – and should, in business's view – improve the general economic and financial environment, but no more.[1]

The public philosophy of the enterprises is centred around the principle of the state's obligation to facilitate rather than hamper the free running of the economy. This implies several major conditions which, although only too familiar, may be re-stated here. One condition is peace in the world, or at least, in Europe. This requirement has been since the First World War particularly significant for British businesses, and through them it exerted an important influence on British foreign policy between the two World Wars. Another condition is that the resources and means of the national economy should not be overburdened by taxation, and should not be diverted into the public sector. Reduction of taxation and of public expenditure are the obsessive slogans of this philosophy.

Business in modern British society requires the state to support, financially and otherwise, projects which are in their view of direct interest to the government. This is the continuation of what Edmund Dell felicitously calls *the imperial tradition*, i.e. the association between British trade and industry and the policies of the empire, with the Foreign Office and the Royal Navy as intermediaries in the joint ventures. But in an industrial-technological society and with government already intervening in the post-war mixed economy, business now expects it to underwrite the participation of enterprises in innovatory technological ventures with massive investments.[2] On

1. To take one example of the classic attitude of business towards modern government in Britain: 'Just as the pre-war economic establishment vastly underrated the ability of the government to influence unemployment by general financial policies, the post-war view vastly overrates its intellectuals. Concepts and ideas have indeed played a role in our troubles – not in solving them but in making them worse.' Samuel Brittan, 'Five fallacies of economic management,' *The Financial Times*, 22 November 1973.

2. 'The loss of empire as an instrument of demand management left Britain uncertain and divided between the *laissez-faire* instinct and the use of state power. But the imperialism was not worked out. If we were not to enjoy the prestige of empire, we would seek prestige through

the other hand, business expects the Government to interfere in the *inter-corporate* relations, the bilateral or indeed triangular relations between business, organized labour and local administration, only by explicit invitation. Thus while business as a whole presses the Government to contain the trade unions' wage push and to keep wages down, individual enterprises usually prefer to use direct means of collective agreement with their workers, even if it means paying higher wages. This applies also to the boards of the nationalized industries, as for instance the NCB.

The means of influencing policy-making that are open to business have been so laboriously examined by modern sociologists that they are now part of the folklore of modern populism. They need only be recalled for the sake of the overall picture. Insofar as the general philosophy of business is nearer to the general philosophy of the Conservative Party it is right to presume that the latter is the political ally of business. Yet this must be taken with the proviso that business is by its own declaration only interested in the party which can create the best economic conditions. When Labour governments seem able to fulfil these basic conditions more easily, and especially to bring effectiveness back into economic life, business collaborates with it as much as with the Tory Party. Moreover, socialist purists recognize with sadness that business has, especially since the end of the Second World War, established informal contacts with the Labour Party as good as those it traditionally had with the Tories.[1]

The socialist purists have also left no stone unturned in the exploration of the occult relations between business and government, especially Tory Government. 'Networks', 'filtrations', 'backgrounds' and 'connections', 'origins and education', of the 'élite' or of the top

---

advanced technology, by becoming leaders in aero-space and nuclear energy. Only with lavish state aid could it be done. Military requirements encourage its doing.' Dell, op. cit., p. 30.

1. See especially Ralph Milliband, *The State in Capitalist Society*, London, 1972.

'decision makers', have been furiously investigated – and the results form a complete atlas of the areas of intersection of political, social and economic personnel, and give a good, if crude, image of the *potency* involved in these relations (for, as in most sociological studies of power, it is only *potency* which is established and not the direct *power* of decision-making). The two most convincing approaches to be found in such studies are those bearing on the interchangeability of political and business personnel, and on the methods of consultation between government and business. Here is one example of each of the approaches, as drawn from *Power in Britain*,[1] one of the most recent exercises of the kind. They were chosen here for the reason that belonging as they do to a work essentially critical of the poor distribution of power in British society, they cannot be suspected of being deliberately benign.

In a study of 'the controllers of British industry', by Michael Barrat Brown, it is argued that with increasing state intervention in industry, the interchangeability of the personnel of industry and government has also increased. Chairmen of companies involved with government contracts such as Lord Chandos of AEI, Lord Monckton of the Midland Bank, Viscount Amery of Hudson's Bay and Lord Kilmuir of Plessey are seen to have come 'straight from cabinet office'. As for ex-ministers going to boards, they 'are legion'. The study underlines the development of top civil servants going straight to industry and finance. It also mentions 'the movement in the opposite direction: Sir Frank Kearton of Courtaulds invited by the Labour Government to head up the NEDC,' etc.[2]

As for the method of consultation, let us look at S. Aronovitch's study on 'The ruling class' in the same volume, which examines the *Minutes of Evidence to the Radcliffe Committee*. From the 1957 inquiry on the bank rate, Aronovitch learned that the cabinet as a whole, the Minister of Labour and the President of the Board of Trade played only a small role in the decision to increase the bank rate, which was actually made by the Committee of Treasury of the

1. John Urry and John Wakeford (eds.), *Power in Britain*, London, 1973.
2. ibid., p. 115.

Bank of England. It goes on to show by whom that committee was formed at the time.[1]

There are also the direct trade associations or promotional organizations from the formidable Confederation of British Industries,[2] the slightly obsolete Chambers of Commerce (but which of late have re-acquired some of their past influence in their dealings with local authorities), all the institutionalized industrial, financial and commercial groups at the national level, and finally the simple propaganda agencies like the *Economic League*, and *Aims of Industry*. With this one comes to the principal *bête noire* of populist, and for that matter, socialist political sociology, the domination of the media by capitalists. The Press Lords are all investigated and their manipulation of public opinion fully exposed. Mr Wedgwood Benn's criticisms of the media as they work now are particularly severe. His conclusion is that all media should be opened up to the participation

1. Ibid., p. 125. 'At the time of the Tribunal they were: C. F. Cobbold, Governor, related to the Hambro family of whom Sir Charles Hambro is a Director of the Bank (but not on the Committee of Treasury); H. C. B. Mynors, Deputy-Governor (whose brother was Temporary Principal H.M. Treasury in 1940, and who is related to the Brand family – of Lazards – and more distantly, to the Colvilles of Rothschilds); Sir G. L. Bolton, Executive Director at the time, who since then has become chairman of the Bank of London and South America, and a director of Consolidated Zinc Corporation, Sun Life Assurance Company of Canada and other concerns; G. C. Eley, chairman of British Drug Houses, British Bank of the Middle East, chairman of Richard Crittal, Director of Equity and Law Life Assurance Company and others; Sir John Hanbury Williams, chairman of Courtaulds – into which family the Hon. R. A. Butler married; Basil Sanderson, chairman of Shaw Saville and Albion Company and of the Aberdeen and Commonwealth Line, director of Ford Motor Company, Furness, Withy, Dalgety & Company, etc. and Minister of War Transport, 1941–45; and finally Lord Bicester, head of Morgan Grenfell, director of Shell, Vickers, etc.'

2. The FBI (now CBI) suggested in 1946 that 'Government give official recognition to effective trade associations and normally use them, and them alone, in dealing with the affairs of their industry as a whole', quoted in Nigel Harris, *Competition and the Corporate Society*, London, 1974.

in policy-making of all employees, including the liftman of the *Daily Express*. It is obvious that the best-selling newspapers are owned by business. But once more, it is easier to ascertain that there is a *potential* relation deriving from this fact of ownership than to establish the actual power of the Press Lords in influencing readers and publishing what they personally want to publish. It is also argued that both the press and the media have more of an entertainment effect than an indoctrinating influence. Threatened as the newspapers are now in their profitability, and therefore their viability as enterprises, they must, and do, concentrate above all on selling more copies and getting more advertising rather than on preaching lessons on economic and political matters. Good sensational stories serve these purposes much better than doctrines and ideologies. Besides, between the power of the advertisers and the power of the editors or editorial boards,[1] the Lords-owners are left with a shrinking margin of *direct* influence. The answer of Lord Beaverbrook to the Royal Commission on the Press in 1945, when he was asked why his papers had insisted until the very last moment that there would be no war in 1939 – that the advertisers wanted the impression of a prosperous peace to continue as long as possible – highlighted how even then, and in a particularly dramatic context, advertising was the most potent influence on the press. Thus more *indirectly* than directly, the general attitude of the national press towards the current government does reflect the business point of view, and originates from it.

What particular criticisms of government have been made by business in the industrial-technological era, say, since 1945? The usual answer to this question is that business, and not only British business, is generally critical of the constant orientation in favour of the public sector, of the seemingly irreversible tendency towards increased public expenditure, and of the handling of industrial relations. British business has also had special grievances. Like British organized labour it has been critical of the performance of British government and of British political personnel.

1. See Colin Seymour Ure; 'Editorial policy-making', in *Government and Opposition*, vol. 4, no. 4, pp. 427–525.

Lack of continuity in national economic policy since the war is due in great part to international events which have blown the national policies 'off course'. But it is also due to the constant internal interruption of national policies and to the constant re-formulation of new policies in contrary directions after short and inconclusive periods of trial. The 'stop-go' British economic policy is the object of business's major criticism of post-war government. 'The pattern of stop-go had been dysfunctional to industry, sharpening the cyclical movements of capital investment and undermining confidence in general. Within specific industries, especially consumer durables, the rapid changes in monetary policy had almost certainly had a deleterious effect on the long-term potential of these industries'.[1] British industry contrasts critically British post-war economic policy with the continuity in effort shown by a non-planning liberal economy like that of West Germany, or conversely by a planning economy like that of France both of which, 'blown off course' as they may have been by the same international events, have a relatively satisfactory record of continuity. It might be argued that in the case of France, this was due precisely to the increased authority of the government over the economy. In Britain it was business which had defeated the attempts of the Labour Government in 1945 to start planning in earnest. But by the sixties some business circles were beginning to have doubts about the advantages of a political system based on the alternation in power of two parties with different if not opposite economic approaches. The national elections, which every four or five years interrupt economic orientation, cause frequent reconsiderations which in turn cause new hesitations and finally new and precarious launchings of new policies in other directions. This explains, at least in part, why both a newspaper like *The Times*, representative of British opinion-forming circles, and Cecil King, a prominent journalist who had been a director of the Bank of England at the end of his career, should have openly expressed doubts, by the end of the sixties, on the effectiveness of the two party system. They drew attention to the disillusion of the

1. Channon, op. cit., p. 78.

British public in this respect and advocated a national or non-political government, and the formation of new, more modern political parties or the rejuvenation of the Liberal Party.

We turn now from the ways in which enterprises can *influence* national decision-making in Britain, to the ways in which they can directly *impose* their decisions on the national economy as a whole.

How enterprises impose their decisions

With the rise of great corporations goes the power extensively to enforce their will on society...and to influence the attitudes of the community and the action of the state.
J. K. Galbraith
Economics and the Public Purpose.

The enterprises or corporations impose their decisions on the national economies in three broad ways:
a) by controlling a national market through their oligopolistic division of it, and by manipulating the consumers through their marketing systems; b) by planning their production investments and supply of raw materials over long-term periods of economic policies of their own, in contrast with the short term, and frequently revised, economic policies of the states; and c) by choosing the country or the products towards which their plans and investments will be directed according to the higher profitability to be obtained from geographic and product-diversification.

These techniques by which the corporations are able to impose their decisions on the national economies have been too well studied to require further examination in detail. An entire literature, initially of American inspiration, has detected the growing impact of the giant corporations on the advanced industrial society (Berle, Galbraith, and Barber) and followed it to the present stage in which (some authors believe) modern society is already trying to 'subordinate' the corporation by means of social control (Daniel Bell, Kenneth Arrow, Milton Friedmann). The study of corporations or indeed of the 'corporate society' (a term under which Robin Marris, Adrian Wood and Tom Burns have gathered an Anglo-American group of authors), is now flourishing in Britain too. To be sure, the sociological-economic terminology of these authors does not directly correspond to the language in which a parallel political reasoning could be expressed, although they do speak, like political scientists, of the 'irresponsible political power' of corporations opposed to the public interest.[1] More specifically, sociological theories aim to comprehend the universal phenomenon of corporate society, without explicitly trying to distinguish the authentic features of corporations in particular countries other than America, for instance Britain.

Yet British corporations, especially when looked at from the point of view of their relationship with the national interest, naturally differ from the American models, and each of the three principal techniques listed above must be approached differently in the British context.

As far as oligopolies are concerned, although in the last decade or so the rhythm of concentration of enterprises in Britain has been significantly intensified, the image still differs greatly from that of the US. Whereas in the US slightly more than 500 firms account for eighty-three per cent of all corporate assets, in Britain in 1968, 1200 companies held seventy-one per cent of total assets.[2] And whereas in

1. 'If indeed the corporation and not the market decides how goods will be allocated, then the corporation's economic power is irresponsible. If the corporation is large then the pattern of these irresponsible economic choices is likely to have political and social consequences. Hence, Kaysen's serious charge that corporations possess irresponsible political power.' Joseph L. Bower, 'On the amoral organization,' in Robin Marris (ed.), *The Corporate Society*, London, 1974, p. 184.
2. Monopolies Commission, *A survey of mergers 1958–1968*, quoted in Channon, op. cit., p. 35. But Graham Bannock, *Juggernauts, the Age of the Big Corporations*, London, 1971, argues that 'the top 100 corporations in Britain probably accounted in 1968 for over fifty per cent of all profits, a considerably higher percentage of total assets, and about one third of total employment of all industrial and commercial companies', p. 39.

the US two-thirds of the manufacturing industries are highly concentrated,[1] in Britain only five industries (electrical engineering, drink, vehicles, textiles and paper, publishing and printing) show a high degree of concentration. Here it must not be forgotten that in Britain the public sector of nationalized industries (steel, coal, telephone, electricity etc.) is exceptionally large when compared to that of the US. Obviously this concentration by nationalization increases the absolute amount of concentration in British industry. But obviously too this very fact renders the fundamental pattern of the relations between the governments and the respective groups of corporations entirely different in the UK and in the USA. This seems to be so obvious as not to need mention, yet it would be as wrong to surmise that public corporations are deprived of autonomy, and therefore to exclude them from the corporate oligopolies, as it would be to accept the premises of the American theory of the corporate 'irresponsibility' as fully valid for the mixed economies of Western Europe as well. Besides, one must reckon with the size and volume of the two economies within which the American and British corporate oligopolies respectively make their impact (for, as Hugh Stephenson points out, 'in almost all the mature industries, the biggest European company is smaller than any of the three top companies in that same industry, based on the US.')[2]

1. Richard J. Barber, *The American Corporation*, London, 1970, p. 23.
2. Here is a selective sample of British and American corporate performance in 1968 in a few industries:

Corporation	Sales	Net Profit	Invested Capital
Steel		(in £1,000)	
US United States Steel	1890	106	1395
US Bethlehem Steel	1193	66.9	785
GB British Steel	1071	−9.3	829
Oil			
US Standard Oil	5870	531	4110
GB/D. Royal Dutch Shell	3840	390	3385
US Mobil	2592	179	1695
US Texaco	2275	349	2258
GB BP	1358	101	1211

The political background must also be taken into consideration. The relative slowness of the British enterprises to organize themselves, like their American counterparts, into unassailable oligopolies, is due in part to economic reasons but also, in part, to the ambivalent attitude of British governments since the war, both Conservative and Labour, towards competition. Two recent books by a Conservative and a Socialist British author have examined the hesitations and the ultimate indecision of their respective political parties towards the problem of industrial concentration and competition. One, by Nigel Harris,[1] describes with sadness the drifting of the purely 'competitive' non-interventionist doctrine of the Conservative Party into a kind of permanent, but half-hearted, interventionism created by the welfare state. The other by Edmund Dell describes the socialist reasons why the Labour Party in power has encouraged competition and intervened against further concentration in industry.[2] Be that as

Automobiles			
US General Motors	9480	721	4065
US Ford Motors	5865	261	2060
US Chrysler	3102	121	1833
GB British Leyland	907	19.2	628
Aerospace			
US McDonnell Douglas	1505	39.5	191
US Boeing	1365	34.6	338
US Lockheed	924	18.6	391
GB Rolls Royce	320	8.8	162
GB British Aircraft	191	4.2	24

Based on material appearing in the 1968 Fortune Directories, © 1968, Time Inc.

1. Harris, op. cit.
2. Dell, op. cit. Mr Dell's book makes fascinating reading, especially in conjunction with Andrew Knight's book on *Private Enterprises and Public Intervention*, London, 1974. Both study the abortive mergers in the textile industry of ICI-Courtaulds and Courtaulds-English Calico. The authors analyse them from opposite points of view; on the one hand the then Socialist Minister having to decide against the mergers, and on the other hand the then executive of Courtaulds interested in absorbing Calico.

it may the fact is that the two parties have produced alternating and intermittent policies, or ultimately, a lack of policy.

Another factor affecting the study of the relations between enterprises and the national interest in the US and Great Britain respectively is that most of the giant multi-national corporations are US-located, and their profits ultimately US-bound. This affects the relations of these corporations with the British national interest and the American national interest in opposing ways. It is true that the British subsidiaries of US multi-national corporations are fully integrated in the general progress of British industry, and moreover that without their participation, the 'growth' of British industry would have been even more anaemic. It is also true that the giant US-based multi-nationals maintain ambiguous relations with the US national economy. It has been convincingly argued that until the late sixties the US-based multi-nationals failed to bring back to their country the whole of their international profits, which amounted to some thirty per cent of their total profits. These accumulated profits accrued to the floating Euro-market, and because of the geographically diversified production of the US multi-nationals US exports as such have steadily declined. Finally it is true to say that the ever-expanding British-based multi-nationals[1] operate as successfully and as ruthlessly outside their own national boundaries as the US-based multi-nationals. But none of these important considerations can change the fact that the US-based multi-national corporations active in the UK have a more independent attitude towards British national interests than the British-owned enterprises have. The cases of open conflict of interest between the British government and Ford on the question of the Ford-Pinto car, which was first to be produced in Britain, then in Germany and finally went back to Ohio; with IBM on their diversification of models between Britain (1970), France, Germany and Spain; with Chrysler when it took over Rootes, and with Reed when it took over IPC, are only a few examples.

1. 'The subsidiaries of British-based companies in other countries were already, by 1970, manufacturing twice as much as the whole of British domestic industry's direct exports.' Stephenson, op. cit., p. 5.

Insofar as planning is concerned, all British enterprises suffer from the fact that, whereas a modern corporation must plan for at least five or ten years ahead, the constant changes and reversals in British economic policies bring uncertainty and incoherence to long-term activities.[1] This compares unfavourably with the situation in the United States, where the overall buoyancy of the economy and the high rate of investment caused by over-capitalization and confidence in the American economy (although US population has increased by fifty million, the per capita income has gone up by fifty per cent in the last two decades), facilitate the long-term 'partnership' between the state and the corporations. Most of the US government's largest programmes in the principal or new areas of production are planned jointly with the corporations to which the respective 'contracts' have been given and with whom the US government shares in various proportions the investment expenses.[2]

This leads to what Galbraith calls 'the planning system' which he opposes to 'the neo-classical market system'. He describes how in the latter the producers who want a modicum of stability must act collectively to influence the government. 'Legislators do not always respond. If action is taken, it is often taken apologetically for it is

1. In November 1960 a Brighton Conference of the (then) FBI, in the presence of the chancellor, demonstrated deep dissatisfaction amongst a group of important businessmen. 'Large firms must plan five to ten years ahead, it was said, but the government did not plan and was thus compelled to intervene in the economy so that company plans were disorganised.' Harris, op. cit., p. 240.
2. To take one example: 'Faced with the missile challenge the Air Force placed full responsibility for overall systems design and technical direction in an outside firm that directed and co-ordinated the work of a number of associate contractors. For this job Space Technology Laboratories, then a division of the Rasno-Wooldridge Corporation, was chosen. By deciding to act this way, the Air Force had effectively delegated the entire job of developing an ICBM system to STL, which literally became a staff arm of the Defence Department. It exercised such intensive control over a family of contractors that for all practical purposes it, not the government, was the manager of the entire Air Force ballistic missile program in its most crucial period.' Barber, op. cit., p. 193.

recognized that the established economies disapprove. In the planning system, in contrast, the firm wins its control over prices automatically...by being large. Similarly over output...there are also things for which it needs the support of the state. But its approach is not to the legislative but to the bureaucracy.'[1] 'The planning system exists in the closest association with the state. The obvious core of this relationship is the large expenditure by the government for its products. The planning system has a powerful commitment to independence from the state except where public action is required.'[2]

Allegorical as Galbraith's description might be, it does, in broad outline, characterize the economic and political situation in the US. But in order to assess the same theory in the British context one has to bear in mind (apart from the specific differences in concentration, planning and impact of the multi-nationals between the two countries) the contrast in the backgrounds of the respective economies, their present conditions and their outlooks for the future.

From the economic point of view, the metropolitan market of Great Britain is territorially small and, with the exception of coal and until the recent discovery of oil in the North Sea, almost barren in industrial raw materials. The overseas market has continually shrunk since decolonization and the subsequent jettisoning of Commonwealth preferences. In contrast with this the US territorial market is vast and rich and its overseas market has continually expanded.

Financially, British capital was in any case insufficient for the formidable task, after the Second World War, of modernizing British industry, already lagging behind that of other national economies. British capital was also reluctant to commit itself to investing mainly in national industry, which threatened to become unprofitable owing to new international competition, and seemed particularly unappetizing because of Britain's system of industrial relations. The formidable political combination of an emancipated trade union movement and a popular Labour Party made investment in Britain a particularly doubtful proposition in the eyes of industrial

1. Op. cit., pp. 49–50.   2. Ibid., pp. 155–6.

profit-seekers. From all these points of view the situation in America was different from that of Britain.

The relative lack of interest in British industry of British capital, the growing technological gap, and the general tardiness in modernization also had a bad effect on the quality of management in Britain. After long and painful hesitations by the end of the fifties action was taken to modernize and improve the performance of British management to make it competitive with other national industries. The American firm of consultants, McKinsey & Co., was called in by company after British company to modernize their managements. America was in the advantageous position of possessing, ever since the beginning of the technological revolution, the most modern management in the world, fully-equipped to deal with new technologies and specially trained to cope with modern methods of diversification and corporate administration.

Finally the massive and gradually expanding public section in the British mixed economy[1] – carving, as it were, out of the body of British industry as a whole some of its principal sectors and branches – accentuates the dissimilarity of the two industries. The homogeneous comprehensiveness of all branches of industry in the American private sector of the economy renders intercommunication in the American capitalist industry much easier than its British or for that matter, Italian counterparts, where private industries are limited to some sectors and are unable to expand in or collaborate freely with the public sectors. Public opinion in Britain as well as in the USA fails to recognize that the growth of the public sector does have the effect of increasingly reducing inequality and social injustice, and thus of rendering the very idea of public interest easier to visualize than it is in the USA (where it is still based on and attained only through the assumption that the growth and profits of enterprise are ultimately beneficial to society as a whole). But the captains of industry find the conditions of work in a mixed economy very difficult.

1. This is discussed at length in Andrew Shonfield, *Modern Capitalism*, London, 1966.

These obvious differences between the conditions of British and American enterprises have been touched on here in order to draw two conclusions. One is that the general theories of the corporation and corporate society, while universally valid in their prediction of the increasing emancipation and power of enterprises in industrial-technological society, must be *comparatively* and specifically applied to the different contexts. For all the particular reasons listed above it is obvious that while both American and British corporations are increasingly able to impose their own decisions on their respective societies, the reasons why they can do so, and their specific relations with their own governments and representative institutions, are entirely different. This applies not only to the differences between British and American enterprises, but also to the specific differences in the activities of the enterprises in West Germany, Sweden, Japan, Italy and Yugoslavia. Although the trend is the same, the rationale differs fundamentally. To be sure, the trend might lead to a sort of final complete internationalization of all the national oligopolies and to the absorption of all multi-nationals of the Free World in a unified floating Euromarket magnified to intercontinental dimensions. While this vision is not implausible, it is at least premature. The national umbilical cord linking the multi-nationals with their respective original economies would have to be severed from the main body, if this final vision, sometimes projected by Galbraith and the other contributors to the general theory of corporation, is to be realized.

Both trade unions and enterprises can use either direct or indirect means to attain their goals. Withholding of services or refusals of implementation are typical direct means. The second conclusion to be drawn is that British enterprise has in the last two decades made its impact felt more indirectly on the national interest by its reluctance to participate in the appeals made by successive governments to all major sectors of the economy to join in a common effort. The relative tardiness of British enterprise, when compared with the great strides made in the same decades by their West German, Swedish, French – not to mention Japanese and American counterparts – was the direct effect of its unwillingness to participate. That the other corporate sectors of the economy were equally unco-

86

operative toward the appeals of the government to produce more centripetal efforts is undeniable. But what can be added here is that the reciprocal withholding of effort of both labour and capital in Britain, because of their mutual antipathy and distrust, has led in the last quarter of a century to the characteristic vicious circle, which in turn has had a grievous effect on the national interest as a whole. Each of the two major corporations, trade unions and enterprises, played negative and positive parts in this vicious circle.

This was very much the case of, when the wings do not hold, the centre falls apart. But here both wings were hiding their responsibilities behind that of the centre. Each of the two wings accused both Labour and Conservative governments of lack of leadership and resolution. One principal argument was centred around the question of the right – or indeed the obligation – of the modern government to intervene in an industrial society. Another argument was conducted around the problem of partnership with the state. The trade unions asked the state to become their partner by nationalizing industries and taking over their management. The private enterprises asked the state to collaborate with them in new initiatives and in launching new industrial undertakings. Both trade unions and enterprises wanted the direct help of the state to finance projects and to protect them against the hostility of the other side, trade unions versus employers, enterprises versus trade unions.

The history of the British economy since the Second World War is littered with the debris of attempts by alternative British governments to set up institutions and instruments by which the opposing interests of the corporations could be reconciled and by which some tripartite decision-making in industry could be achieved. Whether the focus was put on growth or on inflation, what was sought was a durable framework for the tripartite agreement of government, enterprises and trade unions. All these institutional improvizations have failed. The last one was the Heath Government's attempt to institutionalize a system of co-ordination of prices and incomes around a counter-inflationary policy. In the previous chapter we have seen the reaction of the trade unions. Now we turn to the attitude of the enterprises and their impact on the policy.

The confrontation of 1974

The pre-electoral crisis and the elections of 1974 proved, among many other things, how independent British enterprises could be in their political orientations, although they had until then been traditionally in agreement with the Heath Government and the Conservative Party. As in the case of the trade unions and the Labour Party, one again found the determination of a socio-economic group to keep its own interests above its political links with a political party and with government. When the two interests happened to follow a parallel direction, or even more so when the Tory Party and government succeeded in espousing the line of the enterprises, the old collaboration emerged again. The fact that the traditionally allied government spoke in terms of national interest that covered all sectors of society was not taken as a categorical argument. For the enterprises would argue that the national interest as seen by politicians was not the same as the national interest seen by them. In their eyes, national interest could be measured by the well-being and success of the enterprises, and economic prosperity was the yardstick of the nation's welfare.

Two different instances of the political centrifugalism of the British enterprises during the confrontation of 1974 revealed the tensions which existed between them and the representative institutions. The first instance had to do with the relationship between all British enterprises, as represented principally by the Confederation of British Industries, and the Heath Government and the Conservative Party. This usually peaceful and confident relationship was subjected to great strains during the crisis. The second instance concerned the relationship between the national interest as a whole and a particular group of enterprises, namely the oil companies. This came dramatically into the limelight because of the energy crisis, and because of the divergencies thus exposed between the oil companies and the British state and indeed of all Western Europe.

Two caveats ought to be made here before embarking on the examination of the two cases. The first is that the 'examination' cannot but be summary, oversimplified and with the accent put on the political aspect, although the entire crisis was primarily of an economic order and could best be grasped in economic terms. The second caveat is that if the analysis, thus lopsided, will lead to critical conclusions of the ultimate confusion in which the crisis of 1974 threw all sectors of society, this is not the same as to say that a critical view is taken here only of the behaviour of the enterprises in both instances. First, it should be made clear that much more than the trade unions which, during the crisis tried to make sufficient or insufficient compromises towards the 'anti-inflationary' policies which the Government described as crucial to the national interest, the enterprises did their best to implement the anti-inflationary policies of the Government. From the very beginning they pledged themselves to observe the restrictions for twelve months. In both instances, British enterprises made exemplary efforts to uphold, under difficult conditions not of their own making, the national interest. The performance of British enterprises during the three-day week will remain one of their 'finest hours'. Equally the successful efforts of the major British oil companies to keep supplies of oil to Britain and Europe going, and to mediate between their own governments and the governments of the Arab states, played a determining part in lowering temperatures and in reducing risks and damages. At the same time, they were making profits higher than ever, while the national economy was suffering one of its worst crises. This demonstrated once again the way in which the enterprises' view of their interests, like the trade unions', may coincide with the national interest – although it equally may not.

The enterprises were that part of the British economy most interested in the attempt undertaken by the Heath Government to stop the wages-push of the unions, and, even more so, to put some order into industrial relations as a whole. They accepted with no false modesty the explicit and implicit praise bestowed upon them for their patient and positive patriotic efforts, compared with the 'shortsighted greed' of the other 'social partner', the trade unions. In all the arguments presented by Messrs Heath, Barber or Carr, the enterprises were given good marks, for there is no reason to think that Mr Heath's incidental sally against 'the ugly face of capitalism' could have shaken the mutual confidence between him and the enterprises. Indeed perhaps the concentration of Mr Heath's critical analysis on the trade unions alone, and the determination of Mr Barber's pre-electoral budget not to hinder the middle classes and the enterprises, were the basic reason why so many floating voters did not rally around the Conservatives.

Throughout the parliamentary struggle to pass the Industrial Relations Bill, and during the functioning of the Industrial Court, the enterprises backed the government and observed (to their advantage) the law. Similarly, when the Government switched its focus to the fight against inflation and proposed its Prices and Incomes policy, the enterprises, dismayed as they may have been by the restrictions on prices, and critical as they were of some aspects of the regulations during the three successive stages, did not demur. This was understandable, as their main concern was to make order, whether legal or of some other kind, prevail in the field of industrial relations, keeping industrial wages to a reasonable and steady level. The national press, reflecting the views of the enterprises, castigated both the direct action of the minority groups in industrial relations and the general phenomenon of social inflation no longer only as an economic danger, but more directly, as a *political* catastrophe, indeed as a threat to parliamentary democracy in Britain. The stand taken by the Heath Government was described as a last-ditch fight against both these disasters, and one of the reasons why Mr Heath personally was praised was precisely because he was the first Prime Minister to grasp this worst nettle of all. It was this fundamental problem which all Prime Ministers since the Second World War, however glorious or successful they had seemed at the time, had left unsolved and allowed to grow to threatening proportions. Not to back such a Prime Minister would have been folly for the enterprises which for two decades had longed for a man with that kind of vision and that kind of courage. A Prime Minister prepared to deal with the trade unions as a constitutional statesman and not as an electoral politician – this is what business wanted. 'The fears that the government may eventually surrender to the miners and thus effectively wreck its own stage three have been only half allayed, for one of the most worrying smoke signals in British politics is when prime ministers start entertaining trade unionists at No. 10', remarked *The Economist* significantly.[1]

Even when, in the dramatic escalation of measures and counter-measures, the Heath Government came to proclaim the three-day week, the Confederation of British Industries, although showing a natural anxiety about the effects of such a drastic step if it were to last too long, approved of the Government's measure not only on the ground that it was directly dictated by the shortage of fuel, but also as a means of making the workers experience directly the iron law of interdependence in an industrial-technological society. Indeed it can be said that at the beginning the trade unions were more frightened than the enterprises by the effects of the three-day week. It was then that private enterprises had an unexpected opportunity to show their mettle. Managers improvised work under the worst conditions, bought their own generators and more often than not found the right voice to convince their workers to work overtime and under very trying conditions. The result was the miracle that according to the CBI's own report of 14 February 1974, output had actually risen in the February period of the three-day week and a large number of companies were reporting normal production.

For the public enterprises the case was, of course, different. For obvious reasons, some of which were noted in the preceding section of this chapter, the boards of management of the nationalized industries were less ready and indeed able to propose and obtain compromises with their own workers. During the whole course of the conflict with the miners, the National Coal Board seemed much less convinced that the methods used by the Government, and the escalation in which it engaged with the National Union of Miners could ultimately produce happy results. But more directly bound to

1. *The Economist*, 1 Dec. 1973. But it is also true to say that *The Economist* remained faithful to its general philosophy on these two matters, and criticized the CBI at the time for vacillating and losing its nerve.

the Government, which indeed had shown in the last years or so a greater determination to intervene in the affairs of nationalized industry,[1] the National Coal Board had to toe the line willy-nilly and could not, like private enterprise, manifest its displeasure with the steps taken by the government.

When in January 1974, the trade unions for the first time made their pledge to advise all workers to implement the last stage of the Heath Government's Prices and Incomes policy provided the miners were treated as a unique special case (a proposal and a pledge on which they subsequently enlarged and which became the hard core of the social contract announced jointly by the trade unions and the new Labour Government) it was the Confederation of British Industries which found the terms much too vague to be acceptable and influenced the Government to refuse them. Yet it was at that juncture that, had the Heath Government adopted less intransigent attitudes and given 'the tripartite partnership' which it advocated a chance to work it might have succeeded.

Once the escalation of events had led to the inevitable general election, the enterprises gradually started to separate themselves from the Government now seeking a renewed mandate. The Heath Government believed that it was representing the National Interest in two ways. First, it was the representative government based on the representative majority of the Parliament of 1970. Secondly, doctrinally, it presented itself as the political party which had condensed most of the economic and social problems of the country into one single political question: Who governs? In other words it posed the question whether sectional minority groups, however potent, should be allowed to obstruct and change the policies and measures

1. The Select Committee on nationalized industries, in a report published in January 1974, criticized the government for interference with the nationalized industries in matters of prices and investment – and for the antiquated way in which it dealt with these conditions, postponing decisions with a long bureaucratic machinery at the top of which stood, inevitably, the Treasury, which scrutinized their requests and proposals. Select Committee on Nationalised Industries, House of Commons, paper 65, HMSO, 1974.

which the majority of the country had adopted and implemented through proper constitutional mechanisms?

Yet, from that moment on, the relationship between the enterprises and the national interest as described by Mr Heath changed. Not only did the economic propositions change (in the eyes of the CBI this happened just before the date of the election was announced, when the CBI received the answers to the questionnaires it had issued on the effects of the three-day week) but after the date of the election had been announced, the *political* relation changed too. The enterprises were now faced with a Conservative Party which, if elected, would have continued, with even greater zest, the hard policy towards the trade unions. The Conservative Party would also have continued the Prices and Incomes policy with which not all managers were in total agreement (indeed some found that Mr Powell was much more in the tradition of genuine Tory *laissez-faire* than Mr Heath who had revealed himself as a new interventionist). Thus the enterprises found themselves again in the situation of choosing between the national interest as seen by the politicians and the national interest as they saw it.

In reality the Confederation of British Industries had come to the conclusion, after reading the 1200 answers it received from its principal members, that it would soon be faced with mass closures, that insolvency would become rampant, and that investment plans, happily forecast by the Department of Trade and Industry in December 1973 to reach the high level of twelve to fourteen per cent in the following year, could in the present circumstances rise to only three per cent or not at all. It was clear that it had been the miners' strike which had made, to use *The Economist*'s expression, 'the bottom fall right out of the CBI's confidence'. The President of the CBI, the intransigent Sir Michael Clapham, said that things had not been so bad since the outbreak of war and asked the Government to increase its cash offer to the miners because 'we cannot get coal by any other means...they have the country in their hands'.

These revelations were not going to help the Conservative Party under Mr Heath's leadership either to win the election or to keep its own morale high. Mr Heath's strongest ally, in that decision-making triangle in which he believed that economic decisions were made, was now, if not yet deserting him, barely concealing its doubts and hesitations. Business, the traditional support of the Conservative Party, was wondering whether the Conservatives were still right. For indeed as the electoral debate evolved and moved away from the miners' strike the issue was no longer simply whether to give the Miners more cash (the wisdom of which the British enterprises had reasons to doubt), but the wider logic of Mr Heath's policy based on the rigid framework of the Industrial Relations Act. Most of the national newspapers which had loudly encouraged Mr Heath to maintain a strong stand gradually became more sceptical and advised moderation and flexibility.

When on 26 February 1974, the very eve of the election, whether, by a calculated or accidental slip, and whether or not with the consent of the Confederation of British Industries, Mr Campbell Adamson declared that the Industrial Relations Act ought to be repealed, it was clear that at least a substantial part of the British enterprises had decided against Mr Heath's idea of the national interest.[1] According to Mr Heath, Mr Campbell Adamson lost him the election.

1. The mystery of Mr Campbell Adamson's statement must be elucidated in the light of the subsequent events, and indeed in the light which was further thrown on the functioning and significance of the CBI as a whole. It was thus revealed that before Mr Campbell Adamson's comments about the Industrial Relations Bill, some companies such as Dunlop and GKN were highly critical of the leadership of the CBI and wanted to suspend their membership in the organization – the structure of which, it was felt, hampered its effectiveness. The Devlin Report of 1972 had criticized the illogicality of the structure and made proposals for a new Confederation of British *Business*. Be that as it may, it was announced on 18 May 1974 that the former President of the CBI, Sir Michael Clapham, had been succeeded by Mr Ralph Bateman, chairman of Turner & Newall, while Mr Campbell Adamson remained in his capacity as Director. Commentators drew the conclusion that this might prove a successful blending of a more conservative chairman with a more liberal director. Yet, when it comes to the *political* orientation of the CBI, it seems that, as in the case of the Trade Union Congress, whereas collaboration with the traditionally

The divergence of interests between the oil companies and the national interests will be examined here only in part, as the same problem will be discussed in the context of the attitudes of the European Community towards multi-national corporations in general (and the oil companies in particular).

The three 'major' oil companies, BP, Shell and Burmah control two-thirds of the gasoline market in Britain.[1] When the Yom Kippur war started, the prophecy which the oil companies had long made, and had frequently asked the British Government to bear in mind, namely that the Arab states would retaliate by raising the price of oil, came dramatically true. The European Commission in Brussels too had constantly warned its member states of this danger to their economies. But the European Commission (unlike the oil multi-nationals which asked for a greater flexibility in pricing and transacting bilateral agreements with the Arab states), viewed the problem

---

allied political party is much easier, and more congenial during the periods when it is in opposition and the other party is in power, the very difficult periods in these relations occur when the allied party is in power. It can even be said that a kind of functional poetic justice made it so that whereas the misunderstanding between the TUC and the Labour Government in 1970 helped the election of the Conservative Government of 1970, the misunderstandings between the CBI and the Conservative Government in 1974 helped the election of the new Labour Government in 1974.

1. The Royal Dutch Shell Group (formed in 1907 out of the Dutch company, Royal Dutch Petroleum and the British company, Shell Transport and Trading) has two centres, a technical one in The Hague, and a financial one in London. British Petroleum, until 1909 the Anglo-Iranian Oil Company, is the largest British-owned oil multi-national. The British Government has a majority holding. Burmah Oil, which also has major share-holdings in BP and Shell, operates mostly in India and Pakistan and in North and South America, and specializes in motor lubricants. In 1914 when Winston Churchill, as First Lord of the Admiralty, wanted to ensure that the oil supplies would not be interfered with by alien interests, the British government acquired a controlling interest in BP, but it is not a nationalized industry.

as an opportunity for a complete reappraisal of the energy policy of the Community. This policy would have the effect of cutting down to size the oil multi-nationals, too strong by now to be controlled by the national states. Only the co-ordinated control and organization of the Nine countries could achieve a more sensible collaboration between them and the 'majors'.

The financial power of the oil companies and their power to fix high prices and high profits everywhere, especially on the European markets, has always been of great concern to financial and economic authorities in Europe. It is significant that the first reduction in prices forced upon the oil companies after the Second World War was due to the intervention of the men in charge of the Marshall Aid Plan in Europe, who were able to see how high oil prices affected the entire European economy.[1] It is true that in view of the losses produced by nationalization in many of the oil-producing countries, which resulted in the expropriation of oil company assets in those countries, and in view of high taxes and royalties paid to the producing countries, the European states have given the oil companies special treatment (BP, for instance, is not subject to direct taxation in Britain).

It must also be remembered that the relations between the national authorities and the oil multi-nationals differ from country to country. It is believed that France keeps the companies under the strictest control, and that the British Government, although more flexible, especially in matters of price, has good working relations with the British-based companies. In the Netherlands and in West Germany there is more controversy in the official collaboration with the companies, and on the form which it should take.

1. 'The oil companies were able to operate on staggering profit margins. By early 1948 Persian Gulf crude oil was selling at $2.22 a barrel, the high point. Exposure, partly by Paul Hoffman, head of the European Co-operation Administration which was running the Marshall Aid Plan in Europe, brought the price down to $1.75 a barrel.' Hugh Stephenson, op. cit., p. 152. Stephenson also recounts how the British Government protested against the inequitable pricing system during the Second World War but 'never discovered the full facts'.

Being the unchallenged middlemen between the oil-producing and the oil-consuming countries of the world, the oil companies became the policy-makers of the oil sector of the European economies. They attributed their position to the pioneering years when, by their technical skill and financial efforts they opened up oil fields everywhere, providing the under-developed oil-producing countries with their principal source of wealth, and the rest of the world with its principal source of energy. (The same situation is repeating itself in the exploration of North Sea oil.) The enterprises explored and developed the fields, controlled the output and fixed the prices. Gradually tension set in, and in their relations with the emancipated Middle East, the oil corporations rapidly began to lose ground. When in October 1974 the OPEC (the new Organization of the Petroleum Exporting Countries) took their new stand, the oil companies lost in the exercise two of their privileges: to fix the price of oil at the production point, and to decide on the amount of production.

Thus the Yom Kippur War directly affected the European Community, which found itself for the first time dramatically split between Britain and France, on one side, and the other seven countries on the other. The split was directly and deliberately created by the degree of preference, or alternatively of persecution, which OPEC reserved for each of the Nine countries. It was understandable that France and Britain held better relations with the Arab states in view of their past colonial links with at least some of the under-developed countries of the region, and on account of the active mediation traditionally provided by the oil-companies, which could exercise their own influence on the Arab states, as well as on London and Paris. Nevertheless one of the ultimate consequences of the dramatic imbroglio at the end of 1974 was that in their own way, and acting in their own interests and according to their views of British and French interest, the oil-companies helped the two Governments to take a line which was in opposition with that taken not only by the European Community as a whole, but also by the United States. The crisis left its deep wounds on all the European economies, which were once more blown off-course by the effect of the high prices of oil which – as shown in Robert

Triffin's calculations of the incidence of oil price increases on import bills[1] – was particularly severe in Western Europe. Indirectly too, the oil companies were toppled from their pinnacles. The Arab states took decisive command of their countries' oil policy. They fixed prices, production and preferential exports. For obvious reasons they preferred direct government-to-government relations as the basis of future relations with the European countries. The role of the oil companies in the Middle East may thus shrink in the future to one of 'transport and trading' as it was initially.

1. Incidence of Oil Price Increases (1974/1972) on Imports Bill of Countries Which Are Net Importers of Crude Oil.

	In billions of dollars					In per cent of			
	Inc. of Imports Bill	1972 GNP	1972 Exports	Oct. '72 Monetary Reserves	Gold Revaluation	Offi-cial Liqui-dity	GNP	Ex-ports	Offi-cial Liqui-dity
	(a)	(b)	(c)	(d)	(e)	$(f = d+e)$	$(g = \frac{a}{b}\,100)$	$(h = \frac{a}{c}\,100)$	$(i = \frac{a}{f}\,100)$
1 United States	15.9	1155.2	49.8	14.4	23.3	37.7	1.4	31.9	42.2
2 Japan	12.8	300.0	28.0	14.0	1.8	15.8	4.3	44.8	81.0
3 Western Europe	39.7		191.4	94.2	47.7	141.9		20.7	28.0
(a) Community	(31.6)	821.6	154.8	71.5	35.6	107.1	(3.8)	(20.4)	(29.5)
(b) Other W. Europe	(8.1)		36.6	22.7	12.1	34.8		(22.1)	(23.3)
Subtotal	68.4		269.8	122.6	72.8	195.4		25.4	35.0
1 Other Dev. Countries	4.2								
2 LDC's	6.7								
Total: Net Oil Importing Countries	79.3								

Source: Robert Triffin, 'Oil, the money muddle and the EEC', in *New Europe*, vol. 2, no. 3, London, 1974, p. 24.

But even were this to happen, as Roger Vielvoye has suggested, it would only mean that the oil-companies would enter what he felicitously called 'an era of powerless profitability...As the profits of all the major oil companies during the past year have proved', Vielvoye states, 'the end of their reign as policy-makers and overlords of the oil scene has not brought financial ruin. A seller's market has enabled them to turn in their best results for years and these conditions have only been created by the overall tightening of oil supplies last year combined with the Arabs' action in restricting production'.[1] It is at this point that the divergence between the interests of the enterprises and the nation reappeared as the leitmotif of the former's ultimate centrifugal interest. Whereas the oil companies' ultimate duty as enterprises is to show profits and achieve maximum returns, in this case such a policy contributes to the general impoverishment of the nation as a whole, and of the individual taxpayers who ultimately have to foot the bill. The contrast between national effort and sacrifice, on the one hand, and profit-seeking and profit-making of the enterprises on the other, had already emerged at the inquiry held by the British government during the Second World War into the oil companies' methods of pricing, and again immediately after that, during the arduous period of the reconstruction of Europe when for the first time the oil companies were forced to reduce their prices. The problem was bound to resurface in the even more dramatic conditions after the energy crisis.

The Royal Dutch Shell group announced in the spring of 1974 that it achieved net profits in the first three months of 1974 of £319 million compared with £114 million in the same months of 1973. Yet Shell communicated at the same time that it would have to seek further price rises and that to this effect 'discussions on price levels are taking place with governments of the consuming countries concerned'. The company explained that the high profits were due to its general operations and not to the increases in prices since the energy

1. Roger Vielvoye, 'An era of powerless profitability,' *Sunday Times*, 12 March 1974.

crisis, and that government price controls in Germany, France and the UK had restricted industry profits to a level where companies were actually selling at a loss if the higher costs of participation were taken into account. But the Organization of Petroleum Exporting Countries suggested in its official studies of the same first quarter of the year that oil companies were making as much as $4 per barrel on crude oil. It accused the Western governments of failing to cream off the companies' profits and warned of a further increase in prices by the producing countries so as to increase their respective benefits.

This did not occur without a general outcry in the political world. In the United States Senator Frank Church, the chairman of the United States Senate Foreign Relations Sub-committee investigating multi-national corporations, on seeing that the increase in OPEC revenues had been paralleled by comparative increases in company profits, came to the conclusion that both groups were in collusion so that both could achieve higher profits. 'It is clear,' he said, 'that the companies and OPEC are partners in profit for the oil being sold at hi-jack prices to the Western World.' In West Germany the Federal Government on 23 April 1974 urged the international oil companies to disclose more information on their prices and profits, stressing that 'states within the state' are not tolerated in West Germany. The Secretary of State at the Ministry of Economics said that as long as full light was not thrown onto the operations and profits of the oil companies it would be difficult to resist the claim that they should be nationalized. The Federal Cartel Office served interim injunctions on BP and Texaco to rescind recent price increases. The correspondent in Germany of the *Financial Times* remarked on 23 April how in response to clearly mounting public concern the criticism of the companies had increasingly spread from the Left to the Right of the political spectrum. Finally, the European Commission of the European Communities again asked that the Communities should enact a common energy policy, as being both of general importance and another means of combating inflation. For it should be noted that the high profits made by the companies and by OPEC not only directly affected prices in Europe, but had an indirectly deleterious effect as oil surplus funds were attracted by the speed and flexibility of the Euro-currency market. In the preliminary discussions held in Brussels in May 1974 the Commission's original proposal met with the resistance of Britain, West Germany and the Netherlands. But of this more later, when we turn to European policy-making.

Like the trade unions, the enterprises have a functional relationship with national interest. In the past their activities normally converged with the national interest within which they worked. But this natural convergence does not exclude the possibility that in cases of divergence the corporations might enhance their intrinsic autonomy, upholding their own limited interest against the more general interest and thus acting centrifugally against the central purposes of the national interest. The evolution of industrial-technological society has accentuated the autonomy of the corporations and has given them new opportunities to impose their decisions on the respective nation-states. The effects of the withholding of collaboration with the governments are much more striking than before because of the specific interdependence of the new society. In the case of the enterprises the internationalization and multi-nationalization of their activities has rendered them more independent of the nation-state, and has enabled them to choose more freely than before whether or not to co-operate with governments.

Chapter Four

Local, regional and national interests

Since 1968, the regions or provinces of Britain, the last of the three
'corporate forces' analyzed in this book, have also been caught in a
frenzy of centrifugalism. Although the strain in their relationship
with the central government had always been there, its manifestations in Britain did not reach the degree of acuteness and indeed of
violence which were reached in Belgium, Italy, Spain and other
European countries after the Second World War. But starting first
in the late sixties in Northern Ireland, where from the beginning it
had a strongly terrorist character, the trend of local centrifugalism
quickly spread to Scotland and Wales. It escalated afterwards into a
general reconsideration of the administrative structure. One of the
forms this took was that of a Royal Commission on the Constitution,
appointed in 1969 'to examine the present functions of the central
legislature and government in relation to the several countries,
nations, regions of the United Kingdom [and] to consider...whether
any changes are desirable to those functions or otherwise in present
constitutional and economic relationships...The Royal Commission
on the Constitution, better known as the Kilbrandon report after the
name of the chairman of the Commission, Lord Kilbrandon,[1] submitted its report early in October 1973. The very appointment of a
Commission on the Constitution was significant, in a state whose
reputation for sound and flexible political structures was epitomized
by the fact that it did not *have* a constitution.

1. *Royal Commission on the Constitution* 1969–73, vol. i, *Report*; vol. ii,
Memorandum of dissent (by Lord Crowther-Hunt and Professor A. T.
Peacock), London, H.M.S.O. Cmnd 5460.

But little as the Commission, like all Royal Commissions, could achieve directly, its ultimate message, that all concerned should take a new and searching look at the deterioration in the administrative fabric of the United Kingdom, was neither superfluous nor premature. Things were happening, and were happening very rapidly, under the surprised gaze of the citizens of the United Kingdom who had until then been unaware of the intensity of the crisis. The intensification of centrifugalism in the relationship between the regions (and local government generally) and central government in Britain was due in part to the same combination of causes which we have seen at work in the cases of the unions and enterprises.

The political changes brought about by the industrial-technological revolution and notably the weakening of the nation-state as a whole, and the demand for participation in decision-making and policy-making of the corporate forces, aware by now of their new importance, were the main causes of the new desire for emancipation of the local corporations and also of the regions. Here, too, the increasingly poor economic performance of central government since the fifties had led to the self-assertion of regional and local interests, and to demands for autonomy. Here, too, the old longing for direct decision-making was revived by the new possibilities offered to corporations (in this case local and regional governments) for taking their decisions independently, thus manifesting – even if indirectly – their insubordination to the central government, and more generally speaking to the representative institutions of the United Kingdom.

The insubordination of administrative units, their defiance of the central authority and of its laws and agents, is the worst nightmare of sovereign governments. For this kind of insubordination takes the ugly and palpable form of territorial mutilations of the state's sovereignty while the ultimate reactions against the danger of such mutilations take the even uglier, and unpredictable, form of military intervention. From another point of view, these forms of insubordination resurrect arguments based on old historical memories, controversies and arguments, which in the case of Wales and Ireland go back to the eleventh and twelfth centuries, and in the

103

case of Scotland to the seventeenth. Finally this kind of insubordination reopens the perennial subject of the legitimacy and feasibility of centralization and central controls, the old opposition of the free communes to the nation-state, now revived in contemporary claims for decentralization and the ultimate dissolution of the 'state' made by revolutionary movements in general.

What the movements toward emancipation of the regions and of local government have in common is their absolute opposition to central controls and to the tendency toward centralization. They also have in common the new 'participatory arguments', and especially the argument that central government is condemned to ineffectiveness and incompetence by the very fact of its remoteness. The interest and the diligence of the 'people themselves', of the 'community itself', is the only solution for positive management. Participation and community work should, in this view, be broadened so as to involve all members of the community. As a corollary to this, once the new collaboration of all the members of the community is ensured the community itself should sever its links of allegiance with the central authority so as not to expose to external influences the decisions thus made in full knowledge and with full unanimity. Regional, and especially local politics are now fed by neo-populist, neo-communist and neo-anarchist ideologies, which are being incorporated in a wide range of models, from the utopian 'communes' to the community work undertaken by political or social groups in conjunction with members of the respective community; or from the ambitiously insulated activities of some local councils in revolt against the central government to the endless variations of *ad hoc* boards and bodies which try to bridge the gap between powerful but indifferent central administration and the zealous but powerless 'communities'.

Finally, what both movements have in common is the fact that their present revival is due, as mentioned above, to the great economic, social and political changes brought about by the industrial-technological revolution. The rise and the decline of heavy industries located in different regions and countries have had direct effects on the welfare of the indigenous populations. The centralization of new industries in England has aggravated the economic problems of Scotland, Wales and Northern Ireland. On the other hand, development of local resources and industry – for instance, the discovery of oil in the North Sea – has increased the sense of independence of the regions.

The conflict between national policies (and especially all kinds of planning policies which are direct sequels to industrial-technological conditions of work) and local policies and interests has been greatly exacerbated by the state's need to 'centralize' all national resources and forces. Such common national efforts, frequently demanded by political parties, parliaments and governments, provide their main hope of restoring some coherence to the politics of a state which is constantly blown off-course by major international developments, and constantly undermined by the separate actions of the sectional interests of the erstwhile national community. At the same time, the local and regional interests, dismayed by the lack of success of the state as a whole, become increasingly inclined to attribute it to perennial incompatibility between national interests and the affairs of the local communities. Inflamed by the new means of direct decision-making, they proceeded to make these decisions themselves regardless of and in opposition to 'national policies'.

But, in other respects, regional and local interests have different and opposed aims and means. The Kilbrandon report had great logical difficulty in linking the two problems together – and indeed ended by treating them separately. One reason for this was that in the case of the local units of administration, from boroughs to counties, the best solution is to intensify their independent participation in the processes of national policy-making; but in the case of the comparatively vast units which are the regions, especially if they are peripheral regions incorporated by various means into the territory of the United Kingdom, the drastic solution of straightforward separation of territories and sovereignties could apply as well. Secondly, the motivations and purposes of the actions of emancipation of the smaller units of local administration – parishes, boroughs or counties and cities – are totally different from those of the regions. What the regions want is to replace national policies prepared, expressed and directed by England, with Scottish national policies in Scotland and Welsh national policies in Wales. This powerful nationalism of the ethnically different provinces is naturally missing from the motivations of the units of local administration.

Their idea of decentralization is parochial and therefore in a sense a-national. The ultimate global link which they might envisage, should their ideal of total decentralization be fulfilled, is that of a national or international federation of communes. Insofar as they are opposed in principle to any central government they should in principle be opposed to any unitary state. The example of Switzerland, the most decentralized democracy, is significant. Small as Switzerland is, the Helvetian Confederation punctiliously observes the sovereign rights of the cantons. To take only one example, it is the cantons which give Swiss nationality to individual citizens.

This sense of local sovereignty (what the Germans call *Lokalismus*) is the characteristic ideology of communes – regardless of whether they are based on communal, indeed communist forms of ownership or on individual, capitalist forms. For this reason it can be assumed that while boroughs and counties in Scotland and Wales might find it easier and more congenial to communicate respectively with Edinburgh and Cardiff rather than with London, this would not solve the basic incompatibility – of both technique and of ultimate constitutional conceptions – between decentralized local administration and nationalist regional administration.

The 1972 Local Government Act which became effective on 1 April 1974, and the 1973 Royal Commission's report on the constitution, together with the abundant literature on public administration which was produced in the wake of these documents, stressed as one of the principal aspects of the modern problem of local administration the change in relationships between local and central government produced by an advanced technological society: broadly defined as a need for planning.

The 'inter-corporate dimension of public planning' is one of the most important aspects of administrative decision-making in this advanced industrial-technological society. It is in this area that the two dialectically contradictory tendencies of modern society – the tendency towards centralization so that overall decisions can be taken effectively, and the tendency towards participation and community action at the local level, clash violently; and this is where local authorities, government departments, appointed agencies, private enterprises and community interests are enmeshed in a common process of decision-making.[1] By now, modern thinking on administrative problems is imbued with the realization that public planning is the corollary of the changes in the industrial-technological society – and that what can be achieved in the private sector should also be achieved in the public one.[2] But it was precisely in this new and determining area of public management that all the clashes of diversified and contradictory interests and approaches have occurred and have until now rendered the entire operation impracticable. Thus, the regional economic planning councils and boards instituted in the wake of the National Plan of 1965 failed to obtain the co-operation of either the higher echelons of central government or the lower echelons of local government (districts and counties) and, at the same time, had their competence and authority continually eroded by the *ad hoc* functional boards and committees. The 1972 Local Government Act drastically reduced the total number of authorities and divided the entire structure into two main tiers, counties and districts (although a third tier of some 8,000 parishes was allowed to continue to exist nominally). But at the same time,

1. See J. K. Friend, J. M. Power and C. Jewlett, *Public Planning, the Inter-corporate Dimension*, London, 1974.
2. Thus, the *Report on the Constitution*: 'It is clear that the pressures will continue and that what the 1970 White Paper described as "the increasingly complex and technical character of the processes of government and administration in modern society" will persist (247). Local government has itself experienced many changes during the course of the twentieth century. As the scope of government has increased, it has acquired many new functions, while it has lost to the newly appointed bodies some of its older traditional functions (258). Many local authorities also resent the fact that the regional economic planning councils are not rooted in local government.' (305). (Numbers indicate paragraphs.)

and by virtue of the same act, local government lost the right to decide on matters pertaining to water, sewage and health. Both these changes could not but make the operations of planning even more difficult and confusing, the two tiers competing with one another and the central government assuming even greater power of decision-making than it had before.

From this point of view, the reservations in the Crowther-Hunt/Peacock *Memorandum of Dissent*[1] against further centralization at the top, against the proliferation of *ad hoc* temporary, administrative bodies as well as against the spread of disorganized, patchy administrative devolution, are particularly relevant. One of the secondary obstacles to Britain's economic recovery has been administrative confusion and the impossibility of co-ordinated policy-making and planning in regional and local administration. In order to stop this permanent disorder, Lord Crowther-Hunt and Professor Peacock proposed in their memorandum that a new and permanent intermediate level of government be found, which would have as 'one of the most important functions' to draw up a strategic plan for its area. This would, of course, involve much more than the traditional 'town and country planning'. It would include 'economic and social planning as well'. And, continues the *Memorandum*:

> Producing such a strategy would involve considering all the planning problems presented by likely demographic projections, technological change, the investment programme of the nationalised and major private industries and the general economic, cultural, educational and environmental changes... Naturally an intermediate level government would draw up its strategic plan in full consultation with all the local authorities in its area...the plan would not, of course, come into effect until it was approved by the UK government. But once that approval was given it would be the responsibility of the intermediate level government to put the plans into effect (332–333).

1. Op. cit. The above-quoted numbers indicate paragraphs.

Whether, when and how this 'intermediate level government', or what the introduction to this book described as 'the new political inter-section of all sectional interests', will be found, is another question – and indeed it is the question on which the next two chapters concentrate. The Crowther-Hunt and Peacock theory will also be more fully discussed in the general framework of the future nature of politics.

But until some new centripetal stability is found, it is on matters of planning that the interests of the different 'tiers' of administrative authority will clash more directly with each other. With the constant decline of the authority of central government, and in an atmosphere conducive to 'direct action' and 'corporate decision-making', these conflicts will lead to increased restlessness within the administrative system, sometimes amounting to insubordination of the local echelons.

The notorious Clay Cross episode,[1] which is considered as the

1. In 1963 a team of young and militant Labour members won control of the Urban District Council of Clay Cross, a little town situated in the depressed mining area of Derbyshire. From the very start, they were determined to go ahead with socialism in one urban district. They were particularly well disciplined as a team, and particularly hard-working – in some six years they cleared nine-tenths of the slums, and built council houses at an exceptionally fast rate. The housing deficit went up vertiginously in spite of the increasingly high rates paid by the rate-payers. The requests of the Council to aid council houses as much as owner-occupied houses were refused by the Labour Government. A district auditor's report was highly critical of the management and policies of the Council. In the 1970 elections Labour again won all the seats. But in June 1970, Labour lost the Parliamentary elections. The opposition of Clay Cross UDC to central government in general was doubled by the accession of a Conservative Government. In September 1972 the Council refused openly and officially to implement the Housing Finance Act. The Government asked the district auditor to inquire. In January 1973 the auditor surcharged the councillors for £6,985, as the increased rent, uncollected in the first six weeks. On 1 April 1974, when the new Act for Local Administration came into being, the Urban District Council of Clay Cross, like all the Urban District Councils, was transformed into a

most symptomatic modern rebellion of local government in Britain, and consequently as a sign of future centrifugalism of this sort, is a typical example of the clash between these two conflicting tendencies: the indecision and imprecision at the top and the quest for direct action at the local level. But from the moment it assumed the aspect of a refusal to implement a law of the land the episode took a turn towards more dramatic interpretations, ranging from the revival of the Poplar case on modern grounds, or indeed of 'Poplarism, writ large' to a 'People's Republic of Clay Cross', or indeed 'socialism in one town'.[1]

The episode, although undoubtedly significant needs to be seen in its true perspective. One of its aspects is political-ideological: upon the failure of the old Labour Party organization in Clay Cross, the new and young team, inspired by contemporary ideas about community action and 'socialism in one town', took upon itself to prove that such ideas can work, especially in solving the housing problem which is of first importance in urban districts. The Council criticized the housing policies of the Labour Government as old-fashioned and right-wing. To that extent Clay Cross should be interpreted rather as another manifestation of the conflict within the Labour Party of two ideological approaches and perhaps two generations.[2]

But its other aspect, more relevant to this study, as a rebellion of

---

successor council and control of housing passed into the hands of the North East Derbyshire District Council which, after certain hesitations and delays, decided to implement the Housing Finance Act. After the elections of February 1974 the Councillors asked the Labour Government to find a way to pay from state or Labour Party Funds the penalty which they had been condemned to pay by the auditors. In February 1975 a parliamentary committee overturned the auditors' decision, and the money was returned. In March 1975 they were exonerated by a new Housing Finance (Special Provisions) Bill, (Hansard, 7 March 1975, vol. 887, no. 83).

1. Austin Mitchell, 'Clay Cross', *The Political Quarterly*, London, April–June 1974, p. 165.
2. See above, pp. 38–9.

a local government against the central government and the Law, took shape from the moment the Council refused to implement the Housing Finance Act. Indeed, during the first phase of the Act it was believed that another forty-two local authorities would defy it. In reality only twelve Councils announced that they would do so, and eleven of them changed their minds. Clay Cross UDC remained alone. 'Poplarism writ large' had not spread so widely as ideological or non-ideological partisans of community action believed that it would under the new social and economic circumstances. Besides, it must also be said that the Clay Cross Council itself tolerated the legal procedures. Its members did not let their insubordination degenerate into mutiny. They did not barricade themselves against the auditors or other officials. They did not repudiate the central institution of government, parliament or party. They did not become a 'no go' area. Their faith was vindicated. On 7 March 1975 the Labour Government presented a Bill to prevent 'surcharges' and to 'terminate disqualifications' of the councillors.

If a single case like Clay Cross can embody so many heterogeneous trends and can be interpreted from so many angles, how much more intricate are the complexities of the three principal regions – Scotland, Ireland and Wales – caught again, in new circumstances and with new motivations, in a wave of intensified centrifugalism.

There were also old motivations, belonging to their weighty heritage. As noted before, whereas the ultimate manifestations of centrifugalism in local government link up with the historical opposition of communes to the State, the main trends of the centrifugalism of Scotland and Wales – and with more peculiar aspects, Ulster – are directly linked with nationalist claims for autonomy, and indeed for sovereignty, of peoples and countries incorporated into the United Kingdom. Each of these three regions has a different historical background, and each of them has different motivations for advancing its demands for independence. From the historical point of view Scotland's case is obviously the strongest as, unlike Wales or Ireland, it had been a nation-state with its own King and Parliament from the eleventh century to the eighteenth-century Act of Union.

But from a geographic point of view, Northern Ireland which, unlike either Scotland or Wales, is physically separated by a sea from the British mainland, could secede most easily. In Northern Ireland, however, as is only too well known, only the Irish Catholic population had initially asked through the Social-Democratic Party for a proportionate share in the policy-making of the province; and later, by the terrorist means of the two IRA revolutionary movements, for reunion with the Irish Republic. During all this time the Ulster Protestants clung fervently to their essential links with, and allegiance to, the United Kingdom. It was only after the 1974 electoral triumph of the Protestant candidates – who were opposed to the short-lived Sunningdale agreements by which a 'power-sharing' system would have been institutionalized in the province – and especially after the strong and successful strike of the Ulster Volunteers industrial workers, that the Orangemen began to think and speak in terms of complete autonomy and even of Ulster sovereignty.

The February 1974 British general election, which carried an implicit message of political centrifugalism (in the sense that the Liberal vote could also be interpreted as a protest-vote against the two 'established' parties who seemed to be being abandoned by the electorate) also carried an explicit message of regional centrifugalism. In Scotland and Northern Ireland, the nationalists were returned with dramatically increased electoral majorities and numbers of seats, while in Wales the Plaid Cymru held its ground successfully and returned two MPs. It so happened also that because of the inconclusiveness of the result these three groups of regional MPs held, together with the Liberals, the balance of power in the new House of Commons. Any minority government, either Labour or Conservative, had to reckon with the vote of these new parties, which were put in a particularly strong bargaining position. Moreover, as the Royal Commission had already disclosed the intention of Westminster to have new assemblies and perhaps governments in Scotland and Wales, the regional MPs considered themselves to be the harbingers of other Parliaments and of other sovereignties to be established or re-established and as the bearers of 'imperative mandates' for one issue alone, the issue of future relations between their 'country' and the UK. Indeed, the trend towards separatism became rapidly stronger both in Scotland and in Northern Ireland. In the latter, the power-sharing institutions favoured by Westminster collapsed. In Scotland the polls, and all other signs, pointed to further and greater successes by the Scottish Nationalist Party.

Now if one links the historical and political backgrounds of the three provinces with the impact of the industrial-technological revolution on the old relationship between the provinces and England, one sees only too clearly how the uneven economic development of the peripheral regions has affected these relations.

At the beginning of industrialization, Scotland (to take one example) was one of the principal areas of rapid industrial development. But the first century or so of industrialization brought with it two evils for the peoples in whose land it took place. On the one hand, the actual pay, the physical condition and the social and political position of the workers were miserable; this was the period which left the working-class everywhere in the British Isles, but especially in Scotland, with irreconcilable memories of exploitation by capitalist owners – who, at the time, were indeed building fabulous fortunes. – The Scottish workers and working class drew precious few advantages from the first industrial revolution. On the contrary, the first industrial revolution savagely despoiled the landscape, polluted the environment and created the 'slums' which until recently have been the stigma of Scottish industrial areas.

As industries in Scotland were heavily concentrated and highly specialized (mining, shipbuilding and textiles) the recession between the two world wars hit Scottish industry particularly sharply. In the thirties a quarter of Scottish workers were unemployed – a percentage considerably higher than in England. Since then, and until recently, the discrepancy between Scotland and England has been accentuated. The effects on British industry of Britain's loss of power in the international arena has led to a continuing economic crisis in Britain – which since the fifties has become a permanent and increasingly evident factor of the international situation. But the crisis, like all crises, affected most directly the weaker parts of British industry, and Scotland, like the other peripheral regions, was already one of the most sensitive parts of the country.[1] The fact that in the meantime the industrial-technological revolution was beginning to give a new impulse to industrial societies but to Britain less than to the USA, the USSR, Germany and France, only aggravated the plight of Scotland and the regions in general. Technological industries, and generally speaking, those modern industries based on electricity, were more concentrated in England, and especially in southern England – while in Scotland the shipbuilding and mining industries declined. Again, unemployment, the thermometer of economic indisposition, rose more steeply in the regions than in the UK as a whole.[2]

Similarly, it is fair to say that sometimes so-called 'national policies' adversely affected Scotland and the other regions. It is a fact that, in different circumstances, and with different backgrounds, the solutions prescribed could have different if not opposite effects. To take the best known cases, deflationary measures adopted for the country as a whole proved to be counter-productive for the three peripheral regions where unemployment was higher than in England. So did the selective employment tax, particularly in Scotland and Wales with their strong dependence on tourism. Finally, the concentration of government departments, boards and agencies, and of the headquarters of industrial enterprises in London, renders the various kinds of decision-making process distant from, and indifferent to, the remote parts of the country – and creates a 'national brain-drain'.

1. In the words of the Kilbrandon Report: 'If people in Scotland and Wales knew more about the present system...they might well accept that their economic problems have arisen mainly from over-concentration on certain heavy industries in an age where there was little economic planning and more recently, from uncontrollable developments such as changes in world markets, the decline of coal-mining as an economic co-operation and the difficulties inherent in building up new industries in relatively remote areas.' Op. cit., 450.
2. In 1970 the percentages of unemployment were 4.3% in Scotland, 4% in Wales, 7% in Northern Ireland and 2.3% in England. *Abstract of Regional Statistics 1972*, table 27.

The perception of such contradictions between 'national interests' and 'regional interests' creates in the peoples of the regions a local antipathy towards 'the English state' or 'London' or 'Westminster', comparable with the social antipathy towards the 'class- or bourgeois-state' or 'the Establishment'. (Often the two attitudes are combined in a double hostility to the English bourgeois state, but there is an inevitable crossroads between the nationalist-traditional and the international-revolutionary orientations.) This basic antipathy makes the peoples of the regions impervious to the argument that, of late at least, Scotland, Wales and Northern Ireland have been the object of special attention in the state's policies of equalization between different areas and official allocation of grants to industry; and that generally speaking the central government spends more on the regions than it gets from them.[1] Such arguments are met with a bitter feeling of 'too little and too late'.

Indeed, since Scotland had the lucky windfall of the discovery of oil in the North Sea, which the Scottish nationalists consider as 'their' sea, the movement towards separatism has forged ahead at great speed. This was a turn of events due entirely to the industrial-technological revolution. The new technical means of exploration and the extraction of oil from the depths of the sea transformed the economic Cinderella of the British Isles into one of the potentially richest of its regions almost overnight. Proposals and appeals to use North Sea oil for the benefit of the entire national economy or, even worse, for that of the European Community, are bluntly countered by the Scottish Nationalists. On the contrary, riding high on this newly discovered 'economic autonomy' of their country, they want to lead their peoples with a vengeance along the path of a somewhat anachronistic Scottish autarchy.

Like Scotland, Northern Ireland suffered especially severely from the decline of traditional British industries after the Second World

1. According to the official calculations examined by the Kilbrandon committee, the expenditure of the central government in Scotland, Wales and Northern Ireland exceeded revenues by a very substantial margin (ibid., 460).

War (as previously noted the percentage of unemployment was higher in the province than in any other parts of the UK), and like Scotland it has been particularly affected by the national economic crisis. To that extent, and with two other highly relevant circumstances which will be examined presently, the industrial-technological changes influenced the evolution of developments in the province, which rapidly took a most dramatic turn. But the different geographic, ethnic, historic, religious, economic and social causes of the Ulster tragedy are so enmeshed that it is very difficult to disentangle them.

Northern Ireland is, for causes too well known to be re-examined here, the most peculiar of all three British regions. It faces the possibility of secession followed by direct union with another country, independent from the UK. Historically, it has been the theatre not only of conflicts with England, but of divisions between its two populations. In religious matters the two populations are opposed to each other by irreconcilabilities between Catholics and Protestants. Nationally, the two populations are divided between those who want reunion with Eire, those who want 'integration' with Great Britain, and those who favour Ulster autonomy, if not sovereignty. Socially, the Ulster Protestants are a dominant élite, and the Irish Catholics a dominated proletariat. These incompatibilities do not add together, but impinge on each other so as to create a total stalemate.

Turning to the two aspects of the Northern Ireland imbroglio relevant to this study, the first was revealed in its full significance only in relatively recent developments of the Ulster drama. This was the strike of the self-styled Ulster Workers' Council in the last ten days of May 1974, which brought down the Faulkner Executive – a power-sharing 'coalition of moderate Irish Catholics and Ulster Protestants', – and together with it the entire structure of the 'Sunningdale agreements' which had been reached with such difficulty. The success of the anti-Sunningdale Unionists in February 1974 had already been a warning against any hope that the agreements might provide a lasting basis for a new political system. But, as in the events which had preceded the February elections in Britain, what overthrew the Executive and shook the constitutional arrangements was the direct action of organized industrial workers.

To be sure, the circumstances were so similar to those of the miners' strike in Britain that the irony of the reversed situations struck most commentators. On the surface it was ironical to see Mr Wilson and the Labour Party, who had encouraged, and ultimately profited from, the miners' strike, condemning as 'sectional', 'mutinous' and 'illegal' the action of the Ulster Workers' Council and considering demands coming not only from within the Labour Party, but from the Left wing of the Labour Party, to call on troops to put an end to the 'illegal' strike. And again, superficially, it was ironic to see the British trade unions, still proud of the political power which they had just displayed in the British crisis, finding their appeals to the industrial workers of Ulster contemptuously ignored and seeing their General Secretary leading a meagre column of demonstrators against the strike through the empty streets of Belfast.

These contrasts were in reality only the most blatant confirmation of the fact that in an industrial-technological democracy power can be exercised unilaterally by any group of industrial producers which can by its direct action bring the functioning of the society to a halt. It also confirms that no matter which party is in power, the functional relation between the Government and the strikers remains the same, the former invoking the law, the latter defying it. It is the functional relation which matters. The ideological aspects attached to it are sometimes incidental and ultimately irrelevant. In the case of the Ulster Workers Council the motives for action were not social at all but exclusively regional and political. Their leaders were not elected or indeed known to the workers, let alone to the international working-class organizations. Indeed their action had been carried out against the will and the injunctions of the trade unions and the Socialist Party – which in the British crises had almost always managed to give the impression that they were controlling, if not leading, the action. The fact that the Socialists called the Ulster Workers Council's leaders 'fascists' did not affect the result of the latter's exceptionally successful industrial action.

So successful was the action of those who ultimately control

Ulster's industrial production and services, that it illuminated two other important aspects. First, it left no doubt that the industry of the province was manned almost exclusively by Ulster Protestants and that, as had frequently been alleged, the Irish Catholic population played little part in industry.

The trade unions both in the Republic and in the Province had during the years of crisis shown an admirable international solidarity and had played a conciliatory part on both sides.[1] But in reality the trade unions and their leadership had no control over the workers who really mattered, the workers in essential production and services. Thus, the Ulster strike highlighted the old, functional opposition of the workers' council to the trade union, already discussed in a previous chapter of this book.[2]

Finally, the Ulster strike demonstrated visibly and painfully that in industrial-technological societies politicians and political parties are dependent on industrial or other organizations which have the means of direct action. The Paisleyites and Craigites who rejoiced publicly at the success of the strike and its ultimate result of bringing down the fragile Sunningdale agreements, were in reality only following the leaders of the industrial activists and were aware of their dependence on the latter. In the opposite camp, the leaders of the Irish Social Democratic and Labour parties realized that the IRA, which has direct terrorist means of action, would again take up the fight. Further progress resulting from the action of militant organizations in both camps might leave the politicians of both sides suspended over a yawning vacuum of public credibility.

The second circumstance in the Ulster situation which links old and traditional ways of action with means which have been changed by industrial-technological action, is the use of violence. Whereas the conflicts between Scotland or Wales and the central government often lead to emotive clashes, terrorist violence does not play the permanent and fundamental part which it has played in the Ulster

1. See Charles McCarthy, 'Civil strife and the growth of trade union unity: the case of Ireland'. In *Government and Opposition*, vol. 8, no. 4, 1973.
2. See above, pp. 31–2.

crisis ever since, after the riots in Londonderry's Bogside in 1969,[1] the Provisional IRA first started to take 'military action'. This in turn pushed the official IRA into action. Gradually an Ulster Defence Association and an Ulster Volunteer Force emerged, no less prepared than the IRA groups to use terrorism and violence as principal means of action. The conflicts between the terrorist organizations led in 1970 to the parcelling out of the territory of Belfast into 'no-go' areas controlled, or indeed 'protected' by those organizations. It took the determined action of the British Army to restore full sovereignty in these pockets of outlawry. Indeed, the British Army became more and more involved in military operations in the Province, with the privilege, sometimes, of having to fight on both fronts.

None of this was new or specific; it bespoke the re-emergence of traits only too familiar in the history of Britain's political presence in Ireland. What was new was the amplification of political resonance which the industrial-technological society provides. The weapons used are easier to obtain and more lethal in their effects. The industrial concentration in large conurbations makes the terrorist action, or, indeed, even threat, much more effective. The interdependence of industrial life transmutes the apparent side-effects of terrorist action into large collective problems. The new means of communication greatly amplify the echo of terrorist action. Violence and organized terrorism have changed so substantially in quantity and quality that they are an entirely different political means. Violence prefigures the possibility of an age of praetorian politics, with a political process in no need of representative institutions, but requiring blind discipline from professional followers of very simplified ideologies. It also brings directly into reckoning the political role of the Army, which is called upon more and more frequently to remove terrorist-created obstructions of even the elementary functioning of the intricate mechanism of industrial society.

The case of Ulster does not resemble that of any other region of Britain. It is unique in its intricacies. But what Ulster brings to mind is the image of a polity reduced to paralysis and ultimately to self-destruction by the stalemate produced within the community by the

1. See Paul Wilkinson, *Political Terrorism*, London, 1974.

irreconcilable, and variously-motivated, centrifugal tendencies of the opposing forces in the community. Ulster long ago reached the point of destroying its own elements of sovereignty. A less centrifugal society would have found the way either of using the old representative institutions or through the long-negotiated Sunningdale agreements of finding a new centre of 'power-sharing'. New forms of representative institutions and corporate participation would have been created which, given time and a modicum of patience, could have been adapted into modern and satisfactory institutional structures. The opposition of the main forces in conflict made such institutions, the embryo-institution of the Province's future sovereignty, unworkable. Ulster now is held back from Civil War only by the presence of the British Army, in direct occupation of the territory of a province which had once enjoyed a certain degree of sovereignty. If the British Army withdraws (and there are no obvious reasons why the growing demand for withdrawal should not prevail one day) Ulster will be left to be devoured by the centrifugalism which has led it gradually to sink into disorganization and disintegration.

Ulster is the tragic model of the a-potent society in which power is so divided among the functional, national, religious and other forces of the society that if no new *political* structures, capable of uniting all these centrifugal forces into one common action, are found, the entire society will come to a terrible end. The division of power in modern societies leads to the neutralization of power by power, which is tantamount to powerlessness, or what is called here the political a-potence of society. Power is now exercised in Ulster only by military, non-political means, and only against opposed armed power. But permanent military conflicts can hardly conduce to the functioning of the industrial-technological society, a society in particular need of positive exchange of services and of dynamic inter-co-operation. The stalemate created by opposing centrifugalisms inevitably spells the end of the state.

With this we turn to the question of whether, and how, the centrifugal tendencies which cut through the political fabric of the United Kingdom can be brought back into some new institutions of political centripetalism.

Chapter Five

Partnerships at the national level: some transitional conclusions

There are of course many other groups and forces in modern society which, like the three corporate forces described in the preceding chapters, have experienced increasing centrifugalism as a result of developments in the industrial–technological society. Racial minorities, like the regions, have felt discriminated against in the affluent society. The mass media have mobilized them for action more effectively than ever before. New means of armed attack and defence have quickly transformed that action into terrorism.

Youth is another centrifugal force. Seldom in history have children been more estranged from, and hostile to, their parents than during the last decades. It was as if an earthquake had split the plateau which they shared with their parents into two cliffs, divided by an abyss. Rendered unusually precocious by the information with which they had been force-fed, and by the coincident revolution in *mores*, the young grew away from their elders, whose world now seemed to them unacceptable. They rebelled against the harsh and claustrophobic industrial society. Some burnt computers, some took to the 'alternative society' and created their own communes and counter cultures. Some found refuge in drugs which enabled them to take 'trips' out of a frightening or depressing reality. Some joined in revolutionary activities, and they too were soon engaged in violence.

Women too felt that the opportunity had come to throw off the shackles of their historically inferior role. In general, groups with all kinds of values and motivations were pushed towards independent action.

If I have concentrated on the three 'corporate' forces, it is because they are, for obvious reasons, the most important and the most accessible to the politics of the changing society. For, while the younger generation must, with the passage of time, in the end be absorbed by the society it hopes to modify, and if women also must, for biological and other reasons, come to terms with the opposite sex in a society which they will have transformed, the case of the estrangement of the corporate forces from the old national interest is quite different. Here the change must be explicit. This *political* estrangement requires a *political* reconciliation with newly institutionalized means of collaboration between representative government and corporate forces.

As this is to my knowledge one of the few works in which the three corporate forces are examined together, I have looked in turn at the trade unions, the enterprises and the regions, and tried to pinpoint, in a deliberately descriptive way, their respective grievances and the irremediability of their respective separation from the old body politic.

The preliminary conclusions which I shall submit in this chapter, as well as the centripetal solutions which I shall here propose as means to enable the corporate forces to share power with the governments, can only be tentative. General conclusions taking into account the full scope of adjustments which representative government will have to make to its manner of functioning must wait for the examination of yet another kind of partnership, the supranational partnership which will be studied in the next chapter. Here I must limit myself to those conclusions and possible solutions which are relevant only to the representative–corporate form of partnership which might be established within the national community.

The first conclusion one can draw from a brief examination of the British political crisis of 1973–4 is that it seems to have brought about a rapid dislocation of the body politic. Left wing ideologists might well describe the situation as a characteristically pre-revolutionary 'duality of power' between the old bourgeois representative institutions and the new revolutionary social forces of 'councils' – workers' councils and local councils. Right-wing ideologists might describe it as a vacuum of power which, if not filled by governments emerging from the parliamentary regime, should be filled by an extra-parliamentary government based on 'law and order'. Neither of these diagnoses, though, takes sufficiently into account the characteristic evolution of politics towards power-sharing.

The second conclusion which can be drawn is that the crisis itself was of what Jeremy Bray has called, in his book of the same title, *Decision in Government*. This crisis was due on the one hand to the fact that the multiple decision-making centres oppose each other to the point of creating administrative deadlocks. On the other hand, it was due to the fact that solutions to national problems were still sought separately in the political-administrative sphere and in the economic sphere. These separate approaches split the global approach to political economy down the middle, though this approach is the only one relevant to, and appropriate for, the inter-dependent problems of governability in the industrial-technological society.[1] Attempts made more recently in Britain to find a better system of decision-making (for, ultimately, most of these examinations since the Plowden Report of 1961 and the Fulton Report of 1965, have been focused upon 'decision in government') fall into two categories. There are those which concentrate principally on economic problems, and especially the problem of growth. And there are those which concentrate more directly on political and especially administrative problems. Finally there are only a few, in the middle, which try to link the two aspects into what is called the study of 'political economy'. This has also been true of academic studies; the economic and political disciplines have kept very much within their 'worlds'. In official inquiries and examinations the maintenance of this dichotomy has led to the overlooking of a significant contradiction: between the need for deconcentration in the political-administrative sphere and the need for concentration in the economic sphere.

1. How diffuse and intricate political-economic decision-making has become in the inter-dependent industrial-technological society can be seen, for instance, from the overleaf organogram of the 'Present forecasting method' of the Treasury, made by the Treasury itself and reproduced in *Decision in Government*, London, 1970, p. 112.

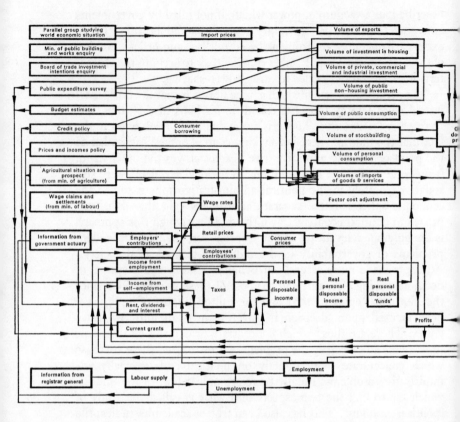

Figure 1: The main exogenous factors and the main relationships taken into account in forecasting domestic developments (from Memorandum by H.M. Treasury in Estimates Committee Report on Government Statistical Services, HMSO, 1966).

Let us take first the political-administrative reforms which have been sought. The conclusions of the Majority Report of the Royal Commission on the Constitution strongly advocated deconcentration by devolution. The contrast between the enormous increase in the activities of government and the pace of change in government institutions was evident and increasing. Most of the complaints about the working of the system sprang from centralization in London, and from practices which led to the weakening of democracy. But the Report noted an opposing view, 'that in an advanced industrial society, government must necessarily be mainly from the centre'. Some of the complaints about the weakening of democracy related to the role of the backbench MP, the party-system in Parliament, the growth of *ad hoc* bodies appointed by the government. The report noted that there was a desire for opportunity to participate in government and a feeling that government was remote. In the regions this dissatisfaction with government had an added dimension of national feeling. The report found both separatism and federalism infeasible in Britain – but strongly recommended devolution. This was defined as 'a delegation of central government powers which would leave over-riding control in the hands of Parliament'. The Report acknowledged that the 'Northern Ireland experience before 1972 is a guide to the technical and practical workings of devolution' but proceeded nevertheless to recommend the 1948 solutions of similar legislative (regional assemblies) and executive and administrative devolution (implementing the Parliament's policies and providing the general administration) to the assemblies and their organs. Finally it proposed setting up regional councils as advisory bodies functioning in *all* regions. As for the general problem of the British political system, the Report regarded 'as particularly important the problem of communication between government and people'.

While the Majority Report of the Royal Commission was limited in the scope of its inquiry to political and administrative problems and in its solutions did not differ very much from the old adjustments already made in the classical structure of British government, the Memorandum of Dissent revealed by comparison a greater sense of contemporaneousness in at least two respects. Although the

Memorandum also limited itself to political-administrative problems and did not link them with the problems of economic policy from which the strongest stresses of present British society originate, it has a sense of historical change. One of its premises is the new fact of British membership of the European Community. This leads its authors to stress that the real problems of sovereignty in Britain should now be examined at the top (national) echelons and at the centre of government, and not only at the lower (regional) echelons and at the periphery. To put such emphasis on British entry into the EEC might in retrospect seem somewhat unwarranted. Britain is, at the time of writing, re-negotiating its membership in the EEC, and the EEC itself has since 1974 taken on a much more pragmatic and international, rather than supra-national character.

But first let us assume, like the authors of the Memorandum, that with ups and downs the EEC will remain a fact of life of the future British political system. In any case, what is fundamentally valid in the Memorandum's approach, is the assumption that, regardless of the forms and of the areas in which the sharing of British sovereignty will ultimately take place, Britain will have to share her sovereignty with some powers, in better or worse conditions according to the opportunities and to her choice. The Memorandum's perception that 'more and more major problems have to be decided in a European context and at a European level',[1] is the right one.

To be sure the authors use this premise to advance the rather lopsided conclusion that Parliament and local government must be strengthened so as to enable them to resist the pull of European bureaucracy. This is a natural view (although a different view from the one that will be taken in this book) precisely because it starts from the initial assumption of the different 'context' in which decisions are and increasingly will be taken. But what the Memorandum questions, albeit implicitly, is the ability of any European nation-state to make its major decisions, and prepare its major policies, without first taking into consideration the European or international dimension. One can rightly consider most of the failures and

1. Op. cit., p. xiv.

reversals of British economic policies in the last quarter of a century as the terrible vindication of the Memorandum's assumption that this can no longer be done.

The Memorandum proposes the creation in the United Kingdom of a uniform intermediate tier of government. It shows that such a tier already effectively exists in the immediate outposts of central government and in the various *ad hoc* authorities, and that even with the larger units of local government since April 1974, this intermediate government will still continue to exist. What the Memorandum proposes is that 'the jungle of boundaries' should be replaced by one set of standard regional boundaries, and that 'a centre of power' should be created in each of the regions of the Kingdom (five of which are English) to cope with all functional problems; and that an Ombudsman, of the New Zealand type, should be empowered to look at the merits of decisions thus taken and recommend redress of complaints of individuals and subordinate authorities.

Again, what is of interest to the argument of this book is not so much the merits or demerits of the regional decentralization proposed by the Memorandum, or the possible contradictions in its reasoning (for it could be argued that if there were to be further transfers of sovereignty to Brussels and further regional emancipation in the UK, the result might well be the creation of a direct and flexible link between the regions and Brussels). What is of great importance and relevance here is the Memorandum's idea of creating new and equal centres of decision-making which can produce in the terminology of this book, a new *centripetal* (in the sense of rallying) and not *centralistic* (in the sense of subordinating) effect on the future political processes of the country.

What is also of importance is that the Memorandum, unlike the Majority Report, accepts the hypothesis that the regional centres may form, together with the old centre of traditional British Government and with whatever new centres of decision-making may emerge, a multi-central chain of decision-making. And the *functioning* of that chain is by implication a continuous process of centripetal politics at all levels, in which forces of the industrial-technological society and all units and sub-units of the administration of Britain can influence each other in a continuous dialectic of decision-making.

But let us now look at the reforms proposed in the economic sphere, of which the purpose, unlike those proposed in the political-administrative sphere, is to achieve greater co-ordination and con-centration in decision-making.

The conglomerate of problems which comprises the 'mixed economy' of Britain is subject to different interpretations, according to whether the interpreters are defenders of the public or the private sector, of the interests of labour or capital, of the interests of local or central administration, of the trade unions or the enterprises, of the Con-servative or the Labour parties[1] (which always renew, while in opposition, their faith in their respective economic and social doctrines, but soon abandon them when faced with the involved problems of governing a mixed economy).

Keynesianism and the test of war-time economy had brought the two parties nearer to a middle-of-the-road position. Keynesian-ism provided an adequate perspective for understanding the mixed economy as it is, as a Western European type, different from both pure liberal and pure statist economies, and with all its inter-dependent economic, social, political and international aspects. But more recently, with the consumer society flooded by inflation, and with the decline of British economic growth when compared, at least since 1950, with that of other European countries, the 'mixed' approach has been increasingly questioned in Britain.

Extreme formulations of the old contradictory ideological pur-poses of free economy (Enoch Powell) versus socialist planning (Anthony Wedgwood Benn) acquired a new lease of credibility precisely because the 'mixed' approaches had, since the fifties, repeatedly failed. But instead of wondering whether these failures had been caused by the insufficiency of effort to carry through one version or another of the mixed economy, the new extremists blamed the system as a whole.

1. 'Britain has a mixed economy which the overwhelming majority of Labour supporters believed in as their definition of democratic socialism.' James Callaghan, 10 April 1975.

The repeated short-lived and half-hearted attempts of Conservative and Labour Governments alike to launch long-term economic policies are usually said to begin with the creation by the Conservatives in 1961 of the National Economic Development Council. Based on the tripartite consultation between government, trade unions and industry, on the research and plans presented by NEDO (the Office of the Council), and on the detailed information provided to it by some twenty-one Economic Development Committees, NEDC was expected to work out long-term economic policies and programmes. It was destined to fulfil, at least partly, the mission successfully accomplished in France by the new planning institutions experimented with in that country since 1946. NEDO's principal achievement was the publication in 1966 of two planning papers, *Growth of the United Kingdom Economy in 1966*, and *Conditions favourable to foster growth*. Growth has remained ever since the principal aim of all British economic policies, and the tripartite system of consultation has also remained, since 1966, the general model of all British endeavours to provide a new framework for the political economy, regardless of the political party in power.

What did differ according to the party in power was the relation between the Government and the Planning Consultative agencies. Whereas the Conservatives left the latter outside the official state machinery, Labour believed that they would begin to work efficiently only if located within the machinery of the State. Thus the Wilson Government of 1964 proceeded by creating a Department of Economic Affairs, incorporating NEDO, which by virtue of its proximity to the seats of decision-making would become more effective than the NEDC to which it was previously subordinated. Moreover, new Economic Planning Councils were created in each region of the land, with the purpose of providing direct information to the government now in charge of planning. Thus the controversies on the theme of consultation versus private interests were passionately renewed.

The British National Plan was produced in 1965 by the new Department of Economic Affairs. It was again aimed at the pursuit of growth, with inevitably inflationary or indeed reflationary rationales. The international currency crisis hit the pound sterling, at the time the most exposed of all currencies, most directly; it caused the Labour Government, which for internal and international reasons had not proceeded earlier with devaluation, to again accept the Treasury's classic deflationary prescriptions. The crisis was partly solved, devaluation was once more postponed. What went by the board though, was the National Plan. The British Government, unlike the French or German governments of the same period, had failed once more to sustain a long-term policy. This incapacity of the Government contrasted unfavourably with the successful planning of the large enterprises, and especially of the self-contained multi-national corporations. As noted in a previous chapter, the enterprises themselves had, since the Brighton conference of 1960, been asking the Government to produce a plan which could be synchronized with their own. The collapse of the National Plan, and subsequently of the DEA, made this commonly acceptable purpose unrealizable.

Compelled to limit itself to less ambitious devices the Wilson Government proceeded to mount yet a new para-governmental agency, the Industrial Reorganisation Corporation.[1] The main purpose of this corporation was to foster mergers in industry where 'production units are small by comparison with the most successful companies in international trade'. But the IRC soon began to turn into another office of industrial policy-making which thus filled, in part at least, the vacuum left by the collapse of the National Plan, and promised, or threatened (according to the party view) to become a state holding company. According to Dell, had the Labour Party been returned in the 1970 elections, it would have enlarged the purposes of the IRC while at the same time submitting it to more parliamentary control. Parliamentary control would have helped to reassure the Confederation of British Industry, which, in spite of its initial hostility to the Corporation, ended up approving of at least some of IRC's activities. Another agency which was beginning to

1. Cmnd. 2889, HMSO, 1966. See also a good description of that institution and of its short life in Dell, op. cit., pp. 74–84.

show its future importance in a society already feeling the effect of inflation was the National Board for Prices and Incomes (PIB) especially as amended by the Prices and Incomes Act 1967 to include cases of industrial action. The latter are also dealt with by the Commission on Industrial Relations, set up in 1969.

Torn from within by the contradictions in the Labour movement as a whole on the subject of industrial relations, and on the twin subjects of incomes and prices, which estranged the trade unions from the Labour Party, the Labour Government fell from power in 1970. The Conservative Government started afresh in the full swing of economic liberalism by abolishing both the Industrial Reorganisation Corporation and the Prices and Incomes Board, but strengthened the Commission on Industrial Relations through the Industrial Relations Act 1971 by creating a National Industrial Relations Court. What followed has been described in a previous chapter.

But while most of the national institutions, plans and long-term policies of economic policy-making were condemned because of their fragility and consequent inconsistency, there was a growth of direct economic decision-making by what, for want of a better name, could best be described as *ad hoc* functional bodies (boards, associations, councils). Such bodies are usually classified according to their legal authority and, more specifically, the extent of their autonomy of decision-making *vis-à-vis* the central or local organs of government. Their relations with these organs oscillate between periods of 'hive-off' and periods of 'control'. Yet, from a policy-making point of view, these bodies are easier to distinguish insofar as they mix in their composition public, elected representatives, socio-economic delegates, and government appointees. This mixture of personnel jointly participating in the making of decisions, as well as the limitation of their sphere of influence to one special range of activities, gives to their decisions and decision-making processes an entirely different, functional, character.

The *ad hoc* functional bodies were first set up as provisional and un-institutionalized organisms, characteristic of the period of transition when the new welfare state was taking upon itself further obligations and responsibilities, for which its old institutions were unequipped both in terms of decision-making (competence and know-how) or in terms of implementation (authority and personnel).

These bodies were *ad hoc* because, first, they did not have legal, let alone constitutional, uniformity across the country. They did not always exist everywhere, and where they did their composition and their competence varied from region to region, and from period to period, sometimes from a Conservative to a Labour period of government, sometimes within the life span of one single government. And, then, partly as a sequel to this alternance in government, but mostly owing to their rapid obsolescence, they were frequently re-defined and re-named, albeit sometimes even then left without an appropriate legal authority. But the more the enlarged and still expanding economic and industrial functions of the state were becoming permanent, the more the *ad hoc* character of these bodies was becoming a contradiction in terms. Indeed, this spontaneous and continuous growth of *ad hoc* functional bodies in economic and industrial matters is one of the major and most symptomatic trends toward centripetalism in both the administrative and economic fields of decision-making in post-war British society. Yet in spite of the significance and perseverance of the trend they remain insufficiently institutionalized. It was therefore natural that in both economic and administrative fields a need was felt to have a network of permanent bodies institutionalized at all levels, which could act legally as intermediate centres of competent and responsible decision-making.

These intermediate bodies should indeed be organized and empowered so as to be able to mediate between the central and local administration, between the higher and the lower echelons of administration, between the experts and the administrators, and finally, between the polity and the economy. The inter-penetration of corporate forces and the representative institutions, which in theory is the alternative to the growing 'confrontation' between these two elements, could be, as in Sweden, France or the Federal Republic of Germany, given fuller institutional responsibility and accountability, even if this would seem to impair the sovereignty of parliament and government. The widespread complaint against the *ad hoc*, functional bodies, that they take illegitimate decisions insofar as they are not elected and representative, is justified while these bodies have a doubtful constitutional authority and an equivocal accountability. But if a constitutional or legal reform were effected it could transform the functional bodies into permanent and official centres of decision-making.

If one were to speculate further one could see other changes in the British constitutional system which would add up to functional reform. The ultimate, but logical consequence would be the advent of functional multi-cameralism. The British bicameral parliamentary system is not new to the idea of constitutional reform. Many of its previous efforts propose new rules and responsibilities for the House of Lords, and even to transform it into a functional assembly of the realm. From another point of view the British parliamentary system has experimented with the Stormont Assembly in Northern Ireland, and seems to be amenable to similar experiment in Scotland and Wales. In these three regions, or indeed in the proposed eight regions a multi-cameralism, is not beyond possibility, each region having its own assembly. But if this kind of geographic decentralization is acceptable, a functional deconcentration of Parliament through subordinate functional chambers should also be acceptable: an Economic Chamber, a Chamber of the Regions, a Chamber for Education and Culture, etc. This deconcentration of Parliament could also answer to the need for expert and specialized decision-making, so indispensable in the industrial-technological society.

To be sure, innovation in such matters would go against the straightforward British political system of one sovereign Parliament with two parties alternating in power on the basis of a 'simple plurality' or 'first past the post' electoral rule. This system had, until now, the advantage of being the simplest to understand as well as the most conducive to strong, homogeneous, party government as against the minority and coalition governments of the other West European states. But, as will be argued at greater length in the final conclusions of this book, one becomes increasingly aware of the indirect political and social disadvantages of this simple system. For precisely because it works in an alternative and clearcut way, which leaves the public without intermediate choices and nuances and without built-in possibilities for compromises, alignments and coalitions, the political system aggravates the main danger of the industrial-technological society, i.e. its divisiveness. The political system concentrates into one chamber all the variegated interests and functional points of view, and into two parties all the choices of these interests and points of view. Thus the political system itself divides society into two camps which, by ideological interpretation, become two classes. A multi-cameral parliament could 'defuse' this added political explosiveness.

The other much more general consequence, and therefore the less susceptible to constitutional reform, is the change at all levels from processes of consultation to processes of concertation. Building all these new institutions would remain an illusory operation if there were no appropriate kinds of action animating them. As a matter of fact, one of the reasons why the attempts at economic and administrative reforms have constantly failed has been the fact that the new institutions which they created (decentralized administrative boards or functional economic boards) were opposed to the traditional nature of the British political system itself, a system of centralized power by means of representation. Non-representative participation and functional institutions are by definition opposed, as we have seen in the first chapters of this book, to a structure of power, which leads to centralization. They need a different political process, based on and leading to the mutual sharing of power, which by the very nature of modern society, would lead to direct and competent decision-making, and direct responsibility and accountability. This political process is the politics of concertation.

Elsewhere I have defined this concept thus: 'The politics of concertation is the range of actions by which modern public organizations endeavour to feed into their processes of decision-making an adequate amount of information from, and participation by, the socio-economic interests. The public organizations which practise the politics of concertation include national bodies, national governments and international or supra-national organizations. The organizations may have a political or an economic focus and they may be geared to systems of either public or private ownership. As is the case with indicative planning (the expression comes from the French *économie concertée* which was one of the ways in which the founders of the French plan described their system) the purpose of concertation is to co-ordinate over a long period of years the socio-economic activities of a community and to direct them toward anticipated targets...the politics of concertation recognize explicitly the need for a preliminary involvement of all the groups and layers of a community in the discussion of policy since their consent and co-operation is required for its implementation. But in the case of concertation it is assumed that those who take part in the making of a decision are more closely involved and committed than they are in the formal process of consultation. In this latter case the authorities reserve the right to choose whom they want to consult, and to accept or reject their advice, while the consulted are free to follow or to desist from a particular opinion. But when the authorities practise concertation they endeavour to take direct account of the opinions of interest groups and to incorporate them and reconcile them all in the formulation of the final policy. And the participants too are more involved in an activity in which the collaboration of all concerned is a *sine qua non* condition of the reaching of a decision.'[1]

The fact that the United Kingdom lags behind in the adoption of the technique of concertation for its economic and social policies constitutes one of the salient differences between this country and not only Sweden, but also France and Germany. These other major European nation-states – which happen to have been more successful in the pursuit of economic growth than the United Kingdom in the last decades – operate two different and indeed opposed economic theories. Germany's official ideology is a staunch defence of pure liberalism and economic competitiveness, while France is by tradition more dirigiste. Most of the modern (indeed rapidly modernized) French economy is centred around the idea of indicative planning – and the idea of indicative planning is inextricably linked

1. *Between Sovereignty and Integration*, pp. 21–22.

with the technique of the 'politics of concertation'. To be sure, it can be said that the politics of concertation and the indicative planning were helped forward in France by the authoritarianism of the Constitution of 1958, in which Parliament was made to 'share power' with institutions of concertation like the Social and Economic Council, the *Commissariat du plan* or the *Commissions de modernisation*. But the example of Germany, which now has a sound parliamentary system, proves the contrary. It was precisely the concept of 'concertation' that the thoroughly liberal, and thoroughly parliamentary German system of politics has borrowed from the French, and has absorbed into its own system of government. This happened in the mid-sixties, when the Federal Republic of Germany was facing a danger of recession – and when the transition towards the '*Grosse Koalition*', uniting Christian-Democrats and Social-Democrats was being effected.

The policy of what the then Minister of Economics, Karl Schiller, called 'the enlightened market economy' and which was described as 'to develop a compatible system which could reconcile systematic consideration of national problems with economic freedom and with an international outlook on the part of socio-economic groups and economic units',[1] was embodied in three acts passed in the mid-sixties. One was the Stability and Growth Act (1965), another the Principles of Sectoral Policy (1966), and the third the Principles of the Federal Government's Sectoral and Regional Economic Policy (1968). The first of these acts introduced to the political economy of Germany the French notion of 'concerted action' or of 'concertedness'. A German analyst of the system describes concertedness as follows:

concerted action on incomes policy had previously been proposed in mid-1965 by the Export Council which had obviously drawn its inspiration from the French model of the *économie*

1. See a penetrating analysis of this policy in George H. Küster, 'Germany', in Raymond Vernon (ed.), *Big Business and the State*, Cambridge, Mass., 1974.

concertée...Concerted action to achieve the aims of stabiliza-
tion policy was described as 'a kind of multilateral gentlemen's
agreement controlled by an enlightened public'. Unified conduct by government and socio-economic groups in the field of
income policy was to be reached through the conviction and
insight of group representatives. The result would be agreement on guidelines for budget, wages and price policy'.[1]

The new 'concertedness' worked particularly well in the period of
recession in 1966-7, when all interests co-operated very actively in
order to avoid the economic crisis, but less well in the ensuing 'boom'
when interests followed their own profit-making in a more selfish
way.

The Act on the Principles of Sectoral Policies in turn organized
state assistance for industries in need of structural adaptation. The
basic principle of competitiveness was carefully observed by *a*)
limiting state intervention only to those sectors of industry in need
of rapid modernization and *b*) gradually withdrawing it as soon as
this could be done.[2] Finally, the principles of sectoral policies
attached important consideration to Research and Development for
which specially large grants were offered, and directly encouraged
the concentration of industry into large enterprises.[3] This helped
towards smoother and quicker concentration in the making of
economic policy. Küster notes that 'the process of concerted action
was highlighted by the techniques of voluntary agreement. The
government in effect made itself the abettor of oligopolistic arrangements by assuring the agreement's immunity from the Cartel Act
and by putting pressure on the small outsiders who had no effective

1. Ibid., p. 70.
2. OECD, *The Industrial Policies of Fourteen Member Countries*, Paris,
1971.
3. 'The Common Market and the trend to world-wide economic integration have created new premises for competition. The Federal government
is concerned to remove obstacles which stand in the way of concentration
of enterprises.' *Stellungsname der Bundesregierung zum Tätigkeitsbericht
des Bundeskartellamtes*, Bonn, 1967.

137

legal protectors. Public functions were thus transferred to large enterprises, and the special state competencies of the public and private sectors were conferred'.[1]

From a general point of view it must be observed that what is original in the concept of 'the politics of concertation' is the fact that it is a political process which combines the political dualism, corporate and representative, characteristic of the industrial-technological society with the economic need of that society for the regulatory functioning of the market and its natural competitiveness. The politics of concertation is the centripetal link between the functional power of decision-making of those who deliver the goods and provide the services in modern society, and the fundamental regulatory role of the market in that society. Thus the politics of concertation is supremely characteristic of the mixed economies of Europe, which when seen *as they are*, are intrinsically different from, and not transitional between, liberal and statist societies.

The reason why the 'politics of concertation' has been introduced at this point of the argument is that it is highly significant that two other European nation-states, both with successful economies but with different economic philosophies, have both of late defined their new approaches to the changed conditions of industrial-technological society as techniques of 'concertedness'. The difference between their adaptability to new political processes, and the difficulties in which the United Kingdom seems to find itself in accepting possible changes in its constitutional conceptions has however deeper causes, which all go back to the strong attachment of the British political system to the concepts of internal and external sovereignty.

If we compare the Federal Republic of Germany, which now has the most successful economy in Europe, and the United Kingdom, which now has one of the least successful economies in Europe, three other differences must be taken into consideration. All three are political and bear a direct relation to the idea of power and sovereignty. The first is that German industry since the sixties practices workers' co-operation (*Mitbestimmung*). This of course is 'concer-

1. Op. cit., p. 75.

tation' at the factory level, and across national industry. The second is that the Federal Republic is indeed a federation and that its *Länder* have, by constitutional right, a degree of autonomy which is much greater than anything that has yet been suggested for regional autonomy in British proposals for constitutional reform. That the *Länder* are gradually losing some of their rights to the federal authorities, is clearly caused by the increasing concentration of functional decision-making which is the other major trend of the industrial-technological society; but even so, this is 'concertation' at the regional level and across national sovereignty. Finally, like France, the Federal Republic of Germany is a full and active member of the European Community: 'concertation' at the international level, and recognition of the limitations on national sovereignty. How much this last factor is operative is the question to which we shall turn in Chapter six.

A further aspect of the trend toward decentralized politics in Britain concerns the sharing of power within the institutions of political representation themselves. Administrative decentralization and economic devolution amount ultimately to 'mixing' political and corporate institutions in the making of decisions and policies. Even the evolutionary trend of the political parties toward increasing domination by the respective interests – labour, business or regions – or the possible evolution of Parliament toward multi-cameralism, are merely syndromes of the trend toward mixed political-corporate methods of making decisions and policies. But could or should not the representative political institutions themselves reflect more adequately, *in their own sphere*, the trends of diffusion of power characteristic of the industrial-technological society?

This question has often recurred in the preceding parts of this study. Often, for instance, I have alluded to the probable need of British politics to grow into a pluri-party system. The trend toward the multiplication of British political parties is already visible. There were six political parties in the British Parliament elected in February 1974, and had it not been for the peculiar British electoral law the final distribution of seats would have been very different.

To be sure, the two-party system had great merits, above all that of lending continuity and consistency to the government in power while ensuring the alternation in power of two parties with different policies and personnel. But neither of these two advantages is exclusively linked with the two-party system. Regular alternation in power of different parties can equally be ensured with many parties, provided the people and the authorities employ fairness in playing by the rules of the constitutional game – a trait for which British politics remain unequalled. Historically, the two-party system has functioned at its best when a European nation-state has had a sufficiently self-contained sphere of policy-making and a society sufficiently under control to ensure that its policies would be implemented. But in post-imperial Britain, with the coming of the modern society, neither of these conditions could any longer be taken for granted.

In the new conditions, the continuation unchanged of an electoral and political system which predisposes toward polarization around two parties alone can prove counter-productive in at least two respects: 1) in terms of the credibility of the system as a whole, insofar as within their respective terms of office both parties are regularly constrained by circumstances beyond their control to go back on their own electoral pledges and programmes; 2) in terms of electoral choice and discrimination, on the one hand because it compresses the ever-widening range of highly specialized problems into grossly over-generalized and partisan slogans, and on the other because it forces the voters, fearful of 'wasting' their vote, to enrol in one or the other of the political blocs which seemingly and allegedly correspond to the class dichotomy of British society.

Thus the two-party system brings about a polarization which blurs equally the issues and the attitudes. A word must be said about the latter. Many students of British politics believe that of late the consciousness of the division in social classes, which is stronger in Britain than in other West European countries, has been further sharpened. In reality what has been sharpened by the industrial-technological revolution is the consciousness of a dichotomy between 'we and them'. But whereas 'them' is more easily identifiable as 'London' (or even 'the South'), 'the establishment' or 'the rich', the 'we' in the proposition differs according to the angle.

The generational, the regional or ethnical, the professional (white versus blue collar), the environmental (town versus country), the religious and many other cleavages cut across the dichotomy of proletariat-versus-bourgeoisie, the *Klassbewusstsein* predicted and fostered by Marxism. Politically this might not make a great deal of difference in a revolutionary situation, one of the side-effects of which is precisely that it brings together all those who are *against* the authority, regardless of what they are *for*. But it is particularly important for the normal functioning of the parliamentary system in an industrial-technological society and for the way in which that system could lend continuity and consistency to the governments which it produces.

The more power it shares with diversified centres of polarization of attitudes, and the more selective and pragmatic are the approaches toward the specialized issues which face modern societies, the *stronger* modern government will grow. This would therefore justify the multiplication of parties. And this would show the hidden advantage of that particularly arduous and humble technique of consultation, improvization and adjustments which we associate in our minds, and critically too, with coalition and minority governments.

A comparison of the record of strength of policies since the sixties of countries which practise coalition and minority governments *v.* those which practise homogenous one-party majority governments is not fully conclusive. The coalition category includes the country with the most stable (Germany) and the country with the least stable (Italy) national economic policy. The one-party category included a country which since the sixties has had a stable record (France) and a country which has had an unstable record (Great Britain) of national economic policy. Thus when it comes to the actual techniques by which economic policies are made, whether by apparently strong executives or apparently feeble executives which conduct hesitating all-round consultations, the choice might be better expressed with the help of a naval metaphor: when you board ship in a choppy sea do you run more risk of being thrown overboard if you walk like a landlubber or if you adopt the rolling gait of a sailor?

More conclusive though is the result of another comparative examination of the politics of Britain and the other West European nation-states. Most of these countries have increased their stability by institutionalizing mechanisms of power-sharing in economic policy-making both at the national and international levels, even at the risk of creating an impression of greater governmental instability. British government has conserved its traditional structures probably at the risk of finding its economic policies constantly frustrated and defeated. This is no reflection on British politics as a whole. Most Western European industrial countries, indeed most of the advanced industrial countries, have seen how their economic policies have been interrupted, diverted or defeated by unpropitious national and international conditions. And the overall record of British politics is as prestigiously high as ever. The fault lies in the tardiness with which the two governmental parties have envisaged, since the Second World War, the necessity to share power both at the national and international (European) levels.

As far as the national level is concerned, the trends and pressures for administrative decentralization and economic devolution have become increasingly evident. But the two post-war parties and their governments have assumed that these operations in decentralization and in devolution were only devices to aid better co-ordination by the central government. In most of the West European countries, consultative planning, medium-term economic policies or prices and income controls are effective instruments of mixed policy-making, with the role of the central government effectively reduced to a proportionate share. It is these socio-economic instruments of power-sharing which reduce instability in Germany, France and Sweden, although the politics of these three countries are considerably different. It is these socio-economic instruments of concertation which ultimately allow for greater political flexibility, for better interpenetration of the centres participating in the policy-making and for more imaginative political techniques and styles.

As for power-sharing at the European level, this is what the next chapter will endeavour to examine.

Chapter Six

The national interests and supra-national partnership

The title of this chapter applies equally well to the two questions which it raises. One is the question of whether by sharing some of the attributes of their external sovereignty within a Community or Union, nine (or more, or less) West-European nation-states could create a more self-sufficient basis and a more independent level of decision-making than their limited national conditions allow. The rationale of union between states, which has always been the pursuit of common strength, has been strikingly enhanced since the coming of the industrial-technological society, with its dominant characteristics: economic concentration and world-interdependence. It is no accident that the two super-powers of this age are both federations and both command vast mainlands and enormous economic resources. But the former European powers, small and impoverished, after the loss of their empires, have found their capacity for decision-making, indeed their sovereignty, increasingly limited.

This chapter, therefore, starts from the point reached by the preceding ones, namely from the realization that even if government-in-partnership were to be feasible at home, it is doubtful if it could work without government-in-partnership abroad. As in the case of government-in-partnership at home, the study looks at the advantages and disadvantages of the European partnership *in principle*. In reality, the European partnership is at a very incipient and controversial stage. At the time of writing, the process of integration is in fact regressing and losing its institutional coherence, although national and international developments continue to point to the European Union as an obvious practical solution.

But, precisely because one cannot know what the practical future will be, it is useful to examine whether in theory the European partnership could help to solve the problems of the advanced industrial countries of Western Europe. The chapter proceeds by a critical analysis of the history of the formation of the European Community and of its system of decision-making (its institutions, policy-making processes and actual policies), with special regard to the relevance of that system for Western Europe seen as a specific region of medium-sized mixed economies. The analysis will be both brief (in order to avoid as far as possible repetition from the vast and well-known literature on the subject) and directly focused on the present problems of government in Western Europe.

But the same analysis will serve also to examine the other meaning of 'the national interest and the European Community', that is the way in which the governments of the member states help or hamper the partnership-in-Europe in the name of the 'national interest'. In the context of this European form of government-in-partnership the Community is the centripetal and the national governments the centrifugal forces. The more the national governments facilitate the working of this new and unrehearsed centre of decision-making (which *could*, perhaps, better than the nation-state, have its decisions reliably implemented, without being continually blown off-course by unforeseen international developments), the more their own country and the community as a whole could profit from a new stability. The more, on the other hand, they persevere in their present 'patriotic' and 'sovereign' ways, the more likely they are to find that their own countries' independence as well as the independence of Western Europe as a whole, is subordinated to other *non-* or indeed *anti-* European interests.

The impact of the Community on the individual states

The principal problem which faced each of the nine future member-states of the European Community after the Second World War was how to preserve, in a world in which individual national power had dramatically diminished, the military, political, economic and cultural independence of their peoples.

From a military point of view they had to achieve a double objective. They had, on the one hand, to make sure that they would never wage war against each other: the two world wars, arising out of conflicts between European powers, had resulted in the destruction not only of European primacy in the world, but of European independence as well. On the other hand, they had to build a system of defence and security sufficient to prevent the other new powers of the industrial-technological world from waging war, at least on European soil.

From a political point of view they had to save, by consolidating and improving, the mixed economic, social and political institutions uniquely characteristic of modern European politics and of its modern embodiment, the welfare state. Also attuned to the European welfare state and characteristic of European politics in the industrial-technological age were its principal political ideologies and its principal parties of government: Labour or Social Democratic parties, and Conservative or Christian Democratic parties.

From an economic point of view the European states were caught between two opposing international trends. One was the rapid technological development of American industry which had proved after the Second World War that it could have such positive effects on growth, productivity and average earnings in the US economy. But if these new achievements of American technology were to be emulated in Europe they would require financial and economic sacrifices of which none of the individual states was capable since, and this was the second trend, all the European powers were rapidly losing their positions in the world. Post-war developments were leading to an increasing loss of European overseas markets; and fierce inter-continental competition, added to the loss of trade through decolonization, was putting European industry in a position of inferiority.

Immediately after the Second World War, there was a revival of faith in European culture both in its separate national forms and as a whole. It was in fact the European writers (André Malraux, Denis de Rougemont, Salvador de Madariaga, Raymond Aron, Stephen Spender, Karl Jaspers, John Wain) who took the initial lead for a

145

European union. The congresses of writers and artists led to congresses of European politicians and economists – which in turn led to congresses of the European Movement as a whole.[1]

The two principal questions which the advocates of some form of European union or integration had to answer from the very beginning were, first, whether their peoples would be able to surmount traditional hatreds, and secondly, whether the old national sovereignties could be absorbed into one new form of European sovereignty and if so, how? The answer to the first question was given by the surprising readiness of the French and German peoples to forsake their old and virulent incompatibilities. Critics of European integration are always inclined to overlook this extraordinary development in European history. Peoples from other European nations, or regions, who pretend that it is beyond them to link their destinies with other peoples who are alien to them, or especially those who 'wronged' them in the past, should look at the new Franco-German friendship, cemented within the framework of European solidarity, as an example and principal proof of the reality of the European idea.

The conceptual and emotional connotations of the transfer of sovereignty from the old nation-states to supra-national European institutions were bound to plague the process of integration. The sovereign is the commander of the armed forces responsible for the defence of the land and the legislative, executive and judiciary powers are responsible for the rule of law in the land. It is therefore significant that even in the present phase of stagnation of European integration the problems of a future European foreign policy and of future European defence have come to the fore again. The history of European integration shows that at the very beginning the most coherent blueprint for integration was the European Defence Community based on the idea of a European army. But, beyond the European army there was to be a European Assembly, to which a European Defence Minister should be responsible. After being signed by the governments of Belgium, France, Germany, Italy,

1. See especially Denis de Rougemont, 'The campaign of congresses', in G. Ionescu (ed.), *The New Politics of European Integration*, London, 1970.

Luxembourg and the Netherlands, the Treaty of EDC was rejected on 30 August 1954 by the French Parliament.

While the European Defence Community was undergoing its long agony, on 25 July 1952 the Treaty for the European Coal and Steel Community was signed in Paris by the same six governments, the British government of the time having refused to participate on grounds of 'national sovereignty'. This was the beginning and first hope of European integration, and led through the Treaty of Rome of March 1957[1] and the Treaty of Brussels of 8 April 1965, to the formation of the present European Community – which on 1 January 1973 was joined by Britain, Denmark and Ireland. The contradictions of this kind of 'functionalistic' integration are constantly revealed in the working of the Community, and cast a doubt on its ultimate viability. On at least two occasions these contradictions have come to the boil. One was the crisis of 1965 on the question of decision-making by unanimity or by qualified majority, partly solved by the Luxembourg agreement of 28–9 January 1966 by which the French Government reserved the right to demand that very important decisions should be taken unanimously, thus in reality obtaining a right of veto for each of the member-states. For this and other reasons the Luxembourg agreement and the earlier Treaty of Brussels are rightly considered by historians of the Community as the turning points towards the institutional predominance of the Council, the inter-governmental organ of the Community, over the Commission and Parliament, which are in theory the future supra-national organs.

The second crisis occurred in 1973–4 and played an important part in the relations between the European Community and the United States. Since its inception the EEC had been favourably regarded and indeed encouraged, by the US government. But, as we

1. The principal article, Article 2, defines the task of the Community as 'by setting up a common market and progressively approximating the economic policies of member-states, to promote throughout the Community a harmonious development of economic activity, a continuous and balanced expansion and increase in stability, an accelerated raising of the standard of living and closer relations of its member-states'.

now know, the progress made by the Community in world-trade and in economic influence since 1957, and the adhesion of Great Britain in 1973, had a stronger impact on the economy and the foreign trade of the United States than the latter probably expected. A change of attitude could be detected in American economic policies toward Europe from 1971. In 1973 American displeasure was officially expressed in the yearly presidential report to Congress.[1] In turn, and perhaps partly because of growing American concern over the growth of the European Community, the US government also worried its Western European allies by unilaterally pursuing the Kissinger policy of 'rapprochement' with the USSR.

Soviet-American bi-polarity, or as it is now called, 'condominium', is the nightmare of European statesmen. It became even more disturbing in 1971–2. The quest for European security and for a European foreign policy was given priority in Community policy-making. A need for co-ordination and for unity was felt. When Dr. Kissinger invited the West European allies to discuss his 'new Atlantic charter' the Nine appointed one single spokesman, Mr Noorgard, the Danish President of the Council, for these negotiations. But the 'linkage' between the US–European economic, diplomatic and military negotiations became only too evident during the oil crisis. The nine members of the European Community, angered by the direct negotiations on Middle East problems between the USA and the USSR on which the Community was not consulted,[2]

1. 'We believed that ultimately a highly cohesive Western Europe would relieve the United States of many burdens. We expected that unity would not be limited to economic integration, but would include a significant political dimension. We assumed, perhaps too uncritically, that our basic interests would be assured by our long history of co-operation, by our common cultures and our political similarities.'
2. 'It is impossible to sympathise or co-operate with a policy if one remains uncertain what that policy is; and it rather looks as though Party Chief Brezhnev had a better idea of it than President Pompidou, Chancellor Brandt or Prime Minister Heath. In the Cuban crisis of 1962, President Kennedy dispatched special envoys – envoys known to, and trusted by, European statesmen to explain his position. Nothing of the kind occurred

148

managed at the beginning of the oil crisis to take a common stand in some respects opposed to that of the USA. But soon two of the member-states, France and Britain, adopted a 'sovereign' line of action in their dealings with the Arabs. Then, at the Washington meeting of February 1974, while Britain and the other seven countries took a conciliatory line towards the United States, France sharpened its attacks against it. Differences of national interest during this second crisis had risked destroying the entire 'communitarian' scaffolding, which was already shaky.

We turn now to the question of how much the European Community of the Six had, between 1957 and 1971, been of help to the individual member-states.

An answer is almost impossible in direct financial terms (or what is called in a French technical expression, *le juste retour*): i.e., how much cash a state puts in, and draws out from the Community. West Germany loses most in direct financial terms – but how can one assess the economic, and, even more, the political advantages which it has derived since it came into the European Community? France and the Netherlands, and now Denmark and Eire are known to benefit directly from the collaboration with the Community and notably from the Common Agricultural Policy. Italy, which immediately after entry into the Common Market experienced an unprecedented 'boom', benefited, when it was hit again in 1974 by, among other things, the oil crisis, from a loan made to her within the

---

on this occasion. Nor does the transatlantic telephone appear to have been used to any effect. All that Europeans could see were a number of diplomatic moves played out as the result of bilateral negotiations between the United States and the Soviet Union – a game of chess from which they were excluded but whose incidental effects might have a catastrophic impact on the welfare of their own peoples. Yet here was an issue where the genuine differences of interest between America and her European allies urgently required discussion...allies should have been able to behave as allies. This was not done, however, and dissension is now out in the open as a political fact whose effect on American-European relations will continue to be felt.' 'The year of Europe?' in *Foreign Affairs*, January, 1974, p. 239.

framework of the Community by West Germany. And how, in such an intricate and integrated operation, can one properly disentangle the interplay of economic interests of the individual Communitarian states: if Danish bacon is subsidised by the Community is it not the British market which benefits from the lower price of this essential commodity?

Two mainly economic assessments were independently attempted in 1972–3. One was undertaken by the British Government, which summarized its findings in a white paper published on the eve of the Parliamentary debate about entry into Europe.[1]

1. 'The Communities together formed a European economc grouping of some 180 million people, with a further 70 million people in their associated states, mainly in Africa, in close economic relationship with them...The formation of the European Economic Community then created an environment within which they have each made further and striking progress over the past decade...The abolition of tariffs provided a strong and growing stimulus to the mutual trade of Community countries...It is estimated that by 1969 the value of this "intra-trade" in manufactured products was about 50 per cent higher than it would have been had the Community not be formed. Those industries which competed with imports faced an intensification of competitive pressure as tariffs fell, obliging them to seek ways of raising efficiency and reducing costs. By the same token, prospects for exporting dramatically improved...Import competition and export expansion were closely associated with a growth in investment...In real terms (i.e. after allowing for price inflation), average British earnings had increased by less than 40 per cent between 1958 and 1969, while in the Community countries average real earnings had gone up over 75 per cent. Similarly, all the Community countries enjoyed rates of growth of gross national product (GNP) per head of population or of private consumption per head roughly twice as great as Britain's...In the period 1959–69, the Six devoted 24 per cent of their GNP to investment, whereas the figure for Britain was 17 per cent... Finally, the Community as a whole have maintained a strong balance of payments position, earning a surplus of more than $25,000m over the period 1958 to 1969; by comparison the United Kingdom had a small cumulative deficit on current account over these years.' 'The United Kingdom and the European Community', Cmnd 4715, HMSO, 1971.

The other was attempted by the Commission itself and entrusted to Monsieur Maillet, Professor at the University of Mons. In order to get as precise an image of the EEC's 'achievement' as possible, Professor Maillet and his team proposed to look at it from four angles: the evolution of the structures of production, influenced both by the abolition of trade barriers and by the initial results of source of the common policies of the Community; the rise in incomes and in the standard of living (although in this field the direct intervention of the Community is naturally more limited); the stability of expansion as assessed in terms of fluctuations of prices and the level of employment (in this field the report believes that the Community has fundamental responsibilities), and, finally, the contribution of the Community to the creation of a world economic order. The fifteen years under survey are divided in the report into two separate periods; the first, eight to ten years, coincides with the creation of the Common Market itself, which followed strict procedure and a precise timetable; the second covers the shorter interval in which the integrated Community, faced with new problems, has had gradually to define its new objectives and tasks. (The same chronological division is used also to the official publication of the Commission, which divides its description of the activities of the Community into, in one section, 'the functioning of the Common Market'; and in other sections, the activities leading 'towards economic and monetary union', i.e. the *policies*, overall and sectoral.[1])

According to the Maillet report, the yearly average growth of the Gross National Product within the Community, 5.7 per cent, was perhaps influenced or stimulated by the creation of the Community, especially by the increase in the rate of investment from 16.4 per cent, in 1958–9, to 19.2 per cent in 1969–70. This growth resulted in an increase of per capita income and consumption of roughly 4.5 per cent per year. The differences in standards of living of the component member states have been reduced, so that the Netherlands gradually reached the Community level, whereas France's advance was comparatively reduced. The odd man out remained Italy which,

1. Sixth General Report (1972) on the activities of the Community, pp. vii–viii.

at the present rate, would require a century to catch up with the rest of the team. But this is a somewhat misleading statistic. The real discrepancy lies between the north of Italy, almost equal in level with the rest of the Community, and the south, which has not reached even half of that level.

Up to 1970 trade within the Community had increased five-fold since the creation of the Common Market, whereas trade with other countries had increased only 2.5 times. Unemployment had fallen from 3.4 per cent in 1958 to roughly 2 per cent over the 15 years. The inquiry is however critically aware of the increase in prices since 1969 (over 5 per cent for all countries) and, even more, of the fluctuations and discrepancies in rates of exchange within the Community. This naturally caused the report to wonder whether the Community could be described as a 'homogeneous economic zone'.

Maillet considers the evolution of the structures of production in terms of specialization and concentration. The report finds that the share of agricultural production in the GNP of the whole Community has decreased by half; that the share of industry has increased in the least industrialized country, Italy, as well as in the most industrialized one, Germany; and that service industries have an increased share in the economic profile of the Community, most noticeably in France, Italy and the Netherlands.

One aspect of these findings is that, relatively speaking, Germany had increased its industrial lead, and Italy had caught up with the more developed countries; but France and Belgium had not made similar progress. Another aspect is that industry progressed simultaneously across the board from the most dynamic industries (the motor industry) to those with a relatively slower growth (textile and food). This was true of all the member states. In fifteen years there had occurred a reduction in specialization of exports per individual country and per categories of products. By now none of the major branches of production is completely absent from any of the countries and no country has an exclusive position in any of these branches. However, this evolution has not completely neutralized the traditional

152

specialization of individual countries in given industries – as, for instance, Germany in the mechanical and electrical industries, France in agricultural and food products, transport equipment and tyres, Belgium in metal and textile industries, and the Netherlands in agricultural production and semi-manufactured goods. Italy's industrial production is more evenly distributed, but is particularly successful in some new branches, as for instance the production of refrigerators.

The report is critical of trends towards industrial concentration within the Community. Mergers have increased more dramatically since 1969, but sixty per cent of the mergers have taken place within the national markets, and in the remaining forty per cent the greatest part has concerned a national industry and a non-Community industry (mostly USA) and intra-communitarian mergers were in a considerable minority.[1] The actual figures were: out of 3,153 mergers and takeovers effected between 1961–9, 1,861 were within member countries, 820 by a non-Community country within a member country, 215 by member countries in third countries and 257 between member countries.[2]

The conclusion drawn in the report on the social effects are that the per capita real national product grew in the Community during the period surveyed by roughly 70 per cent, i.e. at a yearly average rate of 4.5 per cent. The average income in 1970 was distinctly superior to that of the United Kingdom, while only half that of the US, a considerably higher European level than fifteen years before. Although it is impossible to argue that these improvements are due exclusively to the creation of the Common Market, the comparison between the Community and the UK suggests that the creation of a Common Market has had considerable impact. Moreover, the growth of trade has given European consumers a much larger choice.

1. See on this problem also André Marchal, *L'Europe solidaire*, vol. ii, Paris, 1970, and Christopher Layton, *Cross-frontier Mergers in Europe*, Bath, 1971.
2. Opera Mundi Commission of EEC in *Memorandum on Industrial Policy*, March 1970, quoted in Layton, op. cit., p. 3, table 4.

Two further questions raised are why public consumption and public investment have declined in the last five years of the fifteen (compared with the average rate of growth of production of 5.7 per cent, public consumption has increased by 3.2 per cent and public investment by 4.9 per cent, while they should have been respectively 4 per cent and 8.5 per cent), and why public investment was considerably higher in the Netherlands and Germany (and in the United Kingdom) than in France, Belgium and Italy. How do these developments tally with the impact of the Common Market? The most likely explanation is suggested by differing fiscal approaches of the respective countries; the countries with a lower rate of public investment are also those with less direct taxation, with less strict fiscal regimes and with less administrative decentralization.

The Maillet report stressed that after the first ten years there occurred a slowing down of the activity of the Community rhythms. It attributes this to the fact that once the abolition of the national customs and tariffs barriers had produced their initial effects, the need for general common orientation and policies, and for integration in depth, began to be felt. This coincided with the shift of the centre of gravity of the Community from the Commission to the Council – of which more later.

The final remarks of the Maillet report – which concern the profound changes that had occurred in the general orientation of the Community after its first nine years – bring us back to the question of the two different phases in the short history of the Community. For John Pinder these phases involved a necessary change from 'negative integration' to 'positive integration'.[1] While the former consisted of the removal of discrimination between the member states – tariffs, barriers, trade restrictions and all other kinds of financial and economic restrictions – 'positive integration' should consist of the creation of communitarian policies linking together entire sectors and lines of action of the Community as a whole. Signor Malfatti, the former President of the Commission, described

1. John Pinder, 'Positive integration and negative integration', in *The World Today*, vol. 24, no. 3, pp. 88–110.

the transition as the passage from the 'legalistic' phase, when the activity of the Community was guided only by the interpretation of the Treaty of Rome and limited to the ways and means of action opened by the Treaty, to the new 'political' phase, when the accent fell on the need to restructure the economies of the member-states around programmed communitarian policies for the future.[1]

At the time of writing, it is indeed difficult to know definitely whether the Community will survive, whether it will survive with Six, Eight or Nine members and whether, regardless of its membership, it will gather enough strength and political will to embark, presumably by achieving economic and monetary union, on the second 'positive' phase of integration. But if it does so, either with or without undergoing a longer crisis of 'disintegration', the following are the roles and the tasks for which the Community is indispensable.

The first is that by acting throughout its first decade mainly as a Common Market, or indeed a magnified Customs Union, the Community has produced much better results for the six countries together, as a trans-national unit, and for each of them separately than they could have achieved for themselves. The fact that the results for the three members who joined in 1973, and for the Community of Nine as a whole since 1973 are far less conclusive is attributable to many other factors, among which the fact that at that moment the years in which the three joined were, as we have seen, years of stagnation of the EEC. The stagnation was in part caused by the delays provoked by their own entry. But it was primarily caused by the hesitations and lack of agreement between the member states when faced with the controversial problems of embarking on the second, 'positive' phase of integration. When, finally, a grave economic crisis hit the Community just as it was passing through this transitional phase and therefore particularly off its guard and vulnerable, the shock was felt even more strongly.

Be that as it may, the fact remains that the question asked by the Commission immediately after the crisis of 1973-4 and addressed to all the member states which might have been tempted to withdraw

1. In a conversation with the author in Rome in May 1973.

during and after the crisis, i.e. 'Is there a single European country which can exercise real influence and carry weight comparable to that of a United Europe?' cannot be answered affirmatively. This is so because if it was to work fully and properly, the European Community, as a whole, could act as a stabilizer, as a co-ordinator and as a modernizer.

It acts as a *stabilizer*: the combined economic and financial resources of the Six or Nine countries can lend greater stability to the member states caught in some crisis than if they were alone or in competition with each other. This has been proved, for instance, in the adjustments which buttressed, within the Common Market the successive 'floatings' of the major European currencies. This is also proved by the new techniques of intra-Communitarian loans, from the loan made by Germany to Italy within the Community framework in October 1974, to the institutionalization in 1975 of the Euro-loan, a common European fund wherefrom one member state, in acute need, can draw with the Community's appoval.

The Community acts as a *co-ordinator*, because it can pool the resources of all the member states, both in situations of crisis-management, and as the permanent supervisor of communitarian programmes, plans and long-term policies. These policies cannot and should not be made at the level of the lowest common denominator of the various national interests. On the contrary, in taking into account the added factors resulting from the pooling of forces and resources, the Communitarian policy must aim higher and more boldly than each of the separate national policies could. In this sense, it can be said that the Community *amplifies* the common targets by reckoning with the multiplied resources and forces. This process of amplification renders the Community's programmes, long-term policies and planning much more realistic and feasible than those of the individual member states. The *stability, co-ordination* and *amplification* produced by the very functioning of the Community give to the European social, technological and other policies a credibility which those of the member states have long since lost.

Finally, the Community acts as a *modernizer*. By allowing for greater competition and concentration in the different sectors of production (restructuring the agricultural sector, for example, by using the resources and needs – manpower for instance – of the industrial sector) and by offering, because of its greater territorial area, its geographical diversity, and its inter-sectorial communication, vast possibilities of redeployment, the Community speeds the replacement of obsolete activities with new and profitable activities and techniques. But this general role of modernization and of 'catching-up' with the industrial-technological development of other countries which the Community as any Community Federation could fulfil, cannot be separated from the *special* modernization which the *European* Community, as a grouping of West European states, should accomplish.

It is important to remember that the EEC can easily become a homogeneous economic zone because, with the exception of some underdeveloped and peripheral regions, (like the south of Italy, the highlands of Scotland, the agricultural northern regions of the Netherlands and Denmark, as well as many parts of Ireland), the member states of the EEC are all industrial societies. But even more importantly, all the economies of the European nation-states are mixed economies. This, as argued in the preceding chapter, is *not* a transitional situation.

This solution is particularly suited to the requirements of European society, which is characterized by the pursuit of political freedom for its relatively enlightened and politically active citizens, and of social equity for its emancipated and politically active socio-economic groups. But the European economic and political system can probably survive only if all the welfare states and mixed economies of Europe integrate into one large Union, comparable in size and in resource to both the other non-European federations.

With this we come to what is now a topical point in the debate about the European community. Partly because, through the Treaty of Rome[1] and as implied by its other designation, 'The Common Market', the European Community is pledged to maintain free trade, the EEC has lately been described as 'a fortress of capitalism'. This

1. See especially Part III, ch. I, on Free Competition.

reputation grew up in great part because in its first decade the Common Market had concentrated on economic and commercial matters – of great import to enterprises – more than on social and regional matters, of great import to the other 'social partners'. Whatever the causes, the fact is that primarily because of this reputation the EEC forfeited the sympathy of the youth of Europe, which had originally been its fervent supporter, as well as that of large sections of the Left within potential member states, especially Norway and Great Britain. But, significantly, the Left in the Six remained faithful to the EEC. Not only did all the continental socialist parties maintain their staunch support, but even the formidable Italian and French Communist Parties have come to consider the EEC as a permanent European fact of life.

The reproach frequently hurled at the EEC that it is a faceless technocratic organization which is of profit to the great, and indeed, as J. J. S. Schreiber has pointed out, to the American enterprises, is valid only to the extent that the other 'social partners' have not yet influenced sufficiently the policy-making of the Community. But even this is an argument of limited validity because it is the socialist parties which form the most active and coherent opposition in the European Parliament,[1] and because, since the Social-Democrats came to power in Germany, the blue-print of social policy, including workers' participation has been bolder and more progressive than most European national policies. More will be said of this later.

Meanwhile the facts remain that an idealistic and internationally-oriented statesman like Willy Brandt was as passionately interested in the success of the EEC as more pragmatic and nationalist leaders like Pompidou and Heath; and that such disparate but powerful bodies as the Confederation of British Industries, the Italian Christian Democrats and the Italian communists, have supported the *raison d'être* of the Community. We can only conclude that its purposes, can transcend separate national, economic and social interests.

1. See Gerta Zellentin, 'Opposition in the EEC', in Ionescu (ed.), *The New Politics of European Integration.*

Policy-making in the Community

All text books on this subject start by reminding that the Treaty of Rome has endowed the Community with five institutions: the Council, the Commission, the Parliamentary Assembly, or European Parliament, the Economic and Social Committee and the Court of Justice. But the text books hasten to add that the two organs of policy-making are the Council and the Commission. Should this be so? – and, if not, how should it be? In order to answer these questions we shall first look at the three non-policy-making institutions.

The Court of Justice, like the Judiciary in a regime of separation of powers, is by definition meant to be above the political process. As such there is nothing exceptional in its position in the institutional set-up of the Community. But precisely because the institutionalization of the Community has been such a difficult and haphazard operation, full praise should be given to the European Court for the continuity of European thinking which its abundant jurisprudence expresses. It is in the realm of law that, thanks to the silent but solid work of the Court, the European integration is most advanced.

The Economic and Social Committee, another of the five institutions, was given by the Treaty only consultative rights. Its members are all appointed by the Council of Ministers from lists presented by the national governments – Great Britain, France, Germany, Italy having each 24 members, and the other countries 12, 9 or 6. A third of these members represent the trade-unions, a third the employers and another third the other, general interests. The Committee is divided into specialized sections according to the principal fields of action: agriculture, industry, transport etc. They are therefore the representatives of what is called with increasing emphasis in the Brussels vocabulary: the social partners. Yet, the Economic and Social Committee is only consultative. Although its right to give advice to the Council has of late been increased, it cannot be said that it actually shares in the decision-making process.

This is one of the most obvious anomalies of the institutional set-up of the European Economic Community. For precisely because it is European (and we know that the principal problem of modern government in Europe is how to make the 'social partners' commit themselves mutually to collaborate in joint policies) and, even more so because it is an *Economic* Community, it would have been reasonable to give to the representatives of the economic interests in Europe a greater part in the preparations of the Community's policies. Moreover, because the Community is, or should have been, the modern supra-national decision-making body, it should have proved from the beginning its supra-nationality by making a direct link not only with the national governments but with the forces which have now across Europe such a powerful influence on the national governments: the emancipated socio-economic interests, or what is called in this book the corporate forces. By relegating, in what should be the most modern decision-making body of Europe, the corporate forces to a position inferior to that which they have acquired in the national processes of decision-making, the founding fathers made a fundamental initial mistake. This then helped to give the impression that the Community was disinterested in, if not hostile to, the European workers.

But the greatest anomaly of the institutionalization of the European Community was that it failed to give to the European Parliament, or Parliamentary Assembly as the Treaty calls it, a properly meaningful role. The European Parliament consists of 198 members designated by the political groups from the national parliaments. Britain, France, Germany and Italy each have 36 members and the other five countries, 14, 10 or 6. The Assembly elects its president and its bureau, has twelve standing committees – and has, according to the Treaty, powers of 'deliberation' and of 'control'. It gives preliminary advice on the decisions to be taken by the Council, and can overthrow the Commission, which presents to the Assembly a yearly report, by a vote of censure with a two-thirds majority (from 1975 the Assembly also has a direct right to control over the purse of the Commission). Article 138 of the Treaty invites the Assembly to prepare for the organization of direct elections by universal suffrage 'according to a uniform procedure in all the member-states.'

It is obvious that the two great shortcomings of such a 'Parliament' are the fact that its members are appointed by the national parliaments, and not directly elected by a European constituency, *not organic* and the fact that the ultimate organ of decision-making in the Community, the Council, is not responsible to the Assembly and cannot be directly censured by it. Thus the process of representation is cut into two essential articulations: between the voters and the members of parliament on the one hand, and between the executive and the legislature on the other. It can of course be argued that by linking the Commission and the Parliamentary Assembly in a direct relation from which the Council is omitted, the Treaty acknowledged the fact that the Council was an inter-governmental institution, whereas the Commission and Parliament were meant to be supra-national. The Council, being formed by national governments which are responsible to their respective national parliaments, could not be responsible to the European Parliament. Only through the creation of a legislative body responsible to the European voter can a new kind of Council be made responsible to it. Even the French government, which has constantly opposed direct elections for the European Parliament, is now coming back to the idea. For the time being, the Community has a double executive with international and supranational components, which answers ultimately only to the *national* Legislatures. This lop-sided situation can only be considered as provisional and transitional – and the sooner the transition can be effected, the sooner the Community will start to function properly. At a moment of crisis like the present, when the entire impetus of integration seems to have halted and the entire institutional machine seems to be working in a vacuum, it is not astonishing that people should go back to square one – in this context, where everything should have begun: the creation of a European Legislature by direct European elections.

The Community has progressed until now on the assumption of what neo-functionalist authors like Haas or Lindberg describe as 'spill-over' – the process whereby 'the initial task and grant of powers to the central institutions creates a situation or series of situations that can be dealt with only by further expanding the task and the grant of power'.[1] What perhaps the spill-over theory overlooks is precisely the fact that the two 'central institutions' are of different kinds, one supra-national and the other international. The relation, what is called in official vocabulary 'the dialogue' between the inter-governmental Council and the supra-national Commission, hides the basic conflict between the national governments which form the Council, and the supra-national bureaucracy which is the Commission. It is this conflict between executives which, in the absence of a European Legislature, can lead so often to deadlocks and immobility. But before we try to describe the present policy-making process of the EEC, a word should be said in a recapitulative way about the two executive or policy-making institutions.

The Council is formed by the representatives of government which, according to Art. 145 of the Treaty, should ensure the co-ordination of the general economic policies of the member-states and *have the power of decision*. Decisions are taken by majority votes. The total vote is 58, out of which Britain, France, West Germany and Italy have each 10 votes. According to the Luxembourg Agreement of 29 January 1966, though, in cases of very important issues the discussion should be continued until a unanimous agreement is reached. The Council creates its own Committees - the most important of which is the Committee of Permanent Representatives, of which more later.

The Commission is the most original of the institutions of the Community. Its functions are to initiate policies and formulate proposals leading to the progress of the integration, to implement Community policies, to control the application of Community acts and regulations by the member states, to issue regulations and decisions. But the Commission does *not* have the power of decision. It is a collegiate body formed by thirteen members, two from Britain, France, Germany and Italy, and one from each of the other five countries. The Commissioners are responsible only to the European Community and may accept instructions from any national govern-

1. N. Lindberg, *The Political Dynamics of European Integration*, Stanford, 1963, p. 288.

Figure 2: Sphere and processes of policy-making in the European Economic Community

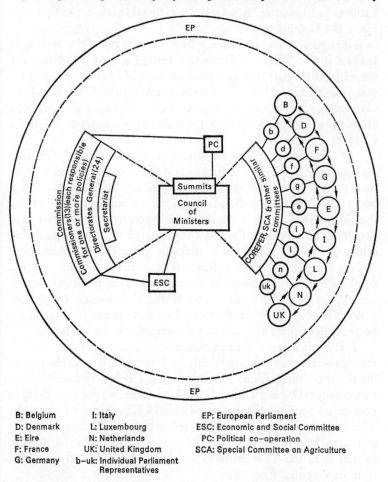

B: Belgium	I: Italy	EP: European Parliament
D: Denmark	L: Luxembourg	ESC: Economic and Social Committee
E: Eire	N: Netherlands	PC: Political co-operation
F: France	UK: United Kingdom	SCA: Special Committee on Agriculture
G: Germany	b–uk: Individual Parliament Representatives	

ments within it. Each Commissioner is responsible for one or more of the policies of the Community; there are roughly sixteen policies, of which more later. The administration is composed of 14 Directorates-General, each responsible to one Commissioner. The staff of some 6,000 employees is responsible to the European Community alone. Like the United Nations staff they have the status of international functionaries. A Secretariat-General oversees the functioning of the Commission.

The figure above shows the sphere and process of the making of policies in the EEC. Its distinctive feature is that it replaces the classic (and official) representation of the EEC policy-making process as a 'dialogue' between a theoretically united Council and the Commission. It stresses the permanent conflictual and bargaining character of relations between the nine nations represented in the Council.

My diagram shows the Council to be the central decision-making body *insofar as it arbitrates* both between individual governments – whose interests might be opposed depending on the policy being considered – as well as between the national governments and the Commission. This is a much more fractured and intricate process of making policies than that represented by federalist-minded critics of the Community as a 'dialogue' between the Commission and the Council. In reality policies are made in the Community by a combination of such causes as a crisis (financial, monetary, social, energy, etc.) in a particular sector of the Community, the special national interest of one or more member-states in one policy, and the personal dynamism and skill of the respective Commissioners.

This interlocking of various executives of different kinds (national, international and supra-national) and at different levels (Commissioners, Commission, Ministers, Council) has resulted in two major trends. One is the trend from Communitarian policy-making to political co-operation – expressions which will be explained presently. The other is the trend of haphazard institutionalization of an organization reacting spontaneously to the tasks which it has been given, as well as to the basic conflicts which it contains – and contained from its very inception.

The trend towards spontaneous institutionalization, and towards the ultimate integrative effect (even if only a side-effect) of institutionalization for practical purposes, can be seen to a certain extent in the unexpected birth and growth of two committees, one within the institutional framework of the Community, and one outside it:

the Committee of Permanent Representatives (COREPER), and the Political Co-operation (nicknamed the Davignon) Committee. (The latter is so informal that it is called after a high official of the Belgian Foreign Office, the Viscount Davignon, who first assembled and chaired it. It is composed of representatives of the Foreign Offices of the nine member states; and the Commission is not represented in it.)

It is significant that an organ as powerful as COREPER was only formally set up in 1965 (by the Brussels Treaty, which established among other things a single Council and a single Commission of the European Communities).[1] This demonstrates the unpredictability of the institutional evolution of the Community, and the idea that it travels, to use Shonfield's expression, on a 'journey to an unknown destination'.[2] The evolution of the Community has always proceeded by unexpected leaps, trials and errors, crises and dénouements, and these often result in the growth of institutional arrangements which differ from the intentions of the Treaty of Rome. To take COREPER as an example: some kind of committee of permanent representatives, as an adjunct to the Council of Ministers, had been authorized by the Treaty of Rome, and finally instituted by the Treaty of Brussels (Art. 4).[3] It would, however, have been difficult to predict then that an apparently insignificant administrative appendage would be transformed into a central institution with the present competence and importance of COREPER. But the formation

1. See Emile Noel and Henri Etienne, 'The permanent representatives and the "deepening" of the communities', in *Government and Opposition*, Autumn 1971.
2. Andrew Shonfield, *Europe: Journey to an Unknown Destination* (The BBC Reith Lectures 1972), London, 1973.
3. The Committee is formed by those permanent representatives of the member-states with ambassadorial rank. The permanent representatives now take part in the work of the Community through the new Committee, thus going beyond their initial duties which were to ensure the communications between the national governments and the Community, and to help towards the co-ordination of the European work of the national administrations.

of COREPER coincided with, and was symptomatic of, the shift of power towards the Council, the non-integrationist element, and away from the Commission, the integrationist element of the Community. Thus the growing significance of COREPER was regarded from the federalist viewpoint as working against the supranational development and further integration of Community institutions. Yet this trend is hardly surprising, for this kind of inter-governmental body is common to every other international organization.

Be that as it may, COREPER's powerful role in European decision-making[1] can be justified on integrative as well as pragmatic grounds. The Committee has proved to be a very useful institutional mediator between the 'communitarian' approach of the Commission and the 'common' crisis-management approach of the Council. Yet, by virtue of their permanence, the Permanent Representatives have been, as it were, caught in the deeper logic of the interdependence of policy-making at both national and Community levels, and have become agents of this mixed process. In this sense COREPER has become a real policy-making institution, though in the future it may take other forms.

The Davignon Committee[2] was also an improvisation, and has also accentuated the trend towards 'political co-operation'. The French, to be sure, tried to use it for their own purposes – to establish a Political Secretariat in Paris. At the beginning the Commission was not even invited to its meetings. But gradually collabora-

---

1. Like other major committees, COREPER is authorized to adopt the convention of placing in a special category, called category 'A', the questions upon which it has agreed and given a decision. The category 'A' decisions are adopted automatically by the Council; when the respective Committees cannot reach agreement, the unsolved questions (category 'B') are sent to the Council for further deliberations. In 1970 it was thought that seventy per cent of Council decisions are taken in this way.

2. Little has been written about this informal committee of the Foreign Offices of the Nine countries. Its work won public attention after its successful coordination of the attitudes of the Nine countries at the European Security Conference in Helsinki, and then in Geneva.

tion between the two organs proved inevitable and a functional *modus vivendi* was established between them. Gradually too the Davignon Committee came to be seen as providing an alternative structural and functional approach to European decision-making. The external relations policy of the EEC, for instance, is initiated in both communitarian and political ways, i.e., in the Commission and in the Davignon Committee. The Commission directly initiates the commercial agreements of the Common Commercial Policy. Complex economic problems like East–West relations and negotiations with the United States have to be, at least in the first instance, assessed and determined by political co-operation. In such matters it is usual that the Community should speak to the outside world through a common spokesman; but individual member states take part in the prior discussion.

Of greater interest to political observers of the Commission is the fact that regardless of where external relations policies originate, when they come to fruition they *can* benefit the communitarian purposes of the Community as a whole. Political co-operation, highly criticized by federalist-minded critics of the Community as a return to simple inter-governmental ways of negotiation and consultation, does as a rule result in an incremental growth of communitarian decision-making. Instruments of integration may result from agreements reached by means of political co-operation: in East–West relations, for instance. And in the wake of institutionalization of these instruments of integration, member states have renounced some of their sovereign rights and transferred them to the supra-national organ. Thus provided (*a*) that the supra-national unit remains in existence and continues to be fully recognized by the member states (which is true for eight of the member states, but is questioned in the case of Great Britain) and (*b*) that the political rationale for participation in the Community continues to be the goal of ultimate integration, the methods of political co-operation do not necessarily run counter to the transfer of parts of the sovereignty of member states to the Community.

The techniques of political co-operation are also called the 'politics of concertation', an expression which we have met before. How well equipped for this technique is the Community? – or alternatively, what obstacles does it encounter in applying this approach? What is the relationship between this technique and the overall process of Community policy-making?

The procedures of trans-national concertation are characteristically intensive within both the Commission and the Council. To take the Commission first: the Commissioners and the Directors-General collaborate in the preparation of decisions as Minister and senior civil servants collaborate in the preparation of decision in the member states. But the trans-national dimension both renders this process more difficult, and ultimately puts more substance into it. A global European perspective is more comprehensive and therefore less partial than the national one. Each commissioner combines with his own national orientation a wider European vision. From the very beginning the national and trans-national views are linked together. This provides a major shortcut towards the attainment of feasible solutions, if it is assumed (as here) that viable political solutions for the major problems of all the Nine European nation-states can now best be reached at the European level. This awareness of the wider Community interest combined with the general trend towards 'horizontalization' of the processes of concertation within the Commission (i.e. the intensive efforts made to link the fields of responsibility of each Commissioner into fewer areas of decision-making) results in a particularly intensive collegiate consultation. The meetings of the Commission are increasingly frequent. The Secretariat too fosters collegiate exchange of information. Above all the *chefs de cabinet* play an important institutional role in ensuring active co-ordination. This intensification of trans-national concertation results in more satisfactory inter-penetration of the points of view of participants in the decision-making.

But there is more to it than this. In order to obtain information and the technical advice required for the preparation of particular proposals, the Commissioners and Directors-General can consult national experts. As European consultants, these experts lend their expertise just as they do to departments of national governments, at

Figure 3: How basic decisions are made

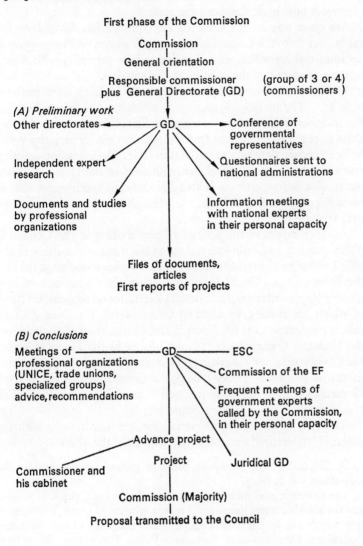

First phase of the Commission
|
Commission
|
General orientation
|
Responsible commissioner   (group of 3 or 4)
plus General Directorate (GD)   (commissioners)

(A) Preliminary work

Other directorates ◄——— GD ———► Conference of
                                   governmental
                                   representatives

Independent expert   Questionnaires sent to
research   national administrations

Documents and studies   Information meetings
by professional   with national experts
organizations   in their personal capacity

Files of documents,
articles
First reports of projects

(B) Conclusions

Meetings of ——————— GD ——————— ESC
professional organizations
(UNICE, trade unions,   Commission of the EF
specialized groups)
advice, recommendations   Frequent meetings of
                                   government experts
                                   called by the Commission,
                                   in their personal capacity

                  Advance project

Commissioner and   Project   Juridical GD
his cabinet

                Commission (Majority)
                        |
Proposal transmitted to the Council

169

a preliminary stage in the formulation of policy. The diagram above illustrates how basic decisions are made.[1]

We come now to the Council. The Council has devised, or has taken over from the Commission, new procedures and techniques of decision-making which we will examine here primarily with regard to their relevance to the politics of concertation.

One of the most original procedures is, for instance, the marathon-meetings. The marathon-meeting concentrates the debate between the member states on one or another European issue, by obliging them to reach an agreement (more often than not by majority vote), before a certain date set out in the timetable. The marathon-meeting resembles to a certain extent the 'guillotine' in the House of Commons. But here the target is an administrative compromise not, as often in parliamentary debates, the triumph of one political ideology over the others.

Another aspect of the politics of concertation of the Council is policy-making by Committees. Among the major committees established either by the treaties or by Council decision one must list first the Economic and Social Committee, then the Committee of Permanent Representatives, the Special Committee on Agriculture (both of which are specifically Council Committees), the Special Committee on Article 113, the Council and Committees of Association, the Monetary Committee (1958), established by the Treaty of Rome, the Conjunctural (or Short-term) Economic Policy (1960), the Committee on Budgetary Policy (1964), the Committee of Central Bank Governors (1964), the Medium-term Economic Committee (1964), and, since 1974, the Energy Committee.

The case of the economic committees created in 1964 with the object of 'concerting' the inseparable aspects of the Monetary Policy[2]

1. D. Sidjanski, 'The European pressure groups', in *Government and Opposition*, vol. 2, no. 3.
2. 'On economic and monetary questions the Council, the Commission and the member states have agreed on the creation of organs of concertation which are largely independent, along the lines of the Monetary Committee (Medium-term Economic Policy Committee, Short-term Economic Policy Committee, Budget Policy Committee etc.)'. E. Noel

(Financial, Economic, Short-term, Long-term, etc.) provides a perfect example of the need for globalization of policy-making within the Community. When Raymond Barre was appointed Vice-President of the Commission he personally co-ordinated the activities of all these overlapping Committees. But it was evident that co-ordination could not be achieved by administrative concertation in the hands of one person alone. The need for regrouping and over-hauling the institutions of the Community on a permanent basis is widely perceived.

On the other hand, the real difference between the economic Committees lies in their power of decision-making. Of all the four, the Committee of Central Bank Governors is most effective in the sense that most of its recommendations are directly implemented. But this is because the Governors can implement decisions formally taken within the administration of the Community by means of their positions within institutions situated outside it. Again, the members of the Committee of the Governors of Central Banks and the Council of Finance Ministers possess a common specialized background which results in a certain unity of opinion. But here too it must be recalled that these two groups have more prior knowledge of each other as institutions and even as persons. They have a double collective, formal identity, outside and within the Community. More often than not their informal consultations carry greater weight, the formal consultations within the Community being mostly a way of officially endorsing agreements previously reached.

The Monetary Committee is formed exclusively by two officials of each member state (one from the Ministry of Finance, the other from the Central Bank) and by officials from the Commission of the EEC. It is responsible both to the Council and to the Commission. Its permanent and basic task is to find a common approach to international monetary problems. After 1968 it concentrated almost exclusively on the different aspects of economic and monetary union.

---

and H. Etienne, 'The Permanent Representatives Committee', in Ionescu (ed.), *The New Politics of European Integration*, p. 119.

This was the result of Barre's proposals for re-organization and of the consequent creation of the three other committees, which together with the Monetary Committee have been charged since then with the task of co-ordinating economic, financial and monetary problems. It is difficult to assess the actual influence of the Committee, or to distinguish between its own official action of 'harmonization', the official actions of the Governors and Ministers of Finance, and the general effort towards harmonization undertaken by the Commission as a whole, under its then Vice-President, inside and outside the Community. The Committee, though, had a direct perception of its own work as distinct from that of the Commission. It saw its task as the harmonization of pre-existing viewpoints held by the different member states, and the provision of compromise solutions both among themselves and between them and the Commission's less flexible formulae.[1] Yet, between the dynamic programme and timetable proposed by the Commission, and the tough negotiations which were taking place outside the administrative area of the Community (among Finance Ministers and Governors of Banks directly and more often than not informally), the amount of exclusive ground covered by the Monetary Committee might prove smaller than expected. But the Committee remains a good example of the functional homogeneity of national experts at work.

More interesting, at least from the point of view of this inquiry, is the work of the new (1971) Standing Committee on Employment. As already mentioned, it is formed by representatives of employers' organizations and trade unions and is meant to become 'an instrument of permanent dialogue and concertation' between the two categories of European producers on problems of employment. The Standing Committee of Employment might become a model of the future Committees for Regional Policy or Industrial Policy.

It was only to be expected that interest groups in Europe would set up their own European organization immediately after the formation

1. William Russell, *The Monetary Committee of the European Community*, a paper presented at the IPSA conference, Montreal 1973.

of the Communities and try to act directly on the European level. To a certain extent this has happened.[1] But three aspects of this development place it in a more modest perspective. First the number of organizations at the European level is still infinitesimal when compared with those at the national level. To be sure, the large European groups contain and represent a vast number of national groups, brought together in this way. Secondly, the evolution of the Communities away from the dominance of the Commission, once believed to be a supra-national body, towards the dominance of the inter-governmental Council, has led interest groups to realize that their action would continue to have greater effectiveness at the national level.

Thirdly, as in the history of the appearance of groups in the industrializing society, of, say, Britain, the employers were the first to set up their European pressure groups. The workers' organizations were slower and more reluctant in spite of the attempts made by the trade unions on the Continent (Italian, German, Dutch, French, etc.) to use the new social and economic environment of Western Europe as a whole to the benefit of the working class. How much the Community actually encouraged the employees' and workers' organizations to participate in its decision-making processes is a moot point. The blame for the failure of the Social and Economic Council to become the organ of representation of the industrial forces and as such one of the most effective institutions of the Community might be laid equally at the door of the national organizations and at the door of the Community. Some cynical observers are even arguing that the rapid economic progress of the Six in the first decade occurred because the working class was caught napping and was unaware of the consequences of integration.

Direct relations between the interests institutionalized at the European level started in earnest in 1958 after the creation of the EEC and because these interests thought that a new 'central power', the Commission, had been born, upon which they should make their

1. Sidjanski, op. cit. This is a useful history of the institutionalization of groups at the European level.

influences felt. But when the Council became the principal organ of decision-making the divisions between the national groups reappeared. The groups, even if acting in a co-ordinated way, found that it was more expedient to exert pressure directly on their national representatives, either through their Permanent Representative or directly, through their national governments.

A new technique of concertation was experimented with, and had mixed results, in the agricultural sector, which is the most highly integrated in the Community. A study by Terkel T. Nielsen,[1] already quoted in these pages throws more light on the institutionalization of the participation of groups in the agricultural policy of the Community. He shows that there are 133 interest groups of relevance to the agricultural sector – of which 15 are the national organizations of the major agricultural producers, grouped under the umbrella organization, COPA. The Assembly of COPA is formed by representatives from the member organizations, and the Presidium by one elected representative from each member state. There are national differences. The Dutch groups are for instance much better organized and represented than the Italian ones. COPA has some thirty specialized sections (working groups) which are either part of the organization or independent European groups. The relations between COPA and the Commission is described in apposite terms by Nielsen as 'a process of feedback and response'. One example of the influence of COPA as representative of the agricultural producers of the member states was its successful opposition in 1968 to the proposal of the Commission to lower the intervention price for butter.

The influence of COPA has of late relatively decreased, for two reasons. One is the shifting of the centre of gravity from the Commission to the Council. COPA has less influence on the latter. Moreover, in the Council it might often be outflanked by the national agricultural groups which exert their influence directly on the national government bodies. The second reason is that after the long

1. Terkel T. Nielsen in Ionescu (ed.), *The New Politics of European Integration.*

years of activity in the making of agricultural policy, and thus in the most integrated sector of the Community, the general conclusion that can be drawn is that, as noted by Nielsen, 'COPA has been more successful in influencing the way in which the CAP has been implemented than in influencing matters of detail or the definition of strategic policy options'.

The Commission itself has of late called in question the way in which the politics of concertation are now practised by the Council. In an important text[1] the Commission criticized the Council implicitly by pointing out that 'experience has shown that the procedure for adopting texts submitted by the Commission must be speeded up'. The Commission was particularly concerned about the increasing delay encountered by its proposals in the Council's process of decision-making; this was to a great extent the consequence of the size of the national delegations' participation in Council sessions, which slowed down the deliberations. Explicitly, the Commission criticized the politics of concertation from a more fundamental point of view. It stated that, 'Concerted action is a method which has its merits but also very clear limitations. It only works really when the fundamental interests of the member states converge, or when the problems do not involve in themselves vital conflicts of interest. This does not mean that concertation must be abandoned. In many cases it represents the optimal sharing of responsibilities, while in others it will be found to be insufficient but necessary for a time for the purposes of transition. Nevertheless, in certain essential matters, the time seems to have come to consider *constraints* and additional means.'

But the most important point made by the Commission seems to this author to be its insistence on the necessity of fostering collaboration between the European social and economic forces and the institutions of the Community, which in itself is only a vast industrial society. Thus in the same document the Commission reiterated its view that 'despite the efforts which have been made the two sides of

1. Communication from the Commission to the Council, 19 April 1973, Com (73) 570, Brussels 1973.

industry have been insufficiently involved in Community decisions. This is all the more worrying at a time when the building of Europe as an end in itself no longer receives unqualified support; people want to know the aims in specific matters, such as the quality of life or the balance between the various forces in society.' And more specifically the Commission demanded that, 'When Community decisions on both general regulatory policies and structural policies are taken the two sides of industry must be consulted more frequently and especially at the preparatory stages. Consultations are already held within, *inter alia*, the Economic and Social Committee and the Standing Committee on employment. There are also informal contacts between the Commission and the major socio-economic groups. The effectiveness of the existing machinery could be increased if the Medium-term Policy Committee were to co-operate closely with both labour and management. For its part the Standing Committee on Employment whose work largely concerns social policy, should also be involved in deliberations on the second stage of economic and monetary union.'

In summarizing the evolution of the political institutions of the European Community we may venture the following conclusions:

1 The institutionalization of the Community, although based on the framework of the Treaty of Rome, has produced substantial spontaneous variations and new and distinctive forms. It is to be expected that the institutionalization will, in the event of Community survival, take unprecedented and unforeseeable forms of organization.
2 On the present evidence it can be surmised that, as long as the member states pursue the common purpose of integration, delayed or diluted as it may seem at times, most forms of institutionalization, even if undertaken solely for pragmatic and national reasons, will have ultimately integrative effects. This, however, does not mean that all losses of sovereignty of the member states because of their inability to cope any longer with some of their traditional obligations will

result in proportionate accretions of supra-national power.

3 Because of the trans-national and collegiate nature of the Community its political processes have an inherent character of 'concertation'. This coincides with the growth of 'concertation' in the national political processes of West European industrial societies. However, there is obviously a need for a greater amount of direct concertation between the European Community *qua* community, and European socio-economic groups representing trans-national interests.

4 This insufficiency in processes of direct European concertation is contrary to expectations insofar as the tradition-free Community might be expected to be less averse to this kind of modern centripetal politics than the ageing European nation-states. It is because of the increasing impotence of the nation-states in making and implementing decisions that trans-national and supra-national solutions are sought. The absence of an effective new centre of decision-making at the European level, as well as the shrewd ways and means by which the member states have channelled the relations between their peoples and the Community were responsible for this.

5 The quest for a new European centripetalism points towards a new form of European Parliament which, in view of the reasons described in points 1, 3 and 4, will probably be multi-cameral (with, in any case, economic and social chambers and a regional chamber) to correspond to the requirements of concertation with newly-emancipated socio-economic groups.

6 But it points above all toward a European Economic Plan and a European technique of consultative planning. Planning, the prerequisite of the functioning of an industrial-technological society, has failed in practically all European nation-states mainly because of the fragility and the instability of the individual national economies. It might well be that even now Europe's size and pool of resources is not enough to give the European Plan sufficient stability. The

monetary crisis has, since 1973, proven beyond doubt that such problems can be solved only by an agreement linking all the major industrial societies of the free world. But only the European Plan can lead to real, positive, integration. Of this more in the Conclusions.

7 In the meantime, however, it still remains to be proved, especially to the corporate forces in Europe, that the social, industrial, regional, and above all economic policies of the Community are potentially more accurate and have a greater chance of effectiveness and feasibility than national policies. Enterprises, regions and trade unions should be able to see whether the respective European policies have more relevance for them, and more credibility in general, than fragmented national projects which are frequently re-styled and seldom carried out. To this question we now turn.

The policies of the Community

The policies of the Community are its least known, and least studied aspect. This may be due in part to an inherent timidity in the information techniques of the EEC. Being under the control of the member states, it is inhibited from attempting to persuade the public directly how much more effective, dynamic and progressive its policies would be, when compared with the hesitating and frustrated national policies. Its subordination to the national governments precludes the European Community from comparing its policies with, let alone opposing them to, the corresponding national policies. The same subordination prevents the Community from showing how its policies are distorted or hampered by the national governments, or how many of the successful policies from which national governments make political capital for themselves are the effect of the actions of the Community.

Partly, too, EEC policies are relatively little known because students of the Community, intrigued above all by the novelty of the quasi-or pseudo-federal structures of the organization, have preferred to concentrate on these institutional aspects. Yet as we have seen during this examination of the working of the Community, while the institutionalization itself seemed to remain half-way in a sort of limbo, some policies did progress and still do.

The policies of the Commission comprise
- the Competition Policy
- the Financial Policy
- the Monetary and Economic Policy
- the Medium-term Economic Policy
- the Regional Policy
- the Social Policy
- the Industrial Policy
- the Common Agricultural Policy
- the Cultural Policy
- the Information Policy
- the Energy Policy
- the Transport Policy
- the Environmental Policy
- the Common Commercial Policy (now renamed External Relations)
- the Development Policy
- the Research and Technology Policy

Most, if not all the policies of the Community have their origin in the Treaty of Rome. Yet some of them are more advanced (the Common Agricultural Policy, for instance) and some are still in embryo (the Environment Policy). Some have been asleep for a long time (the Transport Policy), but some have been the object either of an intermittent institutionalization (the Social Policy) or of active reconsideration and reformulation (the Regional Policy). In general, all policies have had an intermittent course or, to put it in more metaphoric terms, a chequered biography.

The causes of the intermittence of the various policies are to be found in a combination of some or all of the following factors. In some cases a policy is re-activated through the special or immediate interest attached to it by one or more member states at Council or Summit meetings. It may also be the result of pressure of national or especially international (European) interest groups. In other cases a policy is reviewed by the more insistent action of the Commission due to the more dynamic personality of a Commissioner (or of a General-Director or Director) who plan their own strategy for pushing forward their objectives. Sometimes the renewed interest is due to the linkage between the policy which is being activated, and other policies with which it naturally progresses simultaneously, or without which it cannot progress at all – for instance, the linkage between the regional and the economic and monetary policies. But one of the most frequent and effective reasons is the occurence of a world – or European – crisis, in the midst of which the original European policy is again unearthed, and presented again as the best and most comprehensive solution.

In the following pages it is proposed to see how some of the policies of the Community might be of greater interest to the national, in our case British, corporate forces, which are disappointed with the failure of the policies at national level. Of the three corporate forces, the British enterprises have the best information on the policies of the Community. On the other hand, people in Scotland, Wales and especially Northern Ireland seem to be insufficiently aware of the direct relevance of the policies of the Community to their national problems. And the leadership of the British trade unions, on the contrary, now view the European Community as a whole with such antipathy that they prefer to ignore its policies, relevant as they might be to their problems and near as they might be to some syndicalist beliefs.

Starting first with the enterprises, to what extent can it be assumed that they will be less centrifugal within the broad communitarian framework than they have proved to be within the narrower national (British) framework? The reasons why one may assume a positive answer to this question are three.

The first is that both the concentration of industrial activities, and the broadening of the area of commercial activities within the geographic boundaries of the Community, place the enterprises in more favourable situations to work and to develop than if they were kept within the national boundaries. This argument has been judiciously presented during the debate on British entry by Professor John Williamson.[1]

In the first place, when trade expansion involves a reorganization of production, it is likely to require additional investment. There is no need to rely on the psychological effects of an improved trade balance (as Kaldor does) to promote investment. A balanced increase in trade would also have this effect – and this can be expected to materialize from entry to the EEC.

Second, there is the possibility of exploiting economies of scale. While there is no reason for thinking that scale is an important factor throughout industry, evidence indicates that it is significant in three major areas. These are the high technology industries (where increased scale enables one to spread R and D costs over a larger output), much of the engineering industries (where learning results in lower costs as batch sizes increase), and a large part of the chemical and allied industries (where plant costs do not increase in proportion to throughput as the size of plant is increased). A bigger industry may also reduce costs through promoting new firms specializing in the manufacture of components.

Third, there is the benefit of greater competition. It seems to me mistaken to equate 'competition' to having firms tottering on the verge of bankruptcy. On average, I see no reason to suppose that firms would be better or worse off in a larger market. What would differ would be the responsiveness of profits to effort. The cosiness of a small market tends to ensure a tolerable minimum level of profits, while exclusion from foreign markets makes it difficult to greatly improve performance no matter how much effort is expended. A bigger market should increase both the penalties for failure and the rewards of success. To the extent that Britain's poor

1. *The Times*, 26 May 1971.

181

growth record reflects the lethargic attitudes of its businessmen, this is surely desirable.

Fourth, there is the benefit of participating in a fast growing market. At present the growth of the progressive section of British industry is probably restrained by the slow growth of demand for their products. To expand faster than the rest of the economy requires increased reliance of exports. So long as exports face a foreign tariff, this is liable to mean accepting decreased profitability. This would change if Britain were in the EEC, since the more progressive sectors could realise their potential by sharing in the growth of continental demand without facing lower profitability.

In the first part of this chapter we noted the positive effects of the first decade of European integration on the industry and trade of the Six countries of the Common Market. It would be difficult to expect any similar assessment of the effects on British trade and industry after only a relatively short period of full membership. Yet, although the reactions of other quarters of the economy were, after Britain's first year, either non-commital or directly critical, it was precisely from trade and industry that the most positive and outspoken testimony was heard. The Confederation of British Industries publicly took a stand in favour of the continuation of EEC membership, and warned the Labour Government against the dangers of withdrawal.

In a survey released in July 1974 by the London Chamber of Commerce, eighty-five per cent of broad spectrum of British firms which had answered the questionnaire were in favour of the continuation of membership. Confirming Williamson's predictions, it was the engineering and the high-technology industries which were the most enthusiastic about the results of the first year and the future prospects. Most of the others acknowledged difficulties (which they attributed to their own unpreparedness to work in new conditions, as well as to the slowness of the European bureaucracy in Brussels) but declared unambiguously their readiness to take advantage of the opportunities offered by EEC membership. The most common reason they gave for this attitude was their belief that an enlarged market and the consequent economies of scale provided the most promising solutions to Britain's economic problems. Thus those

British enterprises which had lately shown a tendency towards national centrifugalism, now demonstrated an appreciation for the broader European field of action and concentration. But this only confirmed the trade unions' suspicion that the Community was mostly a shield for European capitalism.

The other two reasons for the positive attitude of the enterprises were less ideal. One was that the Community was in a better position, and also more inclined than some of the individual nation-states to control the activities of the multi-national corporations. The other was that the Community, if it were now to work more effectively, would both be in a better position and more inclined than some of the individual nation-states to work out long-term policies and economic plans for the entire Community. It could assess from its more realistic 'commanding heights' the entire perspective of the economy and assign to the enterprises economic and social roles corresponding to the general orientation of the European economy.

To take the second first. Because of the enlarged market in which it could operate, and because of the enormous pool of common industrial resources on which it could draw, as well as because of the possibilities of massive selective investment which the European Monetary Fund could offer, the Community would be in a position to propose an industrial policy. A policy was proposed (in part at least because of the resoluteness of the new Commissioner for industrial policy, Altiero Spinelli)[1] in March 1970.

In that month the Commission submitted to the Council a memorandum on industrial policy, known also as the 'Colonna memorandum'. This presented industrial problems facing the Community on a 'global' level, and significantly, coincided with two other memoranda on regional and technological development. The five

1. See especially Altiero Spinelli, *Agenda pour l'Europe*, Paris, 1973, as well as his *Etat d'avancement des travaux en matière de politique industrielle dans la Communauté*, a report at the conference 'Industry and Society in the European Community', Verona, 1972. For the part he personally played in the history and pre-history (the federalist movement) of European integration, see his contribution in Ionescu, *The New Politics of European Integration*.

principal recommendations of the memorandum were; 1) to remove the remaining barriers to the establishment of a single market embracing the whole Community; 2) to create a unified business environment, including the harmonization of company law and taxation, and the creation of a Community capital market; 3) to reorganize European industry, so as to take account of the dimensions of the Common Market; 4) to promote technological progress in the Community; and 5) to recognize the social and regional aspects of industrial development. The memorandum was examined at great length by a new committee on 'Industrial Policy' which delivered a report on 30 March 1971. At the end of April 1971 the Commission proposed that it should itself set up an 'Industrial Policy Committee'. Since then this memorandum has been examined several times by the Committee of Permanent Representatives, but it has not yet been dealt with by the Council itself, a clear symptom of the difficulty of harmonizing different national points of view.

Broadly speaking the attitudes of the various national governments towards a common industrial policy can be described as follows. Some, notably Italy, call for a prior definition of a comprehensive industrial policy before agreeing to take the specific actions of implementation of the industrial policy proposed by the French and the Belgian governments. Italy's argument is based on the view that an agreement on regional policy should come first. (This argument, together with the entry of Britain into the Community has helped to promote the issue of regional policy, which became more topical if not more advanced than the industrial policy). Another disagreement concerned the establishment of the Committee for Industrial Policy. The French Government was reluctant to base such a committee on the Commission, in line with its standard institutional approach to the Council–Commission dialogue. It argued that such matters should be co-ordinated by the senior national officials. In addition, the French Government advocated that *specific* and *concrete* industrial actions should be taken provided they were approved unanimously beforehand. Other member states, notably Germany, criticized this attitude as a *à la carte* industrial policy and as leading to a French type of dirigism and interventionism (thus reopening the old and confusing Franco–German dialogue on liberalism versus dirigism in the Community). Most member states expressed the opinion that any sacrifice of their own practices and interests could only be justified to public opinion at home as furthering integration (an example of common versus communitarian policies).

The Commission in the meantime proceeded with the consultation of European industrial circles and public opinion. A special conference was organized in April 1972 in Venice.[1] Altiero Spinelli introduced the subject and argued that the need for an industrial policy was felt throughout the European Community, that the 'negative' lifting of barriers was not sufficient in itself. The formation of European companies, the opening of the public markets, the integration of technological instruments and the restructuring of some traditional industries were the main tenets of a European industrial policy. The Commission then prepared detailed memoranda on the implementation of Community industrial development, the opening up of a public sector, and the creation of an office for closer relations between industrial firms. The draft Industrial Policy was fully endorsed by the Summit Conference of October 1973. Yet the industrial policy is still practically unborn.

The reasons for this sad state of affairs are manifold. Perhaps the most important is the question of 'globalization'. The industrial policy can not be launched and implemented until other policies have also advanced: the agricultural policy (also in need of structural reforms), the social policy and the regional policy (with which it is closely bound up). But the two policies on which the industrial policy most depends are policy referred to as the Economic and Monetary Union, which is rightly diagnosed as the nexus of all the other economies, and the energy policy, which as was so dramatically highlighted in 1973–4 directly affects the functioning of European industry. Yet the energy policy too, because of the procrastination of the member states, exists only in embryo. Its saving grace was that in the light of the energy crisis of 1973–4 the Community showed

1. See Spinelli, report at the 1972 Verona Conference (op. cit.), and 'Commission programme of industrial and technological policy', 3 May 1973.

itself much more aware collectively of the imminent dangers facing all Western European states, than any one of them had individually.

The failure of the industrial policy to materialize has been justifiably criticized by the European Left as the major proof that national capitalism obstructs the work of European integration[1] – and that ultimately the EEC works mostly in the interest of the multi-national corporations, which are both un-European and imperialistic. But let us now turn to the contrasting possibility, suggested earlier by industrial opinion, of the EEC exercising control over the multi-nationals.

The view taken by the Community of the activity of the multi-national corporations in Europe is realistically discriminating.[2] It distinguishes between the need for concentration in larger enterprises, preferably European enterprises, and the conflicts of interests that inevitably arise between large extra-European enterprises and European economic interest. The Commission had constantly remarked[3] that too many European industrial enterprises 'were slow in adapting themselves, in size and location, to the new European economic area'. In 1970 it had submitted to the Council a proposal for the formation of European companies.[4] As has been seen from the Maillet report[5] the mergers which took place, especially since the 1960s, were however mainly between enterprises of the same nationality, or between European and extra-European (Canadian, Australian and especially American Enterprises.

In the meantime multi-national corporations continued to expand their activities in Europe. The Commission took the view that 'the

1. See Michel Rocard, op. cit., pp. 83–87, and Edgar Mandel, *Europe versus America*, London, 1970.
2. See a communication of the Commission to the Council on *Multinational undertaking and community regulations*, of 7 November 1973, and the debate in the European Parliament of 24 April 1974.
3. See *Memorandum on Industrial Policy*, May 1970.
4. See Mariano Pintus's report on the European Company Statute to the legal commission of the European Parliament, of 3 March 1972.
5. See above, pp. 151ff. See also Christopher Layton, the *European Advanced Technology*, London, 1969.

growing hold of multinational undertakings on the economic, social and even political life of countries in which [they] operate... demands the attention of the public authorities'. Insofar as its task is to co-ordinate, harmonize and if necessary supplement the policies of member states, the Community saw itself presenting the degree of effectiveness and cohesiveness necessary to form the framework into which a counterweight to these multinational activities could be introduced.

But the direct measures proposed were of course parallel with the general solutions which the Economic and Monetary Union and the standardization of European taxation might bring to the problem of relations between the extra-European and the multinationals. More-over they were considered to become effective only when they will be co-ordinated with world-wide actions to be taken by the United Nations and the OECD.

The measures proposed were divided under different headings as follows: *Protection of the General Public.* Here the first and most important problems were in the area of taxation. The nationally devised systems supplemented by bilateral agreements were seen as inadequate for taxation problems of this size. New European legis-lation was recommended in order to reduce tax avoidance and to improve international assistance and co-operation relating to in-formation, supervision and recovery. Special attention was also drawn to the problem of security of supply of essential resources.

In this connection a timely reminder was given that 'in the sphere of energy the Commission proposed to the Council measures in-tended to improve the Community's security of supply, in particular the concerting of action between the member states and with the participation of the undertakings concerned on their hydrocarbons supply policy'.[1] This is a telling example of the Community's advantages of the individual nation-state in terms of political fore-sightedness. The oil crisis would not have taken Europe by surprise had the project of an energy policy for the Community been given

[1]. 'First orientation for an energy policy of the Community', Communica-tion of the Commission to the Council, i, 18 December 1959.

the consideration it deserved, and the role of the 'major' oil companies been assessed in advance. Moreover after the crisis, the Community was much more eager to enforce a 'code of conduct on multi-national oil companies' than were some of the member states (notably Britain, West Germany and the Netherlands). Under the proposals of the Commission in 1974 the oil companies would have been obliged to give governments detailed information on investment programmes, distribution costs, and ex-refinery prices. An Energy Committee was set up by the Council of Ministers on 30 January 1974. The old proposal for an energy policy was reworked into a 'new energy policy strategy' by which, if applied, nuclear energy could by the end of the century cover fifty per cent of the total energy Europe needs, and the Community could be dependent on coal and oil to cover no more than approximately one quarter of its energy needs. The Energy policy, as frequently mentioned in this study, is one of the foundations of the construction of Europe.

On monetary questions the Commission sought a solution to the problem of short-term disruption of capital movements, part of which is attributed to the activities of multi-national companies. Insofar as international investments play an important part in the implementation of the regional policies of member states, the Commission drew attention to the fact that the multi-national corporations, being among the first to decide on the location of investments, could place the member states in competition.

Another heading is *Protection of Workers*. The Commission considered the setting up of multi-national trade union counterweights as essential for a balanced solution to the problem – and recommended that they should be encouraged by the Community. It made direct proposals on *a*) measures against large-scale dismissals; *b*) protection of employees' interests in the event of mergers or rationalization; *c*) harmonization of national laws on mergers; and above all, *d*) stressed the necessity of adoption by the multi-nationals of the European Company statute.

Yet another heading is *Maintenance of Competition*. Most multi-national enterprises control substantial sections of markets, and are thus in a better position to restrict competition. Rules of competition should be maintained and strengthened by active surveillance in accordance with the Community's regulations on oligopolistic situations. Under other headings the proposals dealt with *Purchasing of Enterprises, Equality of Conditions of Reception,* conditions of *Establishment of Multi-national Companies in Developing Countries* and the better *Provision of Information,* in each case with special regard to *a*) funds invested, re-invested and transferred to the country of origin; *b*) composition of capital; *c*) the number of jobs created and abolished; *d*) declared profits and taxes paid, as percentages of turnover; *e*) expenditure on research and income from licences.

These proposals were bound to meet with the resistance of many member states – which cannot be blamed either for protecting their own 'champion' corporations, or for continuing their traditional and positive relations with American-owned and -located corporations. But the proposals signify the *possibility* of the Community acting, and of its *willingness* to act in a field where individual European states have proved their inability or lack of will. Like the European states, the Community sees the beneficial aspects of multi-national corporations in the modern economy, and encourages their activities in Europe. But unlike the European nation-states, the European Community is capable of exercising control over the large territory wherein the multi-nationals can profit, to the detriment of Western Europe as a whole, from national divisions and a lack of co-ordination. In August 1974, for instance, it was announced that the directorate of the Competition Policy of the Commission was to investigate IBM's behaviour in Europe, to determine whether the firm had infringed Article 86 of the Rome Treaty by abusing its dominant market position in the Community.

The preceding section has tried, however sketchily and superficially, to show that by offering the industries in the European states conditions of stability, expansion and predictability which they cannot get from the individual nations, and by being better equipped to control their integration in the common European interest and economic policy, the Community can orient the enterprises more centripetally than can be done at the national level. In this section we will consider the potential relationship of the European regions to the Community in the same light. The regional policy, like the social and industrial policies, was only just beginning to develop when the breakdown of 1973–4 occurred. The proposals discussed (and never adopted) provided for the immediate establishment of a Regional Development Fund, which would ultimately evolve into a new Regional Development Committee charged with the co-ordination and unification of national regional policies. The unexpected revival of the regional policy, which had long been the Cinderella of the Community's policies, was for three reasons. The first was the special interest in a Community regional policy shared by certain member states (as noted above, primarily Italy among the founders and Great Britain and Eire among the new members). The second reason was that the process of rethinking or 'globalization' caused by the evolution of the Common Agricultural Policy and the Economic and Monetary Union had made more apparent the interdependence of both with a regional policy.[1] The third was the appointment in January 1973 of George Thomson, a man of particular influence and ability, as Commissioner for Regional Affairs.

Thus, with the enlargement of the Community, a regional policy had become one of its most prominent and topical aims. What follows is a general and all too brief account of the way in which this policy has evolved to date.

The legal foundations of the Commission's initiative in the field of regional policy are set out in the Preamble of the EEC Treaty,

1. Thus in the Summit Communiqué of 1972, 'The heads of state or of government agreed that a high priority should be given to the aim of correcting in the Community the structural and regional imbalances which might affect the realization of Economic and Monetary Union... From now on they undertake to co-ordinate their regional policies.' This was expressed even more forcefully in the subsequent *Report of the Commission on the Regional Problems in the Community* (Com. 550. 3 May 1973): 'No member state can be expected to support the economic and monetary disciplines of Economic and Monetary Union without Community solidarity', ibid., p. 7.

which states that 'discrepancies in the agricultural regions should be reduced' (Art. 39). A number of Community actions in other sectors, notably in those dealing with the support of railways and transport, have paid some attention to regional factors. Grants from the original funds of the Community (social, agricultural and European Investment Bank funds) have come to be increasingly subject to regional criteria.

In April 1967 a General Directorate was created for the purpose of 'preparing a regional policy for the Community and responsible to the new Commissioner for Industrial Affairs. On 17 October 1969 the Commission submitted proposals to the Council[1] recommending that the Commission should at once determine which member states were in 'urgent need' of development plans. The criteria for 'urgent need' pointed to predominantly agricultural regions in which the principal industries were declining, frontier regions, and regions where unemployment was a characteristic feature. The proposals called for the establishment of a Community Fund for regional expenditure and of a Regional Development Committee. Both the European Parliament and the Council approved the proposals, although the Italian Government criticized them as inadequate. However, after the initial debate, the file was shelved, partly because it required more study, partly because of the deadlock already produced by divergent attitudes among the different member states.

The causes of this deadlock were to be found in the fact that at the time only one of the six states approached formidable regional problems as if they could be solved by specific regional measures. This was Italy, where regional problems were more acute because of the exceptional discrepancy between its industrialized north and its under-developed south, combined with its traditional administrative centralization. The 1971 administrative reform had tried to establish regional autonomy in Italy on a more coherent and modern basis. The other five member states had, of course, their own regional problems, as the migration balances (Table 3) and the following map of gross domestic products show, but by contrast with

1. Secretariat, *Supplement to Bulletin 12/1969*, p. 53ff.

Table 3

| Countries | Periods | Migration balances | | |
| | | For the whole | Annual average | |
		period thousand units	thousand units	% of population
United Kingdom	1961–1970	− 115	− 11.5	− 0.02
Ireland	1961–1971	− 141·6	− 14.2	− 0.50
Denmark	1961–1969	+ 23.7	+ 2.6	+ 0.06
Germany	1960–1969	+ 2691.6	+ 269.2	+ 0.45
France	1962–1968	+ 1333.6	+ 222.3	+ 0.45
Italy	1960–1969	− 517.9	− 51.8	− 0.10
Belgium	1960–1968	+ 183.5	+ 20.4	+ 0.21
Netherlands	1960–1969	+ 80.2	+ 8.0	+ 0.06
Luxemburg	1960–1969	+ 8.3	+ 0.8	+ 0.25

National statistics of each country. Source (also figures 4 and 5): *Report of the commission on Regional Problems in the Community*, Annex, p. 14.

Italy, they were less acute and less easily distinguishable as regional problems from national economic and social problems. Britain and Ireland, when they joined the Community, were a different case. Their governments – less than the Italian, but more than say, the German – were accustomed to interpreting some of their outstanding economic and social problems in terms of regional disequilibrium. This difference in attitudes was afterwards to crystallize into two major controversies, i.e. 1) how to define 'central' as against 'peripheral' regions, and 2) whether regional solutions should be sought for the more widespread phenomenon of the 'declining industries' for which there were other causes.

The importance and topicality of the regional policy were reasserted only after the Economic and Monetary Union had been seriously discussed and seen in all its implications and ramifications. The Commission had always affirmed that medium-term economic policy, including its regional aspects, should be considered in a total

Figure 4: Gross domestic product per head of population (Index: average of Community of Nine equals 100)

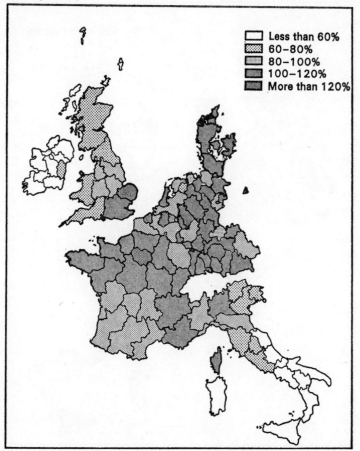

	Less than 60%
	60–80%
	80–100%
	100–120%
	More than 120%

context. Further influenced by Italian criticism of the EMU's failure to deal with regional imbalances, it linked the proposals on regional policy made during Malfatti's term as President with the first stage of the Economic and Monetary Union. On 30 June 1971 its proposals were sent to the Council.

However, at its meeting on 29 October 1971 the Council found it

Figure 5: Unemployment

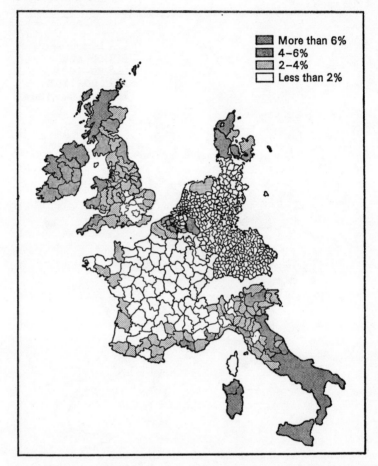

impossible to reach agreement, mainly because of the reluctance of the German, Dutch and to some extent the French governments. At the meetings of 6–17 March 1972, the Italian government, its hand now strengthened by the imminent enlargement of the Community, put progress towards a regional policy as a condition of its acceptance of EMU. A compromise was reached in March 1972 in the form of a resolution proposed by the French that the FEOGA[1] fund be used for regional development purposes. It was also proposed that either a Regional Development Fund be created, or failing this, that a system of joint use of some of the Community's resources should be established for regional purposes. At the Paris summit of 1972, after the enlargement, the heads of state took a clear stand in favour of the promotion of the regional policy.

In the meantime, George Thomson was appointed Commissioner exclusively in charge of regional policy. Both his prestige and his expertise were to exert a great influence on the preparation of the policy.

In his new role Thomson was also called upon to see that British regional policy was consistent with the new projects for a European regional policy. One of the guide lines of the new Community regional policy was that 'it cannot be a substitute for the national regional policies which member states have been conducting for many years.[2] The harmonization of national policies and of national attitudes in regional matters were to be one of the Community's tasks. The new approaches have been criticized by the French, the Germans and the Dutch, who felt that the application of a regional policy to the problem of declining industries stretches to illogical dimensions the policy's potential role.

The proposals presented by the Commissioner were principally concerned with the Regional Development Fund and the Regional Development Committee to be set up by 31 December 1973. He reiterated his proposals to the Council that the FEOGA Guidance section should be used for the creation of industrial employment in agricultural priority areas, and that consideration should be given to such measures as the establishment of a regional development company and a European guarantee system for loans. The Regional Development Fund should be devoted entirely to medium- and

1. The Guidance and Guarantee fund set up under the Common Agricultural Policy. Its two main functions are to support prices on the agricultural market and to help finance the structural improvement of agriculture.
2. See *Report* (Com. 550, 3 May 1973), p. 42.

long-term programmes to assist the less developed and declining regions within the member states. It had to be of sufficient size to reduce effectively the structural and regional imbalances in the Community which might affect the EMU, most probably in the region of 500 mill. u.a.[1] But the proposals did not confront specifically 'the determination of the geographical areas of application of the Regional Development Fund'. As far as the co-ordination of the national regional policies was concerned, the proposals endorsed the Council's opinion that a Regional Development Committee should be created on the lines of the existing Monetary Committee and the Medium-Term Economic Policy Committee, with a representative from a member state as Chairman and the Secretariat provided by the Commission.

The principal policy-makers in the European Community are more divided amongst themselves on the question of regional policy than on many other questions. From the very beginning the Commission and the Council have not seen eye to eye on this. The former was more interested in the regional policy on account of its implicit and explicit importance for the entire process of integration.

In the Council itself the member governments have been divided on the regional issue – the German, Dutch and French governments afraid that they would have to subsidize heavily a policy from which Italy, Britain and Eire would profit, directly and primarily. In the political and administrative structure of each of these three states, regional problems have an explicit context. The federal structure of the German Federal Republic by nature involves sharp contrasts in economic development or in standards of living between regions. Each Länd being also a region, proper schemes for regional action were adopted in Germany only in 1969 and signified 'the start of a more advanced co-operation phase on regional economic policy measures applied jointly by the Fund and the Länder, without, however interfering with the Länder who, until 1969, remained responsible for the Federal Republic's regional policy.[2] In France, the

1. A unit of account – the value of the dollar before the 1971 devaluation.
2. Ibid., p. 230.

solution of regional problems is linked with long-overdue national administrative reorganization. The principal regional problems are the achievement of a better balance between Paris and the provinces, the development of the west, south-west and the Massif Central regions and the conversion of the north and east regions. The former is seen as a major operation in economic and administrative decentralization, and the development of the three, and the conversion of the two regions are considered as going 'hand in hand' with changes in the industrial and agricultural sectors. Consequently French regional policy is regarded by the French as a natural part of the Economic and Monetary Union, but not as a preliminary and separate condition for the setting up of the EMU.

The German Government in its turn felt that regional problems should be treated in the national economic perspective. It feared that its contribution to the new Fund would represent a further sacrifice by its tax payers for the benefit of the people of other countries within the Community; and it questioned the attempt to find piece-meal, haphazardly functional and partial European solutions to some economic and social problems before a proper political structure has been provided for the European Community. These differences came into the open in the most unfortunate moments of the EEC and British crisis of the winter of 1973–4. Under pressure from Rome, and having already taken a non-Communitarian attitude on the oil problem, the Heath Government chose that moment to twist the arm of the Community by refusing to discuss any issues unless the Community gave Britain more substantial help for her regions. This attitude only further antagonized the other member-states. The regional policy collapsed in the fracas of the double crisis in the EEC and in Britain.

There are two more political perspectives opened up by this discussion which can be touched on only briefly here, both because it would take volumes to do them justice and because they are still in an embryonic state. Yet they have some relevance to the future, 'unknown' politics of industrial Europe and might have far-reaching consequences for a modern regional policy.

The first is the possibility that a Community regional policy might appeal to the regions within the member-states, over the heads and behind the backs of the governments concerned and regardless of whether these governments approve or disapprove such a policy. Some regions in the European member states have a tradition of frustration with and antipathy for their central governments. They might evolve into strong pressure groups, active at both the national and the European level in promoting a regional approach. It is not inconceivable that the German Länder could take a more direct interest in European Regional Policy than the current Federal Government. This, in more general political terms, would be a strong confirmation of the trans-national impact of the groups on modern forms of policy-making.

The second perspective is even more distant – but it has great albeit latent significance. This is the question of whether the result, or even the condition, of a real European integration will not be the shifting of the actual decision-making processes from the nation-states to the new socio-economic-ecological regions, which would assert themselves within the new trans-national political structure and communicate directly with the European organization. An entire school of federalism is founded on the view that European federation can only be achieved by the decentralization of policy-making by the nation-states. Regions, provinces and communes will in this view need to wrest the operation of integration from the nation-states and handle it themselves with or against the nation-states.[1] An independent Scotland, for instance, would surely apply for membership of the Community. The principal objection now held by some sectors of Scottish public opinion to British membership in the EEC is the fact that it makes the central government on which Scotland depends even more remote, giving London and Whitehall further opportunities to administer 'from the centre'

1. See especially, Denis de Rougemont, 'Vers une fédération des regions', and 'La region n'est pas un mini-état nation', in *Bulletin du Centre Européen de la culture*, Geneva 1967–8 and 1969–70. H. Bourguinat *Espace economique et intégration européenne*, Paris, 1967, *Regional Development in the European Economic Community*, London, 1962.

funds and incomes which belong to the regions. (Indeed, a school of thought in Whitehall claimed that any money coming to Britain from the Regional Fund should be absorbed in the national accounts of the Treasury as compensation for the contribution paid by the United Kingdom to the EEC.)

There is here a seemingly paradoxical conclusion to be drawn. This can be expressed as the axiom that one geographical unit's centrifugalism, is another unit's centripetalism. By projecting this axiom on to the regional question one can say that whereas the regions are centrifugal within the national framework, they are not necessarily centrifugal within the continental (European) framework. Moreover, if the nation-state is centrifugal towards the continental or the federal unit to which it belongs, then the centrifugalism of the regions in regard to the nation state might coincide with their centripetalism in regard to the Federation. For regional federalists the nation-state can be seen as the ultimate villain both towards the region which it oppresses and towards the Federation which it sabotages. The same people predict that a European Federation will be born and made effective only when the nation-states are sufficiently weakened as to allow federalization by the territorial and socio-economic forces which they can no longer dominate.

With this we come to the third and last of the 'corporate forces' which are centrifugal within the nation-state in the industrial technological society: the trade unions. Could the trade unions, within a broader communitarian framework, find it to their advantage to become, like the enterprises and the regions, less centrifugal within that framework than they have grown to be in the nation-state? In theory the answer should be in the affirmative, and for many reasons, starting with two which have already been discussed in this book.

The first is that if European integration succeeded in creating in all European member states a more prosperous and more stable economic situation, and if standards of living and real wages were to grow, and if industrial workers were increasingly to 'concert' in the management of their enterprises, the opposition of the trade unions, no matter how militant their leadership, would be less virulent than in the present situation. Since the mid-sixties the working-class, as well as all other groups in society has quickly lost confidence in any government which has not worked effectively. Successful governments and successful managements, on the other hand, have the effect of dissociating the long-term opposition of the working-class and its ideological leaders to the bourgeois state as such from the immediate anxiety and indignation caused by inefficacious governments and managements. This is too obvious, and has been so well confirmed by all experience (compare even now the attitude of the German trade unions with that of, say, Italian trade unions) to require more discussion. Therefore, if a European administration were to solve the problems of the Community as a whole better than the separate national administrations solve the problems of their states, the centrifugalism of the trade unions would be proportionately reduced. (Besides, and this again is a proposition touched upon in a previous section of this book, trade unions pressing for overall nationalization and state-control would regret the coming in Western Europe of a monolithic state, as much as the trade unions in Russia and Eastern Europe have reason to regret it there. The more genuinely decentralized and federal the European administration, the better the trade unions should logically fare.)

The second reason is that, just as industry concentrates itself into giant multi-national corporations which devise different industrial approaches for the different nation-states in which they operate, the trade unions too must organize themselves as a 'multi-national counterweight' to these new organizations. Great progress has been made in this direction[1] on the international plane as a whole. Less progress, though has been made at the European level, because of the weakness of the Economic and Social Council within the structure of the Community on the one hand, and because of the unco-operativeness of the British trade unions in European Community matters on the other.

But beyond these two reasons, the overall interest of the trade

1. See Charles Levinson, *International Trade Unionism*, London, 1972.

unions in the growth and success of the Community ought to lie in the achievement, at the higher European level, of a more realistic and progressive social policy than can be achieved in the individual nation-states.

A history of the social policy of the EEC could be summarily outlined as follows:—

Articles 117–128 of the Treaty of Rome declare the interest of the Community in improving working conditions and living standards, and in harmonizing the six different social systems, through equal pay across the entire Community, organized occupational mobility, and a common framework of social security. A social fund was established to provide direct help towards these objectives. But in spite of this constitutional scaffolding the Social Fund was a limited affair: from 1964 to 1969 it allocated grants worth 116 million units of account,[1] of which 109 millions was used for the training of workers.

Since 1968 there have been demands for a stronger social policy arising from causes outside the Community, as for instance, the impact of the events of May 1968 in France and in Western Europe as a whole, and from causes within the Community, such as the acceptance of full employment as a central objective of the Economic and Monetary Union, and changing views of the common agricultural policy. It must also be noted that the European Parliament, in which the socialist parties concentrated much of their well-co-ordinated effort on the social problem, exerted a particularly great influence and even pressure on the Commission and the Council.

This orientation was even more pronounced after the coming to power of the Social-Democrats in Germany in 1969. The German Government argued that social policy should be given a higher

---

1. Italy was rightly the chief beneficiary and received 45 m. u. a. for almost 700,000 workers, followed by Germany with roughly 34 m. u. a. for 300,000 workers, France 24 m. u. a. for 125,000 workers, the Netherlands 7.5 m. u. a. for 12,000 workers, Belgium roughly 5 m. u. a. for 9,000 workers and Luxembourg 13,000 u. a. for 700 workers.

priority and insisted on this being formally stated at the Paris Summit of October 1972. The Italian Governments had until then been the somewhat lonely champions of the priority of social problems in the EEC. It might well be that the demands of Italy, as the member state with the lowest indices of living standards, were viewed by other governments (that of the Netherlands for instance) with the natural suspicion that 'harmonization' and 'standardization' of social measures might lead directly to a dilution of the standards of living in those states which had the highest levels. In March 1971 the Commission presented its first overall programme on social policy, entitled 'Preliminary Orientations for a Communitarian Social Policy'.

At the Paris meeting of October 1972 the heads of states emphasized that they attached as much importance to vigorous action in the social field as to the achievement of Economic and Monetary union. They thought it essential to ensure the increasing involvement of labour and management in the economic and social decisions of the Community. They invited the Community institutions to draw up by January 1974, in consultation with labour and management, a programme of concrete measures with an indication of the corresponding resources required.

The new importance attached to European social problems was explicitly manifested by the face-lift given to the Social Fund. Originally the fund's resources came from direct contributions by the member countries, but from 1972 it has been supplied from the Community's own independent resources. The transition from the old fund to the new will continue at least until 1975, and is to be completed by 1976. For the 1973 financial year the European Social Fund has been allocated a budget of 240 m.u.a. of which 60 m. is for the continuation of the original fund.[1] In its new form it is no longer an equalization fund at the disposal of member states, mostly to assist the unemployed workers, but has become a direct attribute of the Community, which conceives it as part of its future employment policy, seeking to promote the structural adaptation of industries and

1. Commission, *Sixth Report*, p. 135.

firms to the requirements of progress. Two types of intervention can be foreseen.[1] The first would result from a Council decision where other Community policies affect the level of employment in a particular area or industry. The second type of intervention would be designed to correct unsatisfactory employment situations and would be concentrated in backward or declining industrial regions and branches of industry. This complex of potential types of action, of which some are directly part of the social policy and others are closely linked to industrial and regional policies, will require a close co-ordination in the Community.

In recent years there have been two developments in particular that have begun to involve management and labour in community policy-making. One is the evolution of the Standing Committee on Employment which has gradually extended its area of concern. This Committee was set up in March 1971, subsequent to a Council decision in 1970. It has been described as an 'instrument of permanent dialogue and concertation' between employers and trade unions within the Community's institutional framework. The Standing Committee will, it is hoped, work through a series of *ad hoc* conferences to establish commissions for collective bargaining at the Community level, thus facilitating the emergence of European trade unions. The second development has a greater political significance. On the insistence of the German trade unions and the German Government the Community must include the German system of co-determination (*Mitbestimmung*) if it is to adopt a common company law. This, of course, is a matter of great concern for the other governments, some of which are very reluctant to see this institution specifically included in Community law.

After the enlargement of the Community in January 1973, a new Commissioner, Mr Patrick John Hillery from Eire, was given the portfolio for Social Affairs. He outlined his programme, which particularly stressed the importance of dialogue between the social partners, respect for differences of custom among member states,

1. Commission, Press and Information D.9. *The Social Fund New Version*. Information Social Policy 6172.

and the importance of Community social action in the context of the Economic and Monetary Union. As for political approaches, Mr Hillery did not foresee an immediate large-scale transfer of power to the Commission and stressed the need for close collaboration between the European Community and the national administrations on these matters.

On the more specific problem of employment he showed that the present average rate of unemployment (2.5 per cent, but in some regions much more) should be considered as an upper limit and insisted that full employment should continue to be a major European priority. This was closely linked to regional policy action, and to the progress made in the application of the industrial policy. As regards migrant workers (a direct concern of many European countries) he advocated the co-ordination of national policies, especially on immigration from non-EEC countries. He also stressed that the Community should continue its retraining programme and the direct subsidy of new jobs, as well as its range of special programmes for elderly or young workers. This could be attained by permanent collaboration between the Commission and the national civil service agencies for employment.

Like the industrial policy, the social policy is in reality only a policy in formation. While it is true to say that the present constellations of government in Europe favour the realization of both policies, and that in some respects (the renovation of the Social Fund) they have of late acquired greater weight and purposefulness, these two policies must develop and stabilize further before making their impact on the collective strength of the Community.

It is significant that in Europe, unlike in Great Britain, the opposition of the Left to the present European Community and its meagre social policy is expressed in terms which aim not at the dissolution of the Community, but at strengthening it, broadening its social foundations and giving it a much more revolutionary orientation. The following arguments, summed up from Michel Rocard's book[1]

1. Op. cit., pp. 145–87.

mentioned above, are listed chiefly to show the over-simplified 'European revolutionarism' popular on the continent. A socialist Europe, Rocard thinks, should be internationally independent in terms of security. It should also be technologically and economically independent. While autarchy is inconceivable in this age of individual nation-states, a Socialist Europe could have sufficient resources to compete with the other super-powers. But while the Community must make a strenuous effort to catch up with the modern technology and economy of other federations, it need not follow the example and evolution of capitalist societies. Growth should remain the major concern.

Workers' management should not only be a way of organizing the enterprises. It should extend to the policy-making of the Community as a whole, of which the enterprises are only one echelon.

A Socialist Europe should therefore take its full responsibilities on the political plane. Instead of merely expressing common anxiety while the USSR and the USA reach an agreement on the future military situation of Europe, a Socialist Europe could play a political role of the greatest importance. It could, if strong enough, play a decisive part in the liberation of oppressed peoples and in the welfare of the underdeveloped countries, concludes Rocard.

We have taken some of the policies of the Community and examined them in the light of their appropriateness to the respective issues in general, and for the special interest of one or other of the major corporate forces in those issues. This, of course, can hardly be an exhaustive investigation of the question whether the European solutions have greater relevance than the national ones. This kind of demonstration would be convincing only if one could assume that (a) the policies of the Community taken as examples are fully at work (and we know that they are not – most of the policies of the Community are now pigeonholed); and that (b) the same individual policies are part and parcel of an *ensemble* of policies which work together synchronically, and which feed each other in a basic enmeshment. For the same reasons as in (a) we know that this is not the case, indeed we know that if some policies continue to advance, the central communitarian policies, as for instance, the Economic and Monetary Union, have been duly suspended.

But the examination, if fully and thoroughly undertaken, might prove to be useful in two respects. (And one of the leit-motifs of this study is precisely that the pro-European organizations should from now on concentrate on a systematic critical analysis of the short-sightedness, selfishness and incompetence of national policies, when compared with the policies proposed by the Community and ultimately sabotaged by the national governments.)

First, it shows, at least *in principle* (as it limited its validity from the very beginning), that the objective reasons for the need to transfer the major responsibilities of national governments in Europe to a supra-national organization are, from a negative as well as from a positive point of view, fully confirmed. From a negative point of view, nothing has proved that the incapacity of the European nation-states to solve directly their major problems – economic, financial, social or diplomatic – has been lessened during the last years. The energy, financial, and diplomatic crises have found the individual nation-states as short of answers and direct solutions as before, if not indeed, worse than before. Therefore in all these recent crises, the tendency of the European states to try to work together has for perhaps negative reasons ultimately prevailed. The individual European nation-state is progressively sinking into impotence. *In principle*, the European solutions might still give to the Nine, or more, or less, European states sufficient effectiveness, if taken and accepted in common.

But, second, the investigation might be particularly relevant to the question of the misinformation of public opinion in the major political problems, at the centre of which is the problem of the passing of the nation-state. In the opinion of this study, one of the fundamental causes of this misinformation is the deliberate attempt by parts of the élites in Europe to cling by whatever means to the traditional forms of national representation (political representation by the national political parties, socio-professional representation by the trade unions, regional representation by the regional political parties, etc.) in which they have an overwhelming vested interest. These monopolistic forces of national representation have deliberately mis-informed their respective public opinions on the grave and rapid decline of the national institutions, and of the nation-state itself, – and simultaneously on the European alternative as a means of strengthening Western European countries, and saving them from the ultimate danger of losing all their national sovereignties into non-European hands.

The actions of two European parties illustrate this strategy of political misinformation. Both are parties of great prestige and might in the political history of their respective countries. But both have misinterpreted for their peoples the real relation between the nation-state and Europe. One is the Gaullist party in France – which, although it knew that France benefited considerably from European integration, and notably from the common agricultural policy, has done its utmost to prevent the same integration from following its indispensable course towards supra-nationality, and has indeed coun-tered it *ad nauseam* with the myth of national sovereignty. Near the end of 1974, when full European integration had been blocked from all sides, and when, in its absence, there was nothing in sight to prevent all of the European nation-states from falling into spiraling inflation and subsequent social, economic and political troubles, the neo-Gaullist government of M. Giscard d'Estaing made proposals to 'relaunch' Europe, going so far as to propose European elections for a new European parliament. Was it already too late?

The other is the British Labour Party (that is, the left wing as against the pro-European opposition of individual members such as Mr Roy Jenkins, Mrs Shirley Williams, Mr Harold Lever, Mr Lawson, Mr John McKintosh, etc.). Influenced by the present leadership of the trade unions, which unlike the previous leadership is against Europe, the Labour Party has played when in opposi-tion, like the Gaullist party in France, the card of the *unreal* national sovereignty and *national interest*, against the *real* situation of inter-national isolation and economic impotence in which it knew Britain to be. Yet, once indisputably in power, the British Labour Government reduced its claims to 're-negotiate' to a few budgetary and organizational proposals to be operated from within the

Community. It also promised that, if the conditions thus obtained seemed satisfactory to the British Government and to the Labour Party, it would then recommend to the electorate that Britain should maintain its membership – it thus revealed its real object of being the *political intermediary* between Europe and the British people. The ease of the 'renegotiations' proved how over-dramatized the Labour attitude in opposition has been.

✓ These two examples have here been singled out only because they are the best known. But they are representative of the technique of the political and social élites in the European nation-states of *interposing* themselves between the European Community and the European peoples, and especially between the Community and the powerful corporate forces now emancipated from their traditional political tutelage. If the European Community's information is not to be strangled by the censorship of national governments it should at once do two things. It should first show to all layers in European society the real state of affairs in each country and in Europe as a whole, and openly compare its own policies with those of the national governments. As long as any information issuing from the European Community is mediated through the national governments, the indigenous peoples will never have the opportunity to understand the fundamental differences between obsolescent national politics and the emerging European politics.

The principal battle that the European Community has to fight is the battle for European public opinion. As long as it continues to allow its information to be censored, and its communications with cross-European interests and groups to be manipulated by the nationalistic élites, the case for European integration will never be fully made.

The future of representative government in Europe

When an author comes to part with a book, especially a book which was deliberately shaped in an unusual way, he feels a special responsibility towards it. This work has confronted me with countless problems, and I am aware that I have solved most of them by cutting Gordian knots. As I come therefore to draw my final conclusions, I shall try to explain some of my problems to the reader.

I deliberately chose, for instance, to condense and inter-relate the information I supplied concerning the recent evolution of the relations of the British Government with the three major corporate forces within British society, and with the European Community. Many works deal separately with each of these subjects and examine the 'trees' in scholarly detail. I have chosen instead to view the whole 'wood', even if in the circumstances the view is hazy and blurred. My task will be better fulfilled by others for I believe that future textbooks of politics will have to embrace this wider scope.

The principal premise of this book is that just as the present society is exceptionally centrifugal, so politics should aim to be more centripetal than ever before. As a result I have had to take a critical view of both society and government. Society is criticized here for its propensities towards a centrifugalism whose most striking embodiment, inflation, threatens to destroy society itself. Representative government is criticized for the lack of imagination and determination it has shown up to now in grappling with the problem of finding modern political methods capable of countering the disruption of society. But the more centrifugal society grows, the less it is prepared to make its own critical analysis. The centrifugalism of industrial-technological society is accompanied by the spread of a populist mentality, which is a mixture of political opposition to authority, psychological self-pity and moral hedonism.

This does not apply, of course, to all the people living in an industrial-technological society, trying to make it work, and indeed to improve it. It is equally untrue of the peoples living in communist industrial societies, whose governments see to it that they do not fuel inflationary claims, indulge in self-pity or hedonism, or engage in opposition or disruption. But I have deliberately chosen to concentrate exclusively on the question of the ability of representative government to survive in the industrial-technological age. I have examined elsewhere the problems of European industrial communist societies,[1] and from a comparative study I have formed a clear view which I shall now submit as my first conclusion here:

1 That representative government answers better to the requirements of industrial-technological society than communist government

Both communist and non-communist Europe face the same problem: the incompatibility of their respective degrees of centralism with industrial-technological society. But if that society proves increasingly ungovernable, it will be the arch-centralistic communist form of government which triumphs, since it has built into its *raison d'être* unlimited resources of state control, coercion and terrorism. Already it has been observed that communist societies show no external signs of inflation or industrial and political unrest; and in some Western European countries the communist parties might emerge as the only disciplined and coherent political force, should representative government collapse.

But if industrial-technological society is to mature without being compressed into political strait-jackets, then its anti-centralistic tendency can best be accommodated by the modification of repre-

1. *The Politics of the European Communist States*, London, 1969; and see also the series *Political and Social Processes in Eastern Europe*, prepared under my general supervision, and published by Macmillan, London.

sentative government through two partnerships – one corporate–representative and one national – supra-national – which are now taking shape in most Western European countries. Neither of these partnerships is acceptable to, or indeed feasible, in communist systems of the Soviet type. Soviet communism is inherently opposed to self-management in industry, to the autonomy of the trade unions, to independent enterprises, indeed to the market where this independence is manifested. As for the national – supra-national partnership, in the light of the Hungarian revolution of 1956 and the Czechoslovak crisis of 1968, such a partnership can only mean the domination of the junior partners by the USSR. If integration was feasible in Western Europe, it was because it was based on the consent – albeit sometimes grudging – of the peoples of not-too-unequal countries. But nowhere in Europe are nationalism and the defence of sovereignty more inflamed than in the Soviet-dominated area.

From the point of view of the difficulty of adapting a centralized economy to the industrial-technological age, Yugoslavia (in the last twenty-five years) and Czechoslovakia (during the first six months of 1968) provide clear examples of market-based, self-managed and pluralistic forms of national communism (and some Yugoslav sociologists argue that because for the last quarter of a century the Yugoslav economy has practised participatory techniques of self-management, it is by now the economy best prepared for 'the future which has begun'[1]). In Hungary too, experiments with some forms of socialist market, and of increasing independence of the enterprises are being made. Even in the GDR, a model of 'democratic centralism', the growth from within the powerful industrial structures of the giant enterprises (VVB) and of the constitutional legitimacy of the trade unions is such that the party controls them now only through the ultimately central allocation of resources and capital, and through the political reliability of the leadership of these organizations. Finally, in the USSR itself, the relations of the party élites with the technocratic, managerial and military élites are a sensitive indicator of the politics of power in that country; and the

1. See Miroslav Pecjulic, *The Future which has Begun*, Belgrade, 1969.

continuing pursuit of the 'reform of the economy' is the symptom of its malformation.

These sketchy examples serve to demonstrate that anti-centralistic forces are at work in Eastern as well as Western Europe. But whereas the representative governments are prepared to meet the challenge through reform, the more structurally rigid Soviet-type regimes may, in the long run, have to pay the price of revolution. The armed intervention that crushed reforms attempted by the Czechoslovak communists, who were endeavouring to meet the requirements of a modern society and economy, dramatically illustrates this reality.

This being said, let us now turn to the question of how European representative governments might adapt themselves to the new requirements, always assuming that there were to be no war or other international catastrophe affecting Europe. My second conclusion, therefore, is:

2 That the two partnerships require the processes of concertation

In this book, I have tried to show that, just as corporations of all kinds must assert their functional autonomy and thus increase the centrifugal character of the society, so the national representative governments, especially in Western Europe, are increasingly induced to share with the corporations the power which hitherto they have held centrally.

Attention has also been drawn to the opposing tendencies in the decision-making processes, towards diffusion (on the one hand) and towards co-ordination (on the other). Which tendency prevails is determined by the kind of decision. In the making of administrative and managerial decisions, the general trend is towards diffusion of power. Insofar as the functioning of the society depends on the participation of all those who possess exclusive technical knowledge (and by now most producers are in this position) it is necessary for all of them to participate in decisions whose implementation depends on their work and their will. But in the making of public policies, the

212

trend is towards greater co-ordination in the preparation of these policies both in the national and international settings. Wider perspectives are required and greater operational stability than the horizons and resources of the individual national economies can offer. Significantly, the common denominator between these two opposed tendencies is that they both act against the former centralistic prerogatives of national governments.

At the point where the connection between internal and external processes of decision-making entered the argument, I invited the reader on a journey through the new, embryonic institutions and processes of the European Community.

What I have primarily sought, at the national and trans-national level, is the kind of politics required by a society in need of protection from its own centrifugalism. In contrast with the functionalist theories of de-politicization, as well as with Marxist theories of the withering away of politics, and taking up in the new industrial-technological context Bernard Crick's 'defence of politics', I have argued that the new mixed representative–corporate and national–supra-national processes of decision-making require an *intensification* of political mediation as well as a change in its character.

This new mediation, which I have called centripetal politics, should consist of the arduous and relatively humble task of seeing that power is shared by, and circulates freely among, the multiple centres of real decision-making. This process has been described as 'concertation'. Its practitioners should be less professional and less interested than are contemporary political parties in the Western democracies, not to speak of the one-party states, but more prepared to commit themselves in decision-making. What political parties have increasingly done has been to channel power towards the central government and expect it to decide everything. The bottleneck of power created by the tradition of national central government is now being opened up in most Western European industrial states in order to allow for new processes of power sharing, both at the national and supra-national levels.

The new political centripetalism proceeds on three fronts. In most of the Western European states, techniques of concertation are increasingly used in the making of decisions at the local and regional levels, as well as in the management of industry. In the United Kingdom the current legislature is engaged in preparing a reform which aims at the transfer by devolution of significant portions of the power of the central government to local and regional authorities.

In Community language, concertation is lately becoming the expression for the techniques of mediation between national and supra-national representative institutions. Within the European Community the national representative governments use the techniques of concertation either through the organs of the Community or through the system of political co-operation, which is intended to remain informal, but has nevertheless acquired of late a new institutional stability. Joint national – supra-national policy-making is superseding, at least in some fields, exclusively national policy-making. The parliaments of the member states of the European Community are also adjusting their sovereignty to the new system of supra-national decision-making.

Finally, we have seen that the supra-national bodies of the Community, the Council and the Commission, have intensified direct concertation with the supra-national interest groups which act as the representatives at the European level of corresponding national groups. The direct participation of the European 'social partners' in the formulation and preparation of some of the policies of the community has increased. This third network of direct concertation, between the Community and the national and European corporate groups, is not a simple juxtaposition of the first and second processes of concertation examined in the preceding paragraphs. It is a distinct, self-contained and particularly characteristic trend of the emerging political process.

My third conclusion, deriving from the above, is:

3 That new European economic, social and political institutions should be established

If representative government is to be kept alive in Western Europe it will have not only to make the two partnerships workable, but to fuse them into a new system of social and political institutions and processes. What this means is that the possible success of the partnerships of the national governments with the social partners, on the one hand, and with the supra-national organization, on the other, is conditioned by the fact that they are inter-related. In other words, neither policy can succeed if the other fails. If it is true that the functioning of the European mixed economy is dependent on establishing a lasting relationship between the representative government and the major corporate forces, it is equally true that individual Western European representative governments can no longer establish such relationships without their economies and their security being established on new and broader foundations. And vice versa, if it is true that the survival of the Western European states depends on the future integration of their resources and means of defence, it is equally true that any kind of integration is unfeasible while the national societies are in a state of social and economic turmoil.

But the European Community has not acquired sufficient legitimacy, nor is it sufficiently institutionalized to be able to cope, at present, with these new problems. It requires new and original economic, political and social institutions and/or instruments to serve its policies.

In spite of the blows of 1973-4, from which many thought that the Community would never recover, the trend towards continuing institutionalization has now revived if in a somewhat different form. On the economic plane, the requiem for the Economic and Monetary Union has been sung with equal conviction by some sectors of European public opinion and by some statesmen. In reality, as the Marjolin report for the EEC Commission has shown, although the EMU must be considered as postponed *sine die*, developments in the monetary field of continental Europe show a new trend of rallying towards the 'snake' (the monetary mechanism by which fluctuations of participating currencies are regulated). Simultaneous steps towards monetary co-ordination are again being taken. The 'snake', which has continued to work between Germany, Benelux and Denmark, has attracted non-EEC countries into it as well. The five

EEC countries practising the 'snake' have shown a better anti-inflationary record than other member states. More important still is the fact that the French franc is now returning to its pre-1974 position, thus making possible, in the spring of 1975, its re-entry into the 'snake'. The 'snake' is of course not the EMU. But it is an instrument of European monetary co-ordination. The extension of the European 'unit of account', the present substitute for a European currency, to some cases of credit exports is yet another future possibility.

These positive, if fragmentary trends towards co-ordination should be projected onto the background of the negative alternatives with which Europe as a whole, and each of the member states in particular, are now faced on the economic plane. In other words, if more drastic measures have to be taken, given the grave economic situation, can these measures still be taken at the national level, or only at the supra-national level? The foremost two-edged problem is the use of state intervention. Since the oil crisis, and the aggravation of the inflationary spiral in Europe as a whole, the economy of the member states has been in such a condition as to be conducive to intensive state intervention in monetary and credit questions, in imports and exports, in the structure of industry and in industrial ownership. More pressure will be brought to bear on the individual governments to take over enterprises and industries which have become too weak to stand on their own.

It is true that such state intervention is now much more sophisticated than before, as for instance in Britain, where the operations of the newly created National Enterprise Board link state intervention with the participation of workers in management. But at the end of the day, the investment required for enterprises partly or totally taken over by the state might prove to be a further cause of inflation. To take the British example again, *The Economist* estimated that in July 1974 British industry was short of £3-4 billion in cash for investment.[1] The journal justifiably commented that 'if the taxpayer is made to foot this bill, the tax system itself could crumble. And that would be the final step towards hyper-inflation.'

1. 'The days of creeping socialism', in *The Economist*, 6 July 1974, pp. 70-1.

The other obvious limitation on state intervention lies in the proportion of nationalized industries to industry as a whole. If the greater part of the economy consists of state property, then inevitably the state assumes direct control of the whole economy. This in turn might ultimately amount to the replacement of representative government by communist 'democratic centralism', and to new forms of autarchy. Indeed, it is the second sense of the expression *nationalization*, that which relates it logically and etymologically to nationalism, which comes to overshadow its social, collectivistic sense. Regardless of whether it is practised by right wing or left wing dictatorships, nationalization has a chauvinistic connotation, from Stalin in the thirties to Gadafy in the sixties. Since the end of the nineteenth century, all attempts to restore autarchy in the states of Western Europe – which are technologically advanced, but dependent on trade – have led only to major international crises and to two world wars. And the experience of the political regimes which autarchy and chauvinism have created is fresh in the memory of the European peoples.

To those who would promptly ask why, in such a case, supra-national or European intervention would be less dangerous and more feasible than the intervention of the nation-states the obvious answer springs at once to mind. Intervention co-ordinated at the level of the Community as a whole is more feasible because the Community as a whole has greater resources in capital and more geographical scope for organized redeployment than the individual state. Intervention co-ordinated at the top level is likely to be less emotional, both from the ideological and nationalistic points of view, than in the nation-state.

But the most important development will be the political institutionalization now being considered in the proposals for European Union and direct elections to the European Parliament. The European Union is crucial to the whole question of European integration. But it is also the issue which stirs up the most highly emotional national reactions. More immediate is the question of holding elections to the European Parliament by direct universal suffrage. The fact that after the failure of the attempt to achieve a higher degree of economic integration in 1972–3 (the postponement *sine die* of the EMU) integration is now pursued directly on the political plane, and indeed on the very issue of European legitimacy, by concentrating on the creation of a European legislature by direct election, can be regarded as the beginning of a new and perhaps more solid approach. The integrationists have been strengthened by the change in attitude of the French Government, which although still based on the Gaullist party, has come round to acceptance of the demands of the other member states that integration should begin with political legitimacy. Sensing the importance of the move, during renegotiations the British government expressed its reservations on this particular subject.[1] Yet the draft convention approved by the European Parliament on 17 January 1975 proposes to hold the first direct elections not later than the first Sunday in May 1978.

Among the controversies over the European Parliament is the discussion whether it should have one or two chambers. In the project submitted by the Christian Democrats of the different member states (the Bertrand Report), a proposal has been put forward for two chambers; the second chamber is conceived of as a 'Chamber of States', a kind of Senate on the American model grouping representatives from the member states, perhaps two from each. This second chamber would presumably replace the Council of Ministers, which it will be remembered is the inter-governmental executive of the European Community, and would thus gradually

1. 'The heads of government of the Community countries, at their meeting in December 1974, expressed themselves in favour of the introduction of direct elections to the European Assembly by universal suffrage. It was, however, made absolutely clear by the United Kingdom that "her Majesty's Government could not themselves take up a position on the proposal before the process of renegotiation had been completed and the results of renegotiation submitted to the British people". If British membership is confirmed, any scheme for direct elections to the European Assembly would require an Act of Parliament. Any revision of the powers of the Assembly would also require the specific approval of the United Kingdom Parliament.' White Paper on Membership of the European Community: Report on Renegotiation. Cmnd. 6003, HMSO.

218

transform the mixed international executive into a new supra-national legislature. Such an evolution would of course imply a rapid progress towards European federalization. The proposal is neither particularly original (it is equivalent to the Bundesrat in Germany), nor particularly convincing, since if the new chamber were to operate concomitantly with the Council of Ministers it would lead to a cumbersome overlapping of competence.

What is more original – and although more speculative, much more in keeping with the broadening of the decision-making process – is the idea of a multi-cameral European Parliament. The idea is seldom discussed now.[1] The rationale of the project is that trade unions, enterprises and regions could be made to participate more fully in the decision-making processes, if what they were offered was participation in a chamber of the regions (the Italian Senate was originally such a chamber) or in an economic and social chamber (an adjunct often proposed for the British Parliament, notably by Sir Winston Churchill). These chambers would be subordinated to the Parliament. Yet by their very existence they would give the corporate forces, at least at the European level, a forum for homogeneous and expert participation in policy making.

The feeling that social and economic groups are peripheral to parliamentary activities, and that individual regions are peripheral to national decision-making, could most certainly be attenuated by these new forms of deliberation. Certainly, at the European level this interpenetration would bring to the fore European perspectives, and European solutions for common problems. This in itself would be a notable achievement from the point of view of those who believe that the socio-economic groups and the regions are by their function in society, and by historical and ideological tradition, the natural agents of anti-nationalism and federalism. But, as I have discussed

1. But in the *Questionnaire* of the Council of the European Communities on the attainment of European Union (document 214/74, European Parliament) question IV/4 asks: 'Should the legislative body consist of a single chamber or of several, and how should the members of this (these) chamber(s) be appointed?'

in Chapter Five of this book, it may well happen that multi-cameralism will become in future, after further devolution and de-centralization, a feature of national parliaments as well. In any case, if the European Parliament were to take the lead, national parliaments might follow suit.

The idea that the European institutions should take the lead has of course many implications. I shall single out one of these in the next conclusion, which is:

4 That the European Commission and the European Parliament should arouse in European society a sense of its own dangers and responsibilities

I have already alluded in Chapter Six to the shortcomings of the in-formation policy of the European Commission and for that matter of the European Parliament. The fact that the information policy of the Community is controlled by the Council of Ministers and the national departments and agencies has had the effect of transforming that information into a formal handbook-like description of the structures and work of the European institutions. Often, too, the official literature likes to point out the help which some regions, or social groups, or cultural institutions in some member states have received from Community funds, expressing implicitly if not ex-plicitly the hope that more will or could follow.

At the same time, as observed frequently in these pages, social policy is the Cinderella of the Community, and it is only recently that the makers of that policy have activated a programme of concertation with the 'social partners'. Of course, social policy is conditioned by the general political and economic outlook. But equally the politics and economics of a given society are conditioned by the behaviour and attitudes of the society itself. Social policy, in the sense of *Gesellschaftspolitik*, is in great part based on the critical analysis that society can make of itself, or that can be made for it by independent observers or 'guardians'. To enlighten society, to direct it away from the danger of self-inflicted disruption and towards finding its own solutions for its problems is in great part the rationale of a *Gesell-schaftspolitik*.

Putting all these things together, I submit that the real information policy of the independent supra-national bodies should be equivalent to a dialogue conducted above the heads of the member states between these bodies and the European society as a whole. The two main reasons why the national governments are not qualified to do this are obvious. One is that because they are national, they are not competent to grasp the entire European aspect of a problem. The second is that in the last decade representative governments, and especially the political parties from which they are formed, have lost a great deal of authority and are, for reasons amply discussed in this book, much more dependent on the emancipated groups of society. Hence the national representative governments or political parties do not dare to act openly as critics of their societies. These same societies, now in a capricious mood and accustomed to being cajoled by politicians (hence the growing success of right wing or left wing demagogues asking for 'the people' to guide them), can mete out instant punishment with their electoral disfavour to those political forces which dare to make criticism a two-way affair. More than ever before, public opinion now uses governments and political parties as scapegoats; yet more than ever before, governments and parties depend on their alliances with groups of public opinion.

In the vicious circle which has thus been created, those situated at the high European vantage point, and above the electoral scramble, should take stock of the situation of European society. But in a friendly and constructive spirit European society should be told the truth about the changes which have occurred and the consequences which these changes might entail. It is on this truth that the dialogue of European institutions with European society should concentrate, for when seen in the European perspective, the common features are more salient, common conclusions are more easily acceptable and common solutions easier to find.

The truth is that after a period of steady advance on all fronts – growth, employment, prosperity, standard of living, etc. – the European mixed economy has entered in recent years a new period of slackening of its rhythm. On this problem and its consequences the European Community should conduct intensive concentration with the trade unions, the enterprises, and the regions of Europe.

Since the war the mixed economy in Europe has had a record of continuous growth and full employment. Standards of living have constantly improved, due to the increase in real salaries as well as to the sophistication and mass availability of articles of convenience. Mass education and mass information have further stimulated the appetite for comfort. This has ultimately led to a mass psychology of rising expectations. Demands for escalating cash-flow have been made on the ground of material interest of innumerable sub-groups of the main categories of workers (job differentials jealousy and the multiplicity of small trade unions are characteristic causes of in-flationary demands in British economy). Demands also have been made on the idealistic ground of the plight of particularly deprived groups in the society (from pensioners to immigrants).

The present real situation in the mixed economy of the Western European states is in sharp contrast with these rising expectations. The labour force will grow, even if unequally in the different member states, among other reasons because of the constant addition to it of women and immigrants. According to an estimate of the Commission of the Community the GNP growth rates will decline in the period 1973–8 by 1½ per cent by comparison with 1968–73. In the meantime there is no reason why price inflation should fall below two-figure percentages in any of the countries of the Community for the next two years. In some of these countries the level is already 20 per cent and over. World trade is depressed, and competition fiercer.

The inherent weaknesses of national governments, trying to solve the social problem of inflation within relatively small national markets and with their populations cajoled by nationalistic political parties, point towards the inherent strengths which lie in action by the Community. The pooling of resources in a European Social Fund of a proper size (together with similarly constituted Regional and European funds) could succeed where cramped national resources cannot begin to reach their targets. Near-standardization of social legislation across the entire territory of the Community would also facilitate the implementation of measures necessary for eradicating inflation, while at the same time maintaining standards of living and preserving the impetus towards social justice which was and is the characteristic of European democracy. The working populations of the nine states might more easily understand the true bases of their common problem, were that problem projected onto the broader and more neutral European canvas.

Finally I conclude:

5 That the European Community should be a symbol of peace in the world

Europe has lost its empires. It has shrunk to less than its initial territorial base. At the same time its power has been reduced by the emergence of two federal super-powers, and it has come to steer its course by the triangular relations thus created. By now, however, the super-powers have relinquished some of that bipolar monopoly of power which they enjoyed at the end of the Second World War. This happened because other centres of power, among them the European Community itself, emerged; but also because the mythology of each of the super-powers has become somewhat tarnished even in its own eyes. The Soviet myth has suffered from the post-Stalinist revelations, the Hungarian and Czechoslovak crises, and the formidable rivalry of communist China. The American myth has suffered from the Vietnam war and the impact of Watergate on its political institutions. An uneasy rapprochement has thus been established between these two powers which answers to the need for peace and stability of the European Community.

Europe thus is learning to live alone again. To do so it will be able to draw once again on its perennial genius, which is made up of ingenuity, frugality and love of freedom. With pooled resources, Europe might bridge the technological gap and become again a leading force in the science of today and in its application to economy and welfare. With a clearer realization of the limitations of their expanding resources, the European peoples, renowned for their sense of proportion, will be able to live and prosper within their means on the fruits of their own labour, which is the real but forgotten meaning of both frugality and thrift. From the days of the Greek polis and the Roman Republic, the love of freedom has persisted down to the present time of mixed economies and welfare states, characterizing European solutions to social and economic problems. Now the peoples of Europe have come again to a turning point in their history. There is no reason why – if peace prevails in their part of the world, and if they consolidate their union based on the freedom of groups, corporations, nations and races, but above all on freedom of the individual – they should not pass this new test successfully.

Index

Rees, Merlyn, 63*fn*
Regions, 102–142, *See also* EEC Regional Policy, Scotland, N Ireland, Wales
Rocard, Michel, 186*fn*, 204
Rokkan, Stein, 23
Rolls Royce Co, 45, 65, 69
Rome, Treaty of, 147, 155, 157, 159, 162, 165, 170, 176, 179, 189, 190–1, 201
Rougemont, Denis de, 145, 146*fn*, 198
Russell, William, 172*fn*

Saint-Simon, Claude Henri de, 6, 7, 121; theory of politics, 7–8
Sampson, Anthony, 124*fn*
Scanlon, Hugh, 38
Schiller, Karl, 136
Schreiber, J J, 158
Schumpeter, Joseph, 6, 13*fn*, 66
Scotland, 102, 104, 105, 106, 111–16, 133, 157, 180, 198, 199; unemployment in, 114*fn*; Scottish Nationalist Party, 113, 115. *See also* Oil, North Sea
Shonfield, Andrew, 14*fn*, 85*fn*, 165*fn* and Donovan Report, 42*fn*
Sidjanski, D, 170*fn*, 173*fn*
Simpson, Bill (Chairman of NED), 32–3
Skinner, Dennis, 111
Society, industrial-technological, 14, 16–17, 23–4
Sovereignty, 2, 4, 54, 105, 106, 116, 120, 126–7, 143, 167; and 'penetrated', 36; transfer of 146–7, 211
Spain, 102
Spender, Stephen, 145

Spinelli, Altiero, 183, 183*fn*, 185, 185*fn*
Stalin, Joseph, 20, 217
Stephenson, Hugh, 80, 96*fn*
Sternquist, Nils, 21, 21*fn*
Suez crisis (1956), 38
Sweden, 9, 15, 16, 33, 35, 86, 132, 135, 142; and corporate state 21–4; and trade unions, 28*fn*
Switzerland, 106
Syndicalism, 28–9, 30, 31–2

Taverne, Dick, 54, 54*fn*, 55, 56
Thomas, George, 190, 195
Thorpe, Jeremy, 4
Times, The, 77, 181*fn*
Tominaga, Professor, 14*fn*
Trade Unions, 1, 4*fn*, 25–39, 27*fn*, 33, 36, 45, 49–51, 84, 87, 88–9, 117, 122, 180, 199–201; as 'irresponsible opposition', 30; and leadership of 41–2; and nationalization, 56–7; political role of, 34–5; and Gormley's speech, 58; and EEC, 180, 188; in Ulster, 118; and collaboration with government (1972) 57; TUC, 38, 58; rejection of White Paper, 43; statement of intent, 43; attitude to government, 38–9; Mr Wilson's Manchester speech, 49; and Parliament, 52
Triffin, Robert, 98, 98*fn*
Trotskyism, 33

Ulster Defence Association, 119
Ulster Volunteer Force, 119
Ulster Workers' Council, 116, 117
United Nations, 164, 187